SO WHAT NOW?

Time for learning in your school to face the future

MALCOLM GROVES AND JOHN WEST-BURNHAM

First published 2022

by John Catt Educational Ltd,
15 Riduna Park, Station Road,
Melton, Woodbridge IP12 1QT

Tel: +44 (0) 1394 389850
Fax: +44 (0) 1394 386893
Email: enquiries@johncatt.com
Website: www.johncatt.com

ISBN: 978 1 915261 23 6

Set and designed by John Catt Educational Limited

CONTENTS

LIST OF TABLES AND FIGURES

TABLES

FIGURES

Deep and profound change, such as that urgently facing our societies, requires equally deep and profound learning, partly in order to respond to the gainsayers, but more importantly in order to find new, just, and equitable responses. To paraphrase Albert Einstein: 'we will not solve the problems of today by using the same thinking and learning that created them.'

The concept central to our analysis is that of *deep learning*, as opposed to the excessive shallowness of much present school-based learning. Bowring-Carr and West-Burnham (1997, p. 28) offer a clear perspective on the most significant elements of deep learning:

> If the learning that has taken place is merely capable of being reproduced at some later date, then what is being learnt is shallow learning only. Deep learning … results in a change of behaviour, a change in the way that the learner sees the world, a change in the reality which that learner is continuously creating.

This book takes this insight a stage further by focusing in on what we will term 'deep learning for future sustainability'. Such learning involves developing both understanding and the caring and agency to act upon it in the common good. It is not enough just to be concerned about climate change — awareness must lead to action based on relevant knowledge, skills, values, and qualities of character. Deep learning for future sustainability thus combines understanding with action, and links both to moral purpose. This is critical to the pursuit of a better and more sustainable future for us all. It also offers a powerful antidote to the continuing marginalisation of the most disadvantaged and vulnerable young people in society.

Schooling is necessarily and rightly focused on learning from the past. It is one of the most important means for passing knowledge and culture down through the generations. It also plays an important role in regard to the present, having a significant part to play in the socialisation of the young, as well as indeed the future, through the citizens and workers that these young people become. However, the focus on the future in schooling has been far less powerful than it now needs to become. Our main purpose here is to explore that missing dimension by developing an approach that integrates personal effectiveness, academic success, community engagement, and moral purpose.

This aspiration immediately lays us open to the accusation that here is yet another burden being laid on the school and its curriculum, already over-loaded, crowded, and stretched. Is it not better for schools to concentrate on doing a few things well, rather than attempting to solve every problem of society? A response to this challenge drives to the heart of understanding and framing correctly both the purpose of schools and the nature of the learning that takes place in them. To succeed, it will require school leaders who have all the qualities associated with positive models of leadership, along with a firm understanding of how a culture of deep learning is established. Drawing on a combination of research, analysis, and case studies of schools currently seeking to 'build back better', we will examine how the task of equipping young people to creatively and positively shape a changed future needs to be re-framed for the post-pandemic world.

We explore how this might be achieved driven by grass-roots efforts within the profession, whilst strongly aware of the reinforcement needed in terms of future national policy change. And we make an urgent call to action from school leaders as the time remaining to succeed is now very short.

We hope this book will serve both as a stimulus and resource for school leaders, middle leaders, classroom practitioners, leaders of MATs, governors and trustees. It is designed to develop your personal and team understanding of the nature of learning, your grasp of the future, and of appropriate models of leadership and governance to enable your school to face that future. It works best seen as an iterative process offering a cumulative range of evidence and ideas to support personal choices in building your own increased confidence and understanding as a leader of learning fit for the future, as well as extending that process to the teams with which you work.

The book aspires to be neither prescriptive nor partisan. We try to avoid simplistic polarities while being explicit about our underpinning assumptions. We would summarise these as:

- Effective education is the result many partnerships working through mutual respect and parity of esteem.

- A core purpose of schooling is to support social justice through the pursuit of equity.
- Strategies and interventions to support learning should be evidence-informed.
- Schools need to be inclusive, caring, and kind.
- Education has to enable democracy and so has to model democratic structures and processes.
- Leadership works best through collective capacity rather than personal status, through consent not conformity.

Our approach throughout is to develop a synthesis drawing on an eclectic range of diverse sources, case studies of actual practice, critical perspectives, and opportunities for reflection. Our overarching focus is the learning of the individual — from before the age of five to well after fifty! Our hope is that you will draw on our synthesis to inform your own learning but also share that with the teams with whom you work.

The book is divided into three parts. In the first, we summarise the evidence for urgency in addressing the challenges facing humankind and adapting our social and economic lives as a result. We also consider the evidence for why schools need to change in response to these challenges, and how our current models of schooling, learning, and assessment may have potentially contributed in small but significant ways to the problem. Whether that is true or not may be debated, but either way we suggest these models are no longer fit for purpose going forward. Finally, we introduce our rationale for a positive model of deep learning for a sustainable future along with the characteristics of schooling that can contribute towards that.

In part two we unpick what we already know about the nature of learning and teaching in order to establish some core propositions and principles fit for the future. We examine the nature and importance of a learning culture in schools at every level and relate this to the need for evidence-informed practice based on a sound understanding of both the potential and limitations of educational research. We consider how school leaders now need to think creatively and imaginatively about some of the basic concepts with which they work, notably assessment, curriculum, personalisation, and pedagogy. This requires deep not shallow change.

The deep learning and deep change we describe here are not something new. They are based on a sound, research-informed understanding developed over a long period of time, and there are a range of established techniques at the educator's disposal. Deep learning and deep change can already be seen in places in schools today.

Finally, in the third part, we draw on case studies of three very different schools, from two different countries, who are all engaged in a process of deep change. We highlight the need to engage in processes of deep listening with all stakeholders as a pre-requisite for change, as well as the tensions for leaders caught between the demands of the present and the challenges of the future. We argue that, while there is certainly a real need for a policy framework that helps rather than hinders the process, it is for educators and leaders to get on as best they can in their own school context to do what is both necessary and right to secure learning fit for a just and sustainable future, irrespective of governmental lead in these matters. However, we also set out some clear evidence-informed principles for school development and leadership that we think are central to the success of that mission.

Each chapter throughout the book concludes with a reflective self-review opportunity for readers to use both personally and, if appropriate, with the teams of colleagues with whom they work.

We have also opted to begin each of the three parts of the book with a personal thought piece from a school leader. We have done this in part to remind ourselves of the connection between theory and practice, which we have sought to blend throughout the book. In doing so, we are trying to balance two important insights. There is nothing so practical as a good theory. Equally, while theory and practice are in theory the same, in practice they are not.

The future does not yet exist. It is not written in stone. It is therefore reasonable to ask how well schools are equipping children and young people to meet the challenges of the future. In fact, of course, there is no one future to fit all, and so perhaps our aim may be better expressed as equipping children and young people to understand and shape their futures. Our contention is that this requires deep learning for future sustainability and that we can and must now move quickly towards that in all our schools.

Let us show you how and why.

PART ONE

WHAT FUTURE?

THOUGHT PIECE: Clare Flintoff, CEO, Asset Education Trust

Leading and managing in a time of crisis

In March 2020 everything changed as we moved into a period of crisis management. My home became the headquarters of our Trust and I sat in the middle of my living room orchestrating change. With constant phone calls, emails, briefings, plans, meetings — every waking hour was a working hour. It was exhausting but I was in my element as I was doing what I know how to do — holding things together for everyone when everything is going pear-shaped, providing calm reassurance, making quick decisions, keeping everyone else as busy and focused as possible. We didn't have time to stop and comprehend what was actually happening, to feel any element of shock, we just got on with what needed to be done hour after hour.

I knew that communication was key. On 18 March the government announced that schools would close from the following Monday, and I wrote immediately to staff, parents, governors, and trustees. The following day I wrote in my journal that I'd spent 12 solid hours at my computer with no breaks and was frustrated with the government as the definition of 'key workers' wasn't out as promised that day. Over the next two days, we sent forms out to staff and parents to gather information about demand for places and availability of staff, ordered vouchers for FSM children, set up google classrooms for every class in all schools and said an emotional 'goodbye' to our Y6 children, not knowing if we would see them back in school again.

At 8.30 in the evening of the first day of home schooling for the majority of children, the UK Prime Minister announced a full lockdown. That was when my own Coronavirus symptoms started!

Looking back on that time, 'crisis management' doesn't describe it sufficiently — it was leadership in a crisis. Every decision was a crucial one. The most obvious solutions weren't always the right ones to take. The implications of decisions needed to be fully considered and I needed to maintain a longer-term perspective. I was also determined that we were going to use this period to make some advancements that would benefit us in the longer term — for example, with the use of technology. We had Google classrooms up and running in the first week of the lockdown. This meant that our teachers were learning how to do remote learning in those first few weeks, something that teachers in some other places were learning months later. For me it was about making the best use of everyone's time. We still had staff in schools photocopying packs to deliver to homes for those children who couldn't access the internet but these were support staff rather than teachers. Later on, we trained up these staff to support families to access learning at home and provided as many Chromebooks as we could afford. We were determined to skill up our own teachers to provide content online in imaginative and interesting ways. A year later, we have teachers who are highly skilled in technology, and plenty of Chromebooks in all our schools.

The last 18 months have taught me that I need to plan thinking and reflection time into my schedule rather than relying on journeys between schools, evenings and weekends! I am a do-er and I get a lot done. I think carefully about what I do and the implications of my decisions, but I haven't allowed myself enough time to think and reflect during the course of a working day. I heard the phrase recently, 'You are not paid to do, you are paid to think', and this has resonated with me more than I would have imagined.

My daily schedule is slightly less frenetic than it was, and I don't have the same inner pressure to fill in all of the gaps with a manic bout of replying to as many emails as I can in 20 minutes! I also spend less time racing around from school to school. When you are in crisis mode, you are juggling hundreds of balls in the air at once and you only have time to catch them briefly and throw them up again. It gets to a point where you can't keep track of where you've got to with each one, and at that point you become overwhelmed and unproductive.

> The extra thinking time has enabled me to set up systems, to delegate more, and to follow through more thoroughly. Some of those balls are best dealt with by others anyway; some were deflecting me away from my core business and weren't worthy of my attention and some were not receiving enough of my attention.
>
> I have realised that far too much relies on me — I am probably the most important 'single point of failure' that we describe in our trust risk register. I think it is known as 'founder's mentality' — the Trust is my baby and I have been finding it hard to let it grow up. We have a strong distributed leadership approach, but it has been too reliant on me — an orchestra of leaders with one conductor. I need the heads of each section to be able to take on the conducting at times, and I will be a better leader if I can empower them to do that.

As we sit and write these words in January 2022, reflecting back on the experience of the last two years as Clare Flintoff has just done for us, we believe we are at a particular moment of *chairos*. The ancient Greeks had two words for time: *chairos* and *chronos*. Whereas *chronos* refers to chronological or sequential time, *chairos* signifies the proper or opportune time for action. In this sense, while *chronos* is quantitative, *chairos* has a qualitative, permanent nature.

This is a particular moment both of great crisis and urgent opportunity. In part one we set out to understand how and why we have come to be here. It is time to face the future.

CHAPTER 1

A VERY PRECARIOUS FUTURE

The young people of today think of nothing but themselves. They have no reverence for parents or old age. They are impatient of all restraint. They talk as if they know everything and what passes for wisdom with us is foolishness with them.

Although these words are attributed by some to Peter the Hermit in the 12 century AD, they reflect a set of feelings recorded over and over again by past generations across place and time. Yet somehow the world has survived! Meanwhile young people have been equally prone to resent the perceived unsatisfactory world they will inherit from their parents and elders. They have hoped to make something better, which somehow never quite fully materialises by the time they in turn become the next older generation critical of young people of their own day.

But it is possible we are now at a point in time where we will break this cycle of repetition, though not in a good way. For both old and young are confronting a future where unprecedentedly urgent change is required of both, and there is no time to worry about the apportionment of blame.

The reality we now face increasingly appears to be a future of multiple, fast-moving, overlapping, and inter-connected crises. The most superficial overview of environmental issues and geo-political trends and issues in the second half of 2020 produces the following list:

- Worst bush/forest fires in a generation in Victoria, Australia and California (https://en.wikipedia.org/wiki/2020_California_wildfires; https://www.bbc.co.uk/newsround/52410744).
- Plagues of locusts in East Africa and India (https://news.harvard.edu/gazette/story/2020/06/researchers-investigate-a-plague-of-locusts-in-east-africa/).
- Widespread famine 'of biblical proportions' (https://reliefweb.int/report/world/un-warns-impending-famine-millions-danger-starvation).
- Water shortages (https://www.theguardian.com/environment/2020/nov/26/more-than-3-billion-people-affected-by-water-shortages-data-shows).
- Conflicts in Afghanistan, Somalia, and Syria, resulting in the flight of refugees (https://www.crisisgroup.org/global/what-s-driving-global-refugee-crisis).
- 2019 and 2020 were the hottest years since records began (https://www.climatecentral.org/gallery/graphics/top-10-warmest-years-on-record).
- In April 2020 the Arctic had around 13.6 million square kilometres (5.3 million square miles) of ice cover, putting it firmly below any other year on record, and nearly two weeks ahead of previous early April records set in 2017 and 2018 (https://earthobservatory.nasa.gov/images/147746/the-long-decline-of-arctic-sea-ice).
- In Antarctica the Amery Iceberg, larger than Greater London, broke off in 2019 (http://www.esa.int/ESA_Multimedia/Images/2019/10/Amery_Iceberg).
- Desertification — the Sahara has grown by 10% since 1920 with significant implications for its northern, western, and southern neighbours (https://www.sciencedaily.com/releases/2018/03/180329141035.htm).
- A climate of extremes — hurricanes and typhoons, wind and rain, drought and freezing and baking (e.g. https://edition.cnn.com/2020/05/18/weather/climate-change-hurricane-tropical-cyclone/index.html).
- Pollution spread and reduced air quality (https://ourworldindata.org/air-pollution).

- Three major pandemics in 100 years (Spanish Flu, SARS, and Covid-19).

Each of these factors has the potential to destabilise our existing norms as well as social and moral assumptions. What is even more concerning, though, is the potential for these factors to become mutually reinforcing and exacerbating.

Describing the potential impact of climate change, Elizabeth Kolbert (2016) argues that there are multiple possibilities in terms of how feedback between different factors will inform the nature of climate change, most notably the unpredictable human factor:

> Perhaps the most unpredictable feedback of all is the human one. With six billion people on the planet the risks are everywhere apparent. A disruption in monsoon patterns, a shift in ocean currents, a major drought — any one of these could easily produce streams of refugees numbering in the millions.
>
> (Kolbert, 2006, p. 187)

David Wallace-Wells (2019) sees even more wide-ranging and damaging implications.

> What lies between us and extinction is horrifying enough — and we have not yet begun to contemplate what it means to live under those conditions. What will it do to our politics and our culture and our emotional equilibria, our sense of history and our relationship to it, our sense of nature and our relationship to it, that we are living in a world degraded by our own hands, with the horizon of human possibility dramatically dimmed?
>
> (Wallace-Wells, 2019, p. 34)

Wallace-Wells might well have added what will it mean for our children? And linked to that, three even more pressing questions drive to the heart of this book. What does this situation tell us about education systems that have inevitably contributed to, or at least failed to prevent us, getting into such a predicament? What especially does it mean for our understanding of the nature of education and the process of learning going forward? And how can schools play their part differently in the task of mitigation and transformation that lies ahead?

For none of this crisis has come about suddenly, and none of it was unforeseen. To give but one example, in 1972 *The Ecologist* magazine published 'Blueprint for Survival', signed by 30 leading scientists of the time and turned into a book which sold 750,000 copies. It argued for radical action at governmental level in order to prevent what the authors referred to as 'the breakdown of society and the irreversible disruption of the life-support systems on this planet' (Goldsmith, et al., 1972, p. 1).

In the same year the Club of Rome report *The Limits to Growth* argued the earth's interlocking resources probably cannot support present rates of economic and population growth much beyond the year 2100, if that long, even with advanced technology (Meadows et al., 1972).

Yet nearly fifty years on at the time of writing, the situation remains in effect the same, except for the sound of a ticking clock growing louder. In terms of climate change alone we have moved from needing to consider how to prevent change to now only how best to alleviate its worst effects. If by 2030 (less than nine years from the point at which we are writing this), we have failed to reduce carbon emissions profoundly, the effects will be even more severe.

Professor Mark Maslin's short book *How to Save Our Planet* offers two visions of the year 2100. One is predicated on limited action for change. The other assumes we take responsible action. The difference is stark.

In his first pessimistic scenario, global temperatures are allowed to rise by over 4°C. Using existing established scientific research as his basis, Maslin foresees a resulting world where it is physiologically impossible to work outside for many days each year; raging wildfires on most continents create major air pollution events and human health crises; prolonged drought affects nearly half the world population; sea levels rise by over 1 meter, rendering 8 major cities with a combined population of over 60 million people uninhabitable; mega-cyclones with sustained wind speeds of 200mph have become commonplace; the ocean food chain has collapsed due to over-acidification of the water; access to sufficient affordable nutritious food has become a major issue for a majority of the world population; and there is mass migration from the tropics and subtropics to more temperate zones, resulting in increased civil unrest, violence, and disease.

By contrast in his more optimistic scenario, significant action starting now limits temperature rise to just 1.5°C through making major positive changes. Those damaging consequences are avoided, and a virtuous cycle of sustainability for the planet has taken root through a combination of new solutions, new social structures, and new economics.

The key that will make the difference, Maslin argues, is the power of individuals, both in terms of the changes they make in their individual lives but also in their involvement in collective pressure to demand change from governments and industry. Yet, while the inspiring leadership of individuals like Greta Thunberg, and the collective protest of groups such as Extinction Rebellion, have made an impact, these have not yet resulted in the pace of change Maslin sees as essential to avoiding catastrophe.

According to the IPCC report of 2018, if we wanted to limit warming to 1.5°C with little or no overshoot, then we would need to reduce emissions by roughly 50% (relative to 2010 levels) by 2030.[1] Some see that 2030 deadline for achieving 1.5°C maximal warming as somewhat illusory at this late stage. We can still limit warming to 2°C if we cut emissions by 20% by 2030. However, shifting to a target of limiting warming to 2°C does not make the situation any less alarming, nor our need to act any less urgent. Limiting warming below 2°C means reaching net-zero emissions within the lifetime of today's school students (i.e. by about 2075). We have yet to take the drastic action required for even that.

One of the reasons for this lack of action lies in the inability of politicians, and sections of the population who vote for them, to understand in depth, to evaluate competing claims, and to distinguish to a degree the difference between misinformation, evidence-based opinions, and established facts. For example, in 2017 researchers found that most adults cannot accurately judge the truth or falsity of an online news story because they automatically assume that content which aligns with their

1. Intergovernmental Panel on Climate Change (2018), *Special report: Global Warming of 1.5 °C*, Summary for Policymakers, section C.1. Available at: https://www.ipcc.ch/sr15/chapter/spm/.

existing beliefs is true.[2] While this can be seen as human nature, our view is that it also represents a major failure of educational systems across the globe to develop critical thinking skills in large numbers of learners.

As a result, despite several decades of debate, there is still no global consensus on what needs to be done about climate change. Basically, policy makers have responded with platitudes. The message is simply not getting through in terms of changing attitudes and behaviours across society. Whether because people are too comfortable, too complacent, or, for a significant but rapidly growing minority, because of their social and economic insecurity, the moral compulsion for change is missing or dormant, and the moral imagination to take responsibility is lacking.

In Britain, where we live, a high proportion of the population enjoys relatively good levels of social safety, economic security and choice in terms of employment, housing, recreation, health, and education. People have choices and are able to exercise these in a wide variety of ways. However, a growing third of the population do not share this security and freedom. For both groups, necessary change poses both a threat and a challenge.

Professor Guy Standing (2014) has drawn attention to the rise of the 'precariat', as he terms them. This precariat lives in economic uncertainty, usually in chronic unsustainable debt, in which one shock, mistaken decision, or illness could tip them over the edge into the under-class, cut adrift from society and probably condemned to social illness or an early death. The precariat is the first class in history to be losing acquired rights — cultural, civil, social, economic, and political.

Standing argues that the income distribution system of the twentieth century has broken down and will not come back. This has generated a new global class structure, a small plutocracy of multi-billionaires with absurd power; a shrinking 'salariat' with employment security; a shrinking industrial proletariat; and the rapidly growing precariat, who are profoundly different in outlook and experience from the proletariat.

2. Goodfellow, J. (2017), 'Only 4% of people can distinguish fake news from truth'. Available at: https://www.thedrum.com/news/2017/02/06/only-4-people-can-distinguish-fake-news-truth-channel-4-study-finds.

The coming together of globalisation and technological revolution, together with reforms promoting so-called 'labour flexibility', has created pervasive insecurity.

An investigation by the *Financial Times* in April 2021 carried out a global survey of 1700 under-35-year-olds.[3] It reports a real sense among many young people that the social contract has broken for their generation. Many describe feeling as if there is nothing solid under their feet. 'Most people my age are paddling so hard just to stay still,' says Tom, an architect. 'It's exhausting — nobody is asking for an easy ride, but all my friends have worked so hard all their lives, and many are losing faith in the system'.

For child development expert Remo Largo, insecurity extends further:

> ... people's insecurity isn't just existential: it is emotional and social as well. They are feeling less and less emotionally secure and increasingly lonely. They lack the emotional security and social support that family and community used to provide.
>
> (Largo, 2019, p. 294)

There seems little doubt that psychological well-being and mental health are major areas for concern right now. According to an NHS study, rates of probable mental disorder have increased since 2017 for children and young people.[4] In 2020 in the UK one in six (16.0%) children aged 5 to 16 years were identified as having a probable mental disorder, an increase from one in nine (10.8%) in 2017. This increase was evident in both boys and girls. The likelihood of a probable mental disorder also increased with age, with a noticeable difference in gender for the older age group (17 to 22 years); 27.2% of young women and 13.3% of young men were identified as having a probable mental disorder.

---

3. O'Connor, S. (2021), 'A New Deal for the Young', Financial Times, 25 April. Available at: https://www.ft.com/content/77d586cc-4f3f-4701-a104-d09136c93d44?shareType=nongift.

4. Lifestyles Team, NHS Digital (2020), *Mental Health of Children and Young People in England, 2020*. Available at: https://digital.nhs.uk/data-and-information/publications/statistical/mental-health-of-children-and-young-people-in-england/2020-wave-1-follow-up.

If this is an accurate indicator and analysis, then it is more important than ever that young people are able to understand and apply the lessons of not only the school curriculum but also their own life experiences. For they will likely be faced with greater uncertainty as well as choices of greater complexity than any previous generation.

From an environmental as well as a moral perspective, the education of the young, who will inherit the current disaster, needs to offer access to a range of knowledge, qualities, skills, and behaviours. These need to be made explicit in what content a curriculum identifies and, in particular, how this prepares students to take better responsibility for the future. But with all the complexities implicit in environmental and social change, there is equally a need to enhance personal qualities, moral confidence, and emotional literacy.

The urgency of the climate crisis also demands that we consider the rights of future generations, as our activity or inactivity will determine the legacy that we bequeath to them. There was an appreciation of this principle in many ancient indigenous peoples, and it is beginning to take root again in countries like New Zealand. Prime Minister Jacinda Ardern, in a speech to the United Nations in September 2018, put it this way:

> In the Maori language there is a word that captures the importance of that role — *Kaitiakitanga*. It means guardianship. The idea that we have been entrusted with our environment, and we have a duty of care. For us, that has meant taking action to address degradation, like setting standards to make our rivers swimmable, reducing waste and phasing out single-use plastic bags, right through to eradicating predators and protecting our biodiversity.[5]

In his book *The Good Ancestor* Roman Krznaric argues that the survival of our species and planet requires us to shift from the short-termism of current political and business thinking to incorporate a much longer-term view of how what we do today will impact on future generations, and that education is critical to this task:

5. Newsroom (2018), 'Full text: PM's speech to the United Nations'. Available at: https://www.newsroom.co.nz/2018/09/27/256105/full-text-pms-speech-to-the-united-nations.

> Education appears to suffer from an inherent time tension. On the one hand it embodies long-term thinking by providing investment in young people the fruits of which may not emerge for at least a decade ... On the other hand, what they need to learn is in a constant state of flux.
>
> There are at least two core skills they should be learning that will stand the test of time. Firstly, relationship skills like empathy, where humans have a big advantage over AI machines ... Secondly, the skill of long-term thinking itself. This is something we will always need in a world undergoing rapid transformation and facing long-term threats. **We need education systems that will forge a bond with the future generations who will inherit the consequences of our actions** [our emphasis].
>
> (Krznaric, 2020, p. 230)

So, our challenge is this. Can we successfully help our young people survive and thrive in a very different future and to form a bond with it? And, even more, can we help them learn to create it in a way that works for everyone? Is the school system up to this challenge?

The answer to these questions requires us to first understand the limitations of the present system, before we can turn to the much more important task of applying the knowledge that we already have about how humans learn to the urgent changes now needed.

Opportunity for self-reflection and collaborative review

- *Do you accept the broad analysis proposed here? Are there valid alternative perspectives?*
- *What is your school currently doing to help your children and young people understand and shape their own and the wider future?*
- *In what ways is your school currently taking account of any of the forces outlined in this chapter that make the future different and challenging?*

CHAPTER 2

WHY SCHOOL IS PART OF THE PROBLEM

Children are the messages we send to a time we will not see.

Neil Postman (1982)

There is a conundrum at the heart of this chapter. We have argued so far that the unprecedented challenges which the young generation will have to face and resolve in their lifetimes requires a new focus on learning, which we commonly assume is the role of schools. Yet the learning provided by schools has neither stopped us from getting into the present crisis, nor prevented the inactivity at both a personal and a global level which has made it worse. So, can schools really be part of the solution?

An alternative way of framing this question is to ask; is it learning which defines schooling, or does schooling define learning? Is the intellectual process of learning in thrall to the social and control dimensions of schooling, or does form follow function? In other words, if we were to design somewhere for people to learn in the best possible way, would we end up with a school?

Schools are, however, what we have. We have no time to reinvent them from scratch. So, if we are to make them fit for the future quickly, we need to understand the barriers to learning they can currently present and figure out how to remove or minimise these. We also need to be crystal clear that there need to be solutions which work for all young people not just some of them. For, certainly in the UK, we know that our system fails a significant minority of those who pass through it, as we will explore later in this chapter.

Another way of understanding the conundrum with which we started can be found in Alison Gopnik's use of the metaphors of carpentry and gardening.

> ... (as) a carpenter ... essentially your job is to shape that material into a final product that will fit the scheme that you had in mind to begin with. And you can assess how good a job you've done by looking at the finished product. When we garden, on the other hand, we create a protected and nurturing space for plants to flourish. It takes a lot of hard labour and the sweat of our brows, with a lot of exhausted digging and wallowing in manure.
>
> (Gopnik, 2016, p. 18)

These images are compelling: compare the precision of the joiner with the creative expression of the artist; compare the discipline and rigour of a formal garden to a wild meadow. These translate almost exactly into models of formal schooling and more naturalistic learning, as seen in Table 1.

Table 1: Comparing schooling and learning

Formal/ Schooling	Naturalistic/ Learning
Curriculum delivery	Learning for understanding
Information transmission by teachers	Knowledge creation by learners
Generic provision	Personal pathways
Summative outcomes	Formative development
Linear and hierarchical organisation	Complex interdependent working
Increasing employability	Enriching humanity
Bureaucratic and hierarchical	Organic
Carpenters	Gardeners

Ideally, of course, there needs to be a balance — sometimes we need to be the carpenter, sometimes the gardener. Intuitively most of us would argue for the blend of control and freedom that characterises effective parenting, the balance of unconditional love with clear, non-negotiable boundaries. Unfortunately, that balance seems to be elusive in terms of both educational policy and professional practice.

For many thousands of years, apes and humans had one key aspect of their lives in common — they survived as hunter gatherers. In certain respects, this way of life has survived, largely intact until very recent years, with the Bushmen of the Kalahari and the Aboriginal peoples of Australia. The search for food, water, and shelter provides some of the earliest evidence in terms of learning — Sapiens were successful in evolutionary terms because of their ability as hunter gatherers, and the reasons for this prowess still resonate in our daily lives.

> Sapiens did not forage only for food and materials. They foraged for knowledge as well. To survive they needed a detailed mental map of their territory... They needed to know which foods were nourishing, which made you sick and how to use others as cures ... Mastery of each of these many skills required years of apprenticeship and practice.
> (Harari, 2011, p. 48)

One of the key indicators of this cognitive revolution was the introduction of specialisation. In hunter-gatherer communities, everybody was either a hunter or a gatherer, usually men and women and children respectively. A major social transition in the lifecycle of traditional societies was the movement for boys from gathering to hunting and, if necessary, fighting, which required similar skills to hunting.

The shift from a hunter-gatherer society to an agrarian one saw the emergence of urban living that required specialised crafts and occupations. Sometimes this even gave rise to the adoption of surnames based on occupation rather than clan or tribe membership. Obvious examples here include Archer, Fletcher, Cook, Cooper, and Smith.

As settlements became permanent so the provision of skills and services emerged. The movement away from a family-based subsistence economy to one based on specialisation and exchange, or primitive capitalism, led to profound changes in patterns of working. Brewing, for example, though often a household task also become a commercial transaction in which people were employed and became specialists. As they specialised, so the need for training increased, as did hierarchies based on expertise, notably apprentice, journeyman and craftsman or master.

We know from the study of the fragile and vulnerable contemporary hunter-gatherer societies that learning in such societies has significant characteristics that resonate with how we prefer to learn now. Indeed, it may be that the collective memory of living as a sapiens informs much of our dissatisfaction with modern industrial society. The key characteristics of such learning include:

- A functional and pragmatic curriculum focused on safety and well-being — the Sabre Tooth Curriculum (Benjamin, 1939).
- Education recognising the need to respond to a changing context.
- The apprenticeship model — learning based on stage not age recognising the emergence of different aptitudes and skills.
- Opportunities for unlimited practice supported by coaching — the transmission of knowledge and wisdom.
- Play and games that mimic adult behaviours.
- Opportunities for success that is celebrated and for 'no blame' failure.

In his study of children's play in Liberia, David Lancy identifies four assumptions that have become widely held beliefs:

> First, children want to learn their culture, so they strive for competence. Second, they learn best without adult direction and at their own pace. They are motivated to learn useful skills in order to 'fit in' and be accepted by their families. And fourth … when they appear to lack this motivation, they will be called to account …
>
> (Lancy, 2017, p. 48)

It would be very wrong to romanticise the lives of pre-historic hunter gatherers. Their lives could be extremely precarious, and they would often be highly vulnerable and dependent on luck in many aspects of their lives, for example finding water, safe childbirth, and just meeting all the most basic needs identified in Maslow's hierarchy. Issues of health and well-being would argue against the life of the hunter gatherer. But there may well be significant advantages in terms of the lives of children in what Jared Diamond defines as 'small-scale' societies:

> A recurring theme is that other Westerners and I are struck by the emotional security, self-confidence, curiosity, and autonomy of members of small-scale societies, not only as adults but already as

> children ... We are struck by the precocious development of social skills in their children.
>
> (Diamond, 2011, p. 208)

So, it might be appropriate to speculate on the extent to which even schools which teach well-being and make provision for mental health support can offer the same potential for emotional security and social competence as children growing up in small tight-knit communities such as in rural Papua New Guinea, or even the shared parenting of infants in chimpanzee communities on the shores of Lake Tanganyika.

Schools have been intentionally developed in their current form in the UK for reasons to do with the way we now live, but we have also paid a price for the shift to a more formalised education. In the process we have lost sight of some fundamental insights about learning. We have become too school-centric in both thinking and organisation, detaching learning from community.

So, the thesis we explore in this book is simply this. Firstly, schools as we have come to understand them in Western society, are part of the problem that has led us into the predicament now facing humankind. That is not to say they are in any way a major causal factor, but rather to ask whether they could have made more of a difference. Secondly, that schools can also be part of the solution. Again, that is not to say they are able to do this alone. It is simply to suggest that they can make a greater contribution to shaping the social and economic changes now confronting us through an increased focus on deep learning to foster understanding, character, and agency in children and young people. However, to do that, they need to change. And it is important to understand why as well as how.

In our previous book *Flipping Schools!* we examined the robust and long-established evidence behind what we call the 50:30:20 model for understanding school impact on educational achievement. The biggest impact, at around 50%, derives from genetic inheritance and personal characteristics, while social and environmental factors account for around 30%, and school the remaining 20%. It is important to stress here, as we did there, that this is not to argue that the school's effect is negligible or unimportant. It is on the contrary crucially important that every school is as effective as it possibly can be for every young person for whom they share responsibility.

Nevertheless, it is a salutary fact that, despite more than a generation of school improvement policies and remedies, more than one third of young people leave the British education system without the five GCSEs (including Maths and English) that are officially regarded as the basic measure of educational success. Education in England is in many respects an organic mess with iteration after iteration of policies designed to work towards ambiguous, often contradictory and contested outcomes. Teachers, school leaders, and governors have spent hours in meetings over the years responding to the latest policy fads (often dictated by political messaging rather than expert opinion and evidence).

One part of the explanation for this lies in the short-term nature of our politics, gripped by the news cycle and the next opinion poll. Another part lies in the resulting failure to grapple effectively with three resulting structural issues. If a school is to be effective in the more future-facing approach we are advocating, then it is important for it to understand these three key barriers:

- A neglect of family.
- A failure of equity.
- A flawed approach to accountability.

We will consider each in turn.

A neglect of family

The years from birth to age seven are absolutely crucial to a child's life chances, in particular their potential for happiness, well-being, and academic success. This simple truth has profound implications for parenting, schooling, and how these interact. Charles Desforges is in no doubt:

> First, a great deal of the variation in students' achievement is outside of the schools' influence. Family social class, for example, accounts for about one third of such variance. Second, parental involvement in the form of home discussion has, nonetheless, a major impact on achievement. Other forms of involvement have insignificant effects. Unlike social class, this form of parental involvement might be open to the educative impact of schools.
>
> (Desforges, 2004, p. 21)

The challenge and the implications of Desforges's findings are further developed in Table 2, showing relative effect sizes.[6]

In essence, the potential personal, academic, and social achievement of seven-year olds is very highly dependent on the quality of their family life. In fact, as shown in Table 2, the ratio of family effects to school effects is to all intents and purposes six to one. This changes over time. Every parent recognises the transition from walking to school hand in hand to being dropped off around the corner to avoid negative comments on the family car. As school becomes more significant, so the family diminishes in significance.

Table 2: Effects of parents/effects of schools (Desforges, 2014; Sacker et al., 2002)

Achievement Age 7	Parents / school effect size
Age 11	0.29 / 0.05
Age 16	0.27 / 0.21
	0.14 / 0.51

If the family really is six times more significant than the school at an early stage (and the data on this is compelling), then a number of very significant challenges emerge. The first issue is school spending per pupil. In 2018–2019 the spending on early years pupils was £3905. In contrast it was £5040 on primary pupils, secondary pupils attracted £6251, and post sixteen students £5870. In terms of investment to secure long-term progress for all, would it not make sense to significantly increase funding into early years and Key Stage 1?

Indeed, a perspective based on prevention rather than cure suggests spending more on the early years than any other phase. Language development in the early years may be one of the most effective antidotes to academic failure.

> The indicator of pre-school effectiveness in promoting pre-reading skills continued to predict academic attainment at the end of Year 11. Higher levels of pre-school effectiveness predicted more GCSE entries

6. Effect size is a statistical methodology that allows researchers to understand how meaningful the relationship between variables or the difference between groups is. It indicates the practical implications and significance of a research data and evidence. Thus, the table provides a quantified relationship between the effects of schools and families. A larger effect size means that a research finding has practical significance, while a small effect size indicates limited practical applications.

> (ES=0.25), better grades in GCSE English (ES=0.31), and having a higher probability of achieving 5 A*–C including English and maths (OR=1.73).
> (Sammons et al., 2014, p. 45)

This research, carried out by the EPPSE (Effective Pre-school Primary and Secondary) Project, found that attending any pre-school, compared to none, predicted better results at GCSE overall, and higher grades in GCSE maths and English, as well as the likelihood of achieving five or more GCSEs at grade A* to C. The benefit of attending pre-school equates to 41 more points at GCSE, the equivalent to gaining seven B grades at GCSE, rather than seven C grades. The *International Early Learning and Child Well-being Study: National Report for England in December 2020* reinforces the importance of pre-school activity:

> At age 5, parents/carers reading to children, helping them read words and sentences, and having back-and-forth conversations is associated with greater development in a range of domains.
> (Kettlewell et al., 2020, p. 11)

Richard Wilkinson introduces a key hypothesis about the possible relationship between early childhood and later academic performance:

> ... responses to stress throughout adult life are affected by what happens early in life. It has been found that rats handled daily between birth and weaning have lower lifetime levels of stress ... Handling seems to make them more relaxed ... The differences between rats that are handled in early life and those that have not increases as they get older.
> (Wilkinson, 1996, p. 194)

The handled rats had significantly higher performance in learning to find their way through mazes as adults. It is a very long way from researching rats to understanding children but the insights from research are compelling in their consistency. Experiences in early childhood are disproportionately significant — but are also highly conducive to intervention strategies that reinforce the centrality of play and relationships.

This view is echoed from a different perspective by an Education Endowment Foundation (2020) study of early mathematics development which concluded:

- It is important for teachers to be aware of the typical early development of mathematical skills and concepts, to understand what may be appropriate for teaching children in the Early Years and Key Stage 1.
- Structured teaching should be balanced with opportunities for children to engage in both free and structured (or guided) play involving mathematical resources and ideas.
- The use of storybooks in mathematical teaching can have a large impact on young children's attainment in this subject.[7]

A key theme of our discussion here is how to prepare the next generation of school leavers to find their way through the unprecedented challenges they will have to negotiate. For some education systems, notably in Finland and Estonia, the answer to this most basic educational issue is simple — start school later, increase the opportunities for varied social interaction, and crucially, provide support in developing children's understanding of their social relationships.

This apparently contradictory policy in the Baltic states is supported by the strong correlation between less schooling and higher performance. Children in Finland and Estonia may start schooling at the age of seven but start education at birth. The evidence is very clear that any potential loss in terms of relative levels of attainment has disappeared by the age of 15. This policy of starting formal schooling later than the norm in many countries therefore liberates seven years for:

> ... a curriculum that aims to develop children's social skills, positive self-concept and ability to reflect on right and wrong. Finnish children are introduced to activities and environments in which they can develop the understanding, skills and attitudes required for learning to read and do maths.
>
> (Crehan, 2016, p. 16)

Crehan goes on to quote from the Finnish national curriculum for the pre-school age group:

7. Education Endowment Foundation (2020), *Improving Mathematics in the Early Years and Key Stage 1*. Available at: https://educationendowmentfoundation.org.uk/education-evidence/guidance-reports/early-maths.

> ... the basis for emerging literacy is that children have heard and listened, they have been heard, they have spoken and been spoken to, people have discussed things with them, and they have asked questions and received answers.

One answer for England may be something akin to the Sure Start programme that operated between 2000 and 2010, setting up children's centres in the most deprived communities:

> Here, ideally, are sited all the services a family might need from midwives to training programmes helping mothers find jobs, from speech therapy for small children to debt advice, from tai chi classes and parenting support to childcare, cafes, chatting and fun.
>
> (Toynbee and Walker, 2008, pp. 126–27)

Toynbee and Walker go on to demonstrate the impact of this approach. Comparing 9000 three-year-old pupils across 150 Sure Start areas with children in similar areas without Sure Start, they found that:

> ... parents showed less negative parenting and a better home learning environment ... three-year-old pupils had better social development, with higher levels of positive social behaviour and independence, than children in similar areas not having a programme.

This policy of the then Labour government was closely linked to the concept of Extended Schools, whereby schools provided a range of activities and services, often beyond the school day, to help meet the needs of its pupils, their families and the wider community.

Lucy Crehan pinpoints making this broader connection as a key element in Finland's commitment to the health and well-being of its children and young people:

> Finnish schools do so much more than teaching children. Finns know that sometimes what causes children to struggle are not learning difficulties but social or emotional difficulties or health problems.
>
> (Crehan, 2016, p. 28)

She goes on to identify the professionals found in every school or cluster of small schools: psychologist, social worker, study counsellor, dentist, nurse, speech therapist, and family counsellor:

> These professionals make up the child welfare team that is a cornerstone of Finnish education, and it is a legal requirement to have one in every school. In big schools, this group meet weekly for a two-hour meeting. During the first hour the group discuss a particular class with the class teacher — each class being discussed twice a year.

In one of the most substantial studies of disadvantaged and vulnerable young people in the UK, Sabates and Dex identify the most significant risk factors influencing the well-being and life chances of children and young people. The ten most significant of these include depression experienced by parents, alcohol abuse, domestic violence, financial stress, and basic skills.

Across Britain, using this model of social disadvantage: about 40% of children experience no risks; 30% one risk; 14% two risks; 7% three risks; 7% four risks; and 2% more than five risks. The impact of multiple risk factors is very clear:

> ... children exposed to two or more risks were likely to have higher average negative outcomes on all dimensions at age three and five than children exposed to fewer risks ... We can see a widening gap in cognitive development, hyperactivity, peer problems and prosocial behaviours for children with exposure to two or more risks compared to one or no risks between ages three and five.
>
> (Sabates and Dex, 2012, p. 18)

On this basis it seems reasonable to extrapolate that some 30% of children are growing up with some significant degree of risk. These are the children who are the most vulnerable and the most disadvantaged, not least because although their parents undoubtedly love them, those parents lack some of the knowledge, skills, and resilience necessary to thrive in a modern society. However, this level of disadvantage runs deeper and wider:

> Many children are brought up amid great conflict and end up lacking the social skills, such as the ability to trust and cooperate, that are helpful during adult life in modern societies. Others grow up in very secure and caring emotional atmosphere that leaves them ill-prepared for a world in which personal ambition, competition, wealth and position count for so much.
>
> (Wilkinson, 2005, p. 267)

Moreover, there can be little doubt that the Covid pandemic has exacerbated societal issues around well-being and mental health and points to the need for clearer strategies and interventions. Between 2017 and July 2020 rates of mental disorders affecting children's emotions, behaviour, and relationships are thought to have risen from one in nine to one in six.[8]

In a now famous TED talk titled 'What makes us sick? Look upstream' Rishi Manchanda — a general practitioner in a deprived part of Los Angeles — argued that, in effect, his patients came to see him not for medical problems but for social and economic reasons.[9] In other words, it was poverty, housing, crime, and unemployment that made people sick. Treat the causes, by going upstream, and you will cure the illness. Manchanda makes the case that we should not spend our energies rescuing children from a river that they have fallen into but should rather investigate why they are falling in, then prevent them doing so.

It seems blindingly obvious that it is far better to prevent than to cure. It might well be that the most powerful vaccination in childhood in terms of educational success is literacy; every child having a reading age that matches their chronological age would be an educational revolution of the highest magnitude. The well-being and educational success of the Scandinavian countries, as well as the Netherlands and Germany, is to a very significant degree rooted in the quality of early years provision. Well-being in childhood and adult life is largely a product of play and language development.

The evidence suggests, with varying degrees of confidence, that the well-being of all people, irrespective of their age or status, has a significant bearing on their potential for a long and healthy life, including engagement

8. NHS Digital's report is based on a survey of 3,570 children and young people up to the age of 22 who were interviewed in 2017 and followed up online in July 2020 during the Coronavirus pandemic. Available at: https://digital.nhs.uk/data-and-information/publications/statistical/mental-health-of-children-and-young-people-in-england/2020-wave-1-follow-up.

9. Manchanda, R. (2014), 'What makes us get sick? Look upstream'. Available at: https://www.ted.com/talks/rishi_manchanda_what_makes_us_get_sick_look_upstream.

with their community, positive social relationships, educational success, and positive mental health. In some ways it is easier to define 'well-being' by saying what it is not (leaving aside general proscriptions against negative definitions). It goes beyond wealth or economic security, as well as mental and physical health. It is also more than just positive relationships. We can define the well-being of students as the interaction of the following elements according to context and prevailing circumstances:

1. Pupils with better health and with significant levels of well-being are likely to achieve better academically.
2. Effective social and emotional competencies are associated with greater health and well-being, and better achievement.
3. The culture, ethos, and environment of a school influences the health and well-being of pupils and their readiness to learn.
4. A positive association exists between academic attainment and physical activity levels of pupils.

According to Alison Gopnik, parenting:

> ... isn't a goal-directed exercise aimed at shaping a child into a particular type of adult. Instead, being a parent is like making a garden. It's about providing a rich, stable, safe environment that allows many different types of flowers to bloom. It's about producing a robust, flexible ecosystem that lets children themselves create many varied, unpredictable kinds of adult futures.
>
> (Gopnik, 2016, p. 233),

It may be that schools need to shift their role away from being carpenters and more towards becoming gardeners if we are all to survive successfully and foster good levels of well-being in an unpredictable future. The best way to do that may be to build a stronger partnership with all parents at a very early stage and then see it through.

A failure of equity

Educational policy in many countries fails to engage with the needs of relatively disadvantaged children and young people because of the underlying subliminal assumptions influencing educational policy makers. In essence, the stereotypes and assumptions of educational policy in England replicate the world view of a Ladybird book of the 1950s — the nuclear family with a working father and a housewife mother, living in suburbia, with two children, a dog called Spot, and a cat called Tiddles.

Life in school is much more positive and potentially successful when it reflects the norms of life at home. Every facet of the stereotypical family and school reinforces a social divide based on language, social norms, economic security, geography, and a historical legacy of dependency and deference. In essence, less academically able middle-class children will eventually outperform academically gifted but socially disadvantaged children.

The negative aspects of social class are persistent and act as a reinforcing factor for all other variables. Yet any discussion of the potential to create a classless society is either naïve, disingenuous, or both. In fact, the most vocal in the aspiration for a classless society are usually the very beneficiaries of the system they seek to end:

> Geography is class. This is almost impossible to overstate: there is a widening gap of wealth and prospects between London and the south-east and the rest of the nation ... we can see it in mortality rates, shockingly: if you are a man living in Blackpool you will die, on average, nine years earlier than a man in Kensington. Overall, people in the north of England are 20 per cent more likely to die before seventy-five than those in the south. Or look at the smoking rates in pregnancy (a sign of education levels, or desperation levels, or self-preservation levels): in London it is two per cent, in Blackpool it is 27 per cent.
>
> (Abel, 2019, p. 316)

Abel's points are reinforced by the data emerging in England from the Coronavirus pandemic. At the time of writing the areas with the highest levels of Coronavirus infections were Sunderland (highest with 493.5 cases per 100k), Gateshead, South Tyneside, Middlesbrough, and Oldham. The areas with the lowest levels were Wiltshire, Devon, Cornwall, Dorset, North East Lincolnshire, and Rutland (lowest with 83.1 cases per 100k).[10]

10. This data can be referenced at https://www.ons.gov.uk/peoplepopulationandcommunity/healthandsocialcare/conditionsanddiseases/bulletins/coronaviruscovid19infectionsurveypilot/englandandwales4september2020#regional-analysis-of-the-number-of-people-in-england-who-had-covid-19.

The frequently voiced argument that social class has become irrelevant is manifestly untrue in a society where death rates are subject to wide polarization, together with regional accents, television viewing figures, holiday preferences, supermarket branding and, of course, educational achievement. The difference between north and south is one of the most significant characteristics of British society. It has proved to be stubborn and deeply resistant to change.

There seems little doubt that education in Britain, and England in particular, is dominated by a hierarchy in which the highest performance is available to the private schools where parents pay substantial amounts of money, often at great sacrifice, to guarantee both academic high performance and social advantage. The very best private schools provide optimum education both in academic and social terms. There is no doubt that the quality of teaching in many private schools is excellent — and so it should be.

> The concentration of the social composition enables private schools to sustain their peer-resource advantages, needed to maintain their level of academic and other successes. By coupling high-quality learning with luxury and the associated expense — something that became achievable in the modern era with rising income inequality since the end of the 1970s — the required social composition is maintained.
>
> (Kynaston & Green, 2019, p. 119)

However, they do this not just at significant financial cost, but also at great social cost in terms of the continuation of a system that exacerbates social difference and perpetuates the lack of equity across the whole of British society.

One piece of academic research has been particularly significant in understanding the impact of social inequality. Originally carried out by Leon Feinstein, it analysed the results of the 1970 Birth Cohort Study, which tracked the development of British children at 22 months, 42 months, and then 5 and 10 years.

Feinstein's conclusions were clear and unequivocal. Children's test scores at 22 months could predict, though not determine, educational qualifications at 26 years and were causally related to family background.

The children of educated or wealthy parents who scored poorly in the early tests had a tendency to catch up, whereas that was unlikely for the low-achieving children of worse-off parents. Early high-achievers from disadvantaged backgrounds were gradually overtaken by early poor-achievers from advantaged families.

> The Guardian journalist Polly Toynbee put it more baldly, contrasting the trajectories of the bright child from a poor home and a 'dim but rich' baby. The two children are already on a steep trajectory in opposite directions: the poor /bright one travelling fast downwards; the rich/dim one moving up as their social backgrounds counteract their inborn abilities.
>
> (Major & Machin, 2018, p. 92)

A significant challenge for the English education system is to develop strategies that minimise, if not eliminate, the negative effects of social class. In one sense this is almost impossible — the prevailing structure of British society is almost one thousand years old and to some extent still reflects the impact of the Norman invasion of 1066. But to move away from the triumph of rich but dim kids, learning must be seen as an aspect of life that is not related to social class, wealth, positional advantage, or inappropriate interest or influence.

What is very clear is that the proportion of private school pupils (7%) and grammar school pupils (5%) does not reflect the composition of the general school population. The academic performance of private schools, grammar schools, and the very best comprehensive schools is world class, but, sadly and unacceptably, this reflects a minority of the general population.

What is intriguing is that while in Britain the highest level of academic performance is the preserve of an elite minority, other education systems have exceptional performance without academic or financial selection. Finland and Estonia achieve high performance and social justice — equity is their defining characteristic. For most of Scandinavia, education is seen as a crucial component in the creation of a modern, liberal democracy with a commitment to social justice and social mobility.

Pasi Sahlberg explains the philosophy of education that laid the foundations for Finland's exceptional performance:

> This philosophy included the beliefs that all pupils can learn if they are given proper opportunities and support, that understanding and learning through human diversity is an important educational goal, and that all schools should function as small-scale democracies, just as John Dewey had insisted decades before. The new Peruskoulu (the nine-year comprehensive school) therefore required teachers to employ alternative instructional methods, design learning environments that enable differentiated learning for all pupils.
>
> (Sahlberg, 2014, p. 30)

There is a very real issue, given the way that educational policy works in England, that the pursuit of what we are terming deep learning for future sustainability for all might actually be corrupted into an elite programme for a few. Deep learning needs to be seen as a strategy to enhance the potential of *every* student as judged against a range of criteria that are primarily concerned with securing human potential.

A flawed approach to accountability

Education is just one of the areas where the social impact of poverty is demonstrated in practical terms, but the impact of poverty on children's potential and achievement is particularly direct and dramatic. There is a clear correlation between levels of poverty and success by a range of educational criteria. What is shocking is the fact that Britain is the sixth largest economy in the world and yet, as the figures show, child poverty is endemic across the UK.

- There were **4.1 million children** living in poverty in the UK in 2017–18. That's 30% of children, or **nine in a classroom of 30**.
- There are expected to be **5.2 million children** living in poverty in the UK by 2022.
- 47% of children living in **lone-parent families** are in poverty. Lone parents face a higher risk of poverty due to the lack of an additional earner, low rates of maintenance payments, gender inequality in employment and pay, and childcare costs.

- Children from **Black and minority ethnic groups** are more likely to be in poverty: 45% are now in poverty, compared with 26% of children in White British families.[11]

Social and economic deprivation is a key variable in many aspects of how education systems work and schools are seen to succeed. But the nature of the accountability mechanisms used will do much to determine the work of school leaders, the professional activities of teachers in responding to the needs of the poorest, and the subsequent experience of learners.

In England, Ofsted, the school inspectorate, may at last be beginning to show signs of acknowledging that the social and economic context of a school will have a significant impact on its potential to meet the standards used to make judgements of their performance. The following quotation comes from a blog by Sean Harford in 2019, when he was Ofsted's National Director, Education:

> Some will be disappointed to see that, so far, schools with more pupils from deprived backgrounds are still less likely to be judged good than those from more affluent backgrounds under the EIF, just as they were under the last framework. There's currently no clear difference in the proportion of schools judged outstanding in deprived areas, but the overall numbers are small.
>
> As I've discussed before ... schools in the poorest areas of the country face a steeper path to providing a good quality of education for their pupils. Aside from high numbers of pupils starting behind others, the recruitment and retention challenges facing all schools are even more acute in these places.[12]

There are a number of significant insights here. Firstly, the recognition of the 'steeper path'. Without pushing the analogy too hard, there is the world of difference between a stroll through the meadows and an uphill struggle built

11. Child Poverty Action Group Facts and Figures. Updated March 2019. All poverty figures are after housing costs. For current figures, see https://cpag.org.uk/child-poverty/child-poverty-facts-and-figures.

12. Harford, S. 'Our latest statistics: a first look at the EIF' (2019). Accessed at: https://educationinspection.blog.gov.uk/2019/12/16/our-latest-statistics-a-first-look-at-the-eif/.

up by years of neglect. Secondly, there is acknowledgement of the diversity of school intakes and the implications that this has for making judgements about performance. Comparative judgements based on a simplistic assumption of homogeneity are no way to work towards challenging the lack of equity in the school system and across society in general. However, an outcome-orientated model of accountability in a culture of performativity, such as we have in England, fails to recognise the most significant variables in terms of making judgements about relative success.

The OECD report *Equity in Education* (2018, p. 30) points to significant disparities in performance from childhood to early adulthood and offers three key lessons:

> First, evidence of large differences early on suggests that initial learning and development are largely influenced by factors related to family background and early environments, including early education and primary schooling.
>
> Second, the evolution of these inequalities, particularly between primary and secondary school, underscores the crucial role that schools, teachers, and education policies and practices can play in narrowing the gaps and equalising opportunities for all students.
>
> Third, a number of countries have unique profiles that do not fit into the average patterns, for example in England, where inequalities in performance grow markedly between adolescence and early adulthood.

The implications of these judgements from OECD would seem to suggest a focus on the social context in the early years, a need to work for greater integration between primary and secondary education, and an impetus to work to minimise variation in secondary education. For despite all of the policies and research and the professionalism and commitment of thousands of teachers and school leaders:

> By the time they finish primary school, only 51% of disadvantaged pupils reach the expected standard in reading, writing and mathematics. This compares with 71% of all other pupils. At 16, the gaps have widened. Only 25% of disadvantaged pupils get a good pass in English and Maths GCSE, compared to 50% of all other pupils. Similar gaps exist under other headline measures, such as

> Progress 8, Attainment 8 and the Ebac average point score. At 18, and particularly at A-level, there is still a significant gap, which continues into students' post-18 destinations.
>
> (Social Mobility Commission, 2020, p. 35)

Yet data such as this is used to make judgements about school success, as well as about individuals in those schools, as if this was all happening on a level playing field.

We have fallen into the trap of valuing what we can most easily *measure* rather than seeking ways to measure what we truly *value*. We have come to use the data by which we misguidedly try to measure success to make apparently firm statements rather than ask powerful questions. This in turn has led us to an overly narrow focus of purpose for schools, located more in the past with a nod to the present but insufficiently broad and flexible to meet the future. As Stephen Gorard observed as far back as 2009:

> School effectiveness is associated with a narrow understanding of what education is for. It encourages, unwittingly, an emphasis on assessment and test scores — and teaching to the test — because over time we tend to get the system we measure for and so privilege.
>
> (Gorard, 2009, p. 759)

This is part of a growing wider critique of our understanding of assessment and accountability, perhaps summarised most engagingly in this quote from William T. Randolph, Commissioner of Education, Colorado:

> To solely use standardised achievement tests is like casting a net into the sea — a net that is intentionally designed to let the most interesting fish get away. Then, to describe the ones that are caught strictly in terms of their weight and length is to radically reduce what we know about them. To further conclude that all the contents of the sea consist of fish like those in the net compounds the error further. We need more kinds of fish. We need to know more about those we catch. We need new nets.[13]

13. For a wider critique of systems of assessment see www.rethinkingassessment.com; W. T. Randolph quoted in Project Zero, Perspectives on *"Assessment Reimagined" from Project Zero's first 50 Years*. Available at: pz.harvard.edu/sites/default/files/AssessmentReimagined_Booklet_0.pdf.

Time to face the future

If we are seriously to send a message of hope into the future through our children, then we need to address these three areas of deficiency, (a neglect of family, a failure of equity and a flawed accountability) and we need to learn lessons fast about how to change. Those lessons lie first and foremost in fostering a sense of community that will support the whole development of children and young people.

> A community identifies itself by an understood mutuality of interests. But it lives and acts by the common virtues of trust, goodwill, forbearance, self-restraint, compassion, and forgiveness. If it hopes to continue long as a community, it will wish to — and will have to — encourage respect for all its members, human and natural.
>
> (Berry, 1992, p. 119)

High quality family lives combined with economic security are significant factors in terms of optimizing social and academic success. But what really compounds the potential for success is the multiplier effect of community. Social capital, expressed through community, creates disproportionate advantage.

> Our survival hinges on social interaction, and that is not only true of the murky evolutionary past ... social integration — the feeling of being part of a cohesive group — fosters immunity and resilience. How accepted and supported we feel affects the biological pathways that skew the biological expression of a disease.
>
> (Pinker, 2015, p. 57)

There are numerous ways of defining the relationship between community/ social capital, education systems, and personal success. The following list would be recognised by most people working in this area:

- High quality, authentic relationships.
- A shared sense of place and common identity.
- Agreed norms and consensual values.
- Democratic and liberal ethos.
- A culture of learning and development.

There is every reason to argue for a causal relationship between social capital and educational success, however defined. There is every reason to have high confidence in the proposition that community is one of the most significant variables that has the potential to make a disproportionate impact on educational achievement. Social capital expressed through community engagement and authentic relationships makes a genuine difference. As Robert Putnam suggests:

> child development is powerfully shaped by social capital ... trust, networks, and norms of reciprocity within a child's family, school, peer group, and larger community have wide-ranging effects on the child's opportunities and choices and, hence, on behaviour and development …
>
> (Putnam, 2000, p. 296)

A study carried out by Ohio State University found that social capital had a three-to-five-times larger effect than financial capital on reading and Maths scores in Michigan schools. The research found a direct correlation between the level of social capital and a school's performance irrespective of levels poverty, ethnicity, and prior achievement:

> Results showed that on average schools that spent more money did have better test scores than those that spent less. But the effect of social capital was three times larger than financial capital on math scores and five times larger on reading scores.
>
> Social capital was not only more important to learning than instructional expenditures, but also more important than the schools' poverty, ethnic make-up or prior achievement.[14]

The research also found a direct correlation between teacher collaboration and improving test scores — demonstrating the potential for improving performance through building social capital internally in a school and, in turn, through collaborative working.

14. UkEdChat (2022), 'Why relationships — not money — are the key to improving schools'. Available at: https://ukedchat.com/20/1810/26/relationships-key-improving-schools.

Cultural capital is closely allied to social capital and serves as a passport to secure an entry into desirable social contexts. In the organisations we work in and the communities we live in …

> … we wheel around in circles which distinguish us from some and align us with others. This basic insight was elaborated by the French sociologist Pierre Bourdieu about the power of what he called 'cultural capital'. He claims that certain kinds of culture have the prospect of generating social advantage and are hence forms of 'capital'.
>
> (Savage, 2015, p. 97)

The process of 'wheeling around in circles' is how we develop and validate a sense of self and engage with, seek recognition from, and align ourselves with others. It provides both personal legitimation and, crucially, the authority to engage. At one level this is distinguishing categories such as napkins and serviettes, or pudding, sweet, and dessert, and at another it is having the vocabulary and the social signifiers to enter elites of various types.

However banal some of these signifiers, we should have no doubt about their practical impact. The Ofsted *School Inspection Handbook* links personal success to 'knowledge and cultural capital', suggesting clearly that knowledge on its own is not enough:

> As part of making the judgement about the quality of education, inspectors will consider the extent to which schools are equipping pupils with the knowledge and cultural capital they need to succeed in life. Our understanding of 'knowledge and cultural capital' is derived from the following wording in the national curriculum …
>
> It is the essential knowledge that pupils need to be educated citizens, introducing them to the best that has been thought and said and helping to engender an appreciation of human creativity and achievement.
>
> (Ofsted, 2019, p. 206)

Cultural capital is the accumulation of knowledge, behaviours, and skills that a person can tap into to demonstrate their cultural competence, and thus their social status or standing. High capital may create a sense of entitlement and authority. Low capital can result in vulnerability or a sense of social inadequacy. It is one of the most significant variables explaining social mobility or its absence. It explains why some people will never achieve high rank in the armed forces and others will never be called to the bar and a lot about those who will achieve fame in the broadcast media. Goleman (2006) argued that Emotional Intelligence (EQ) is more important than IQ. In fact, EQ is just another manifestation of cultural capital.

Cultural capital is made up of a range of personal qualities, behaviours, knowledge, and skills. For example, in terms of language there are a range of cultural manifestations such as the size and scope of a working vocabulary, the use of words and phrases that are idiomatic to a particular community, the accent and vocabulary used, and the social responses of the participants in a conversation. These elements serve a dual purpose in providing a means of defining social differences, thereby helping to set an agenda for social mobility and aspiration.

For such reasons, some parents will go to great lengths to attempt to secure social mobility for their children by sending them to fee-paying schools or living in the catchment area of a very high performing grammar or comprehensive school. What is significant is that the most academically successful maintained schools perform on a par with the independent sector in terms of GCSE and A level performance. The financial expenditure on independent education in England is largely to secure cultural capital — the networks and relationships, the language and, perhaps more than anything else, confidence and a sense of entitlement to success.

> The desire for the 'right' peer group can often be dissected into two strands, one to do with social class the other with academic or intellectual development. Some appear to want their children to grow up in a refined and segmented corner of society, and to have an exclusive entrée to the world of high-flying dreams and influences, replete with the expectation of — sense of entitlement to — high achievement …
>
> (Kynaston & Green, 2019, p. 133)

Our challenge if we are to really face the future is to draw on this same strength of aspiration but bend it towards a different purpose, not for social mobility and personal advancement but for the future of humankind together.

Schools, because of their loss of focus on community, and because of the barriers to learning within the wider system, are part of the problem we have to solve. But schools also, if they can understand and start to tackle these issues, carry the seeds of the solution. This is where we place our focus in this book. That is not to say school can meet this challenge on their own, but rather to argue they have an important part to play.

Whether schools can make the necessary changes is first and foremost within the power of educators. It is about rebalancing school and community. And it is about rebalancing our focus on the past and the present with a greater focus on the demands of the difficult future which we are necessarily having to pass on as our inheritance. It is time for schools to really face the future and to send it a different message through our children

Opportunity for self-reflection and collaborative review

- *Do you agree that schools are 'part of the problem'?*
- *To what extent are you a carpenter or a gardener? Why have you adopted this stance?*
- *What meaningful steps to make your school more ready to face the future would you prioritise to take meaningful steps to address the three systemic weaknesses of neglect of family, failure of equity, and flawed accountability in your own context?*

CHAPTER 3

DEEP LEARNING FOR A SUSTAINABLE FUTURE

A future-building school is a school that takes seriously its responsibility to equip its students for the future. It recognises that the old measures of future success — the accumulation of certificates, exams, positions on league tables — are no longer adequate to the task of driving a school's contribution to its students' and its community's well-being. Instead, it takes on the more exciting, albeit more challenging, task of creating a meaningful debate with students and communities about the futures that are in development and the futures that they might want.

Keri Facer (2011, p. 107)

What do we mean by a more sustainable future?

There can be no single prescriptive notion for this, but we do need some frame of common reference. The UN Sustainable Development Goals provide an important starting point.[15] However, we have chosen for simplicity and visual understanding to adopt here the complementary image of a doughnut drawn by economist Kate Raworth (see Figure 1).

15. United Nations, Department of Economic and Social Affairs (2015), 'Sustainable Development Goals'. Available at: https://sdgs.un.org/goals.

She uses this doughnut image to illustrate her notion of establishing 'a safe and just space for all' as the basis for a new economics (Raworth, 2017, p.38). The doughnut pictures a future that can provide for every person's needs while safeguarding the living world on which we all depend.

Figure 1: Kate Raworth's image of a doughnut economy

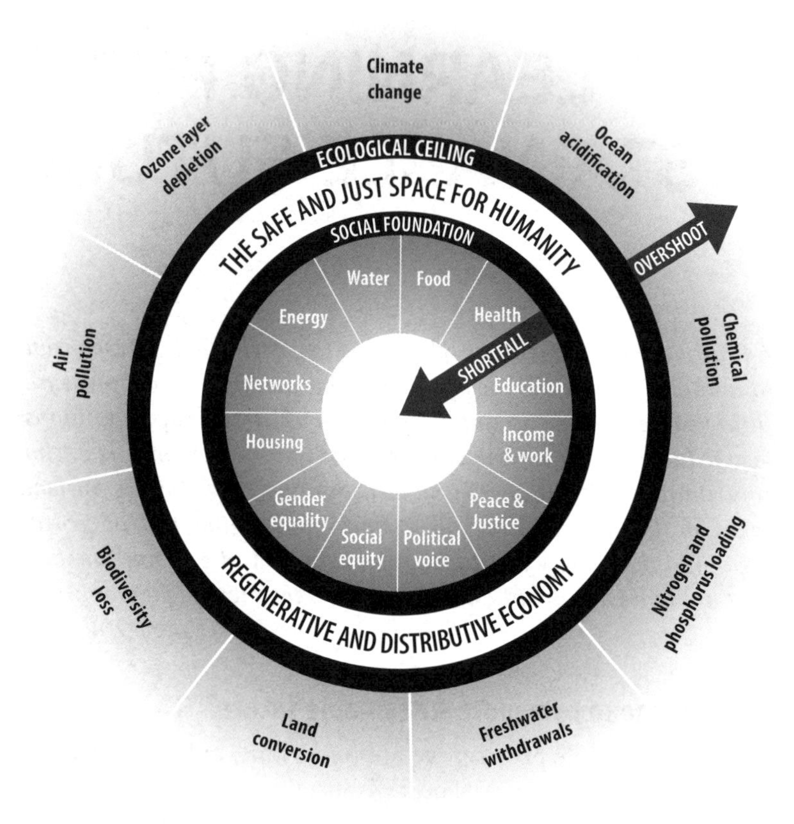

This means addressing both the ecological ceiling that we are at the moment overshooting as well as providing a proper social foundation for every individual. As we have already seen in chapter 2, this foundation is also something in which our society, and the contribution of schools, is currently falling far short.

The doughnut is a vision of the economics we need for a sustainable future. We suggest an equivalent vision is needed for schools, an educational sustainably safe and just place for all, if you like a form of Doughnut Education. In this chapter we will try to develop an outline of such a model.

Education, like much of the public sector in Britain, has been subject to a succession of often contradictory policy changes. There are very few examples of sustained, integrated, and logically coherent policy-making. The period since 1945 can rather be seen as an era of disjointed incrementalism — the antithesis of coherent planning.

> The moment has come, especially for those living in wealthy nations, to recognise a disturbing truth: that we have colonised the future. We treat the future like a distant colonial outpost devoid of people, where we can freely dump ecological degradation, technological risk and nuclear waste and which we can plunder as we please.
>
> (Krznaric, 2020, p. 6)

In sharp contradistinction to these colonists of the future, incurring debts that will never be paid off, literally mortgaging the future, there are those who take a longer view, recognising with Greta Thunberg that 'it will take cathedral thinking to tackle the climate crisis'.

What does 'cathedral thinking' mean? The cathedral nearest to where John lives, Lincoln, was started in 1072, and in spite of spires collapsing, fire, earthquake, poor design and workmanship, the cathedral remains one of the glories of the Middle Ages. The Victorian critic John Ruskin declared:

> I have always held ... that the cathedral of Lincoln is out and out the most precious piece of architecture in the British Isles.

Like a great deal of its contemporary architecture, Lincoln Cathedral has been work in progress for almost a thousand years. The stonemasons of Lincoln knew that there was no possibility that they would ever see their work completed. They provide a powerful antidote to our prevailing short-termism, U turns, and the instant gratification of much policy-making. We are not advocating a time frame of 1000 years: 25–30 would be good, if only we had that amount of time left. Although we are looking to a long-term future, we have to get started very quickly indeed!

Our view of learning to that end is based on three central propositions. Firstly, learning involves understanding, not just factual recall. Secondly, knowing is not enough. It must also develop personal attributes and values which make one disposed to consider the common as well as the personal good. Thirdly, caring must lead to the ability to act on and to apply what is being learned, both individually and collectively. In summary, and by way of shorthand, we will term these elements *understanding*, *character*, and *agency*. Together, they can make possible deep learning for future sustainability.

The foundations of deep learning

It is difficult to establish a precise genealogical tree for the emergence of deep learning as a concept. The website www.deeplearning.net in 2015 defined deep learning as:

> ... a new area of Machine Learning research, which has been introduced with the objective of moving Machine Learning closer to one of its original goals: Artificial Intelligence.

Although there will almost certainly come a time when Machine Learning, and deep learning in this sense, are important in designing learning strategies for use in schools, that is not our current focus here (although chapter 10 does explore in part the link between learning and the increasingly widespread development and adoption of artificial intelligence in computing).

Renate and Geoffrey Caine were early advocates of brain-based learning, and drew direct links between personal engagement and understanding and awareness of neurological functioning:

> The search for meaning is innate: The brain's/mind's search for meaning is very personal. The greater the extent to which what we learn is tied to personal, meaningful experiences, the greater and deeper our learning will be.
>
> (Caine & Caine, 1994, p. 96)

According to Sims (2006), the term 'deep learning' first came into common usage in the 1980s, when Marton, et al. (1984) published research that distinguished between deep and surface learning. They identified the following characteristics:

Surface approach: Intention: to cope with course requirements.

- Studying without reflecting on purpose or strategy.
- Treating the course as unrelated bits of knowledge.
- Memorising facts and procedures routinely.
- Finding difficulty in making sense of new ideas presented.
- Feeling undue pressure and worry about work.

Deep approach: Intention: to understand ideas for yourself:

- Relating idea to previous knowledge and experience.
- Looking for patterns and underlying principles.
- Checking evidence and relating it to conclusions.
- Examining logic and argument cautiously and critically.
- Becoming actively interested in course content.

Most of these components will appear in different guises and more detailed definitions throughout this book. Their relevance for schools is reinforced by Bowring-Carr and West-Burnham (1997, p. 77):

> The problem for schools is to move from shallow to deep learning. So much of what we learn in school impinges on us as a person not one whit. Students imbibe vast quantities of 'facts' and live their lives entirely unaffected by them. Their learning is not only shallow, it is also symbolic; it is needed to pass on to the next stage, at which point it is forgotten or rejected.

Ken Leithwood and his colleagues provide a detailed and systematic account of the relationship between learning and understanding:

> At the deepest levels, understanding of an important theory or work of art should change the way we perceive and experience the world. It should become part of our personality rather than only something we can bring to mind in appropriate contexts.
>
> (Leithwood et al., 2006, p. 15)

A more recent significant initiative for deep learning in education is the *New Pedagogies for Deep Learning* initiative. In their book describing this, Michael Fullan and colleagues argue that deep learning is made up of six C's:

1. **Collaboration.** The ability to work interdependently and collaboratively with others, with strong interpersonal and team-related skills.
2. **Creativity.** Being able to weigh up opportunities in an entrepreneurial manner and ask the right questions to generate new ideas.
3. **Critical thinking.** Being able to evaluate information and arguments and identify patterns and connections to construct meaningful knowledge and apply it in the real world.
4. **Citizenship.** The ability to consider issues based on a deep understanding of diverse values and a worldview, as well as a sincere interest to solve complex real-world problems.
5. **Character.** Traits such as grit, tenacity, perseverance, and resilience; as well as the ability to make learning an integral part of living.
6. **Communication.** Being able to communicate effectively through a variety of methods and tools (including digital) to a range of different audiences.

(Fullan et al., 2018, pp. 16–17)

The development of these competencies is seen as the key to transforming education, rather than 'trappings and structures' and 'policies and mandates'. This approach might be described as transformation through empowerment — placing deep learning at the heart of all educational endeavours.

The reality of course for many learners is that their education is too often a succession of largely irrelevant facts that are forgotten and rejected but are given a significance and status that is rapidly lost. Millis (2014) provides a clear example of how to distinguish shallow and deep learning:

> ... Surface learners study the material superficially and uncritically, searching for facts — often unconnected and unquestioned — that

> they can commit to memory. Not surprisingly, students who study this way rarely retain the material or understand its genuine meanings ...
>
> *In contrast ... deep learners read for both comprehension and understanding, seeking to integrate conceptual ideas. These learners connect the new knowledge with relevant prior knowledge.*
>
> (Millis, 2014, p. 143)

Surface or shallow learners will either lack engagement and be seen as 'difficult' or 'lacking interest' and 'poorly behaved,' or will be almost totally focused on the detail and minutiae of so-called facts. For some it is much more gratifying to organise data and information rather than struggle to create understanding and knowledge. By way of contrast, Michael Fullan and his colleagues offered a powerful practical insight into the impact of deep learning:

> Stop by a deep learning classroom and you will see students who are voraciously curious and who are encouraged to ask questions ... There is a constant buzz of conversation as students grapple with solving problems or investigating ideas ... you will find students who are able to articulate what they are doing and why.
>
> (Fullan et al., 2018, p. 15)

Throughout this book we aim to develop a model of an approach to learning that sees such deep learning as the necessary and optimum aspiration in education, in contrast to the prevailing emphasis in much schooling on surface or shallow learning. We believe this has the potential to be one of the most significant contributions a school can make to securing a sustainable, safe, and just future for all.

Shallow learning of course has its place in any model of learning, but it is not sufficient. It is seriously limited in describing the full extent of human potential. The issue here is that however valuable shallow learning is, it does not:

> ... in any fundamental way alter our outlook on the world. It does not make us better people. Every once in a while, something does break through. We encounter a powerful idea or read a powerful book or hear a powerful piece of music that changes us, that radiates through our whole person ... Needless to say, such education would not be

> imposed on the learner. It would make contact with the deepest wellsprings of the learner's thought and feeling; natural processes would take it from there.
>
> (Leithwood et al., 2005, p. 15)

Deep learning cannot be taught — it has to be learned using a range of strategies and techniques (we will discuss some of the most important later in part two). It takes us into greater knowledge and understanding than we would normally encounter. It is about wisdom and insight, the higher manifestations of creativity and artistry. Deep learning helps us understand personal authenticity and spirituality, but it is also reflected in exceptional performance in the arts and sport, as well as mastery in a wide range of contexts.

Our discussion of deep learning has so far drawn out its prime characteristic of understanding and insight. But if we are to achieve future sustainability in our world, this quality needs to be balanced with two further complementary elements which are also developed in the deep learner. *Understanding* has to be linked to both moral purpose and to action, or as we are choosing to put it: *character* and to *agency*.

Character

The last decade in English education has seen a resurgence of interest in the notion of character education. One leading advocate, the Jubilee Centre for Character and Virtue at the University of Birmingham, defines character education as 'all the explicit and implicit educational activities that help young people to develop positive personal character strengths or virtues'.[16]

Examples of positive personal character strengths, or virtues, include honesty, resilience, courage, perseverance, and compassion (see Figure 2). The aim of character education is to equip children and young people to lead flourishing lives, by supporting them to develop these traits.

Their Framework draws from Aristotle's discussion of the development of a moral person in the *Nicomachean Ethics*, as summarised in its most

16. The Jubilee Centre (2013), *A Framework for Character Education*. Available at: https://www.jubileecentre.ac.uk/527/character-education/framework/.

well-known form by twentieth-century American philosopher, Will Durant:

> Excellence is an art won by training and habituation. We do not act rightly because we have virtue or excellence, but we rather have those because we have acted rightly. We are what we repeatedly do. Excellence, then, is not an act but a habit.
>
> (Durant, 1961, p. 87)

Figure 2: The Jubilee Centre model of character education

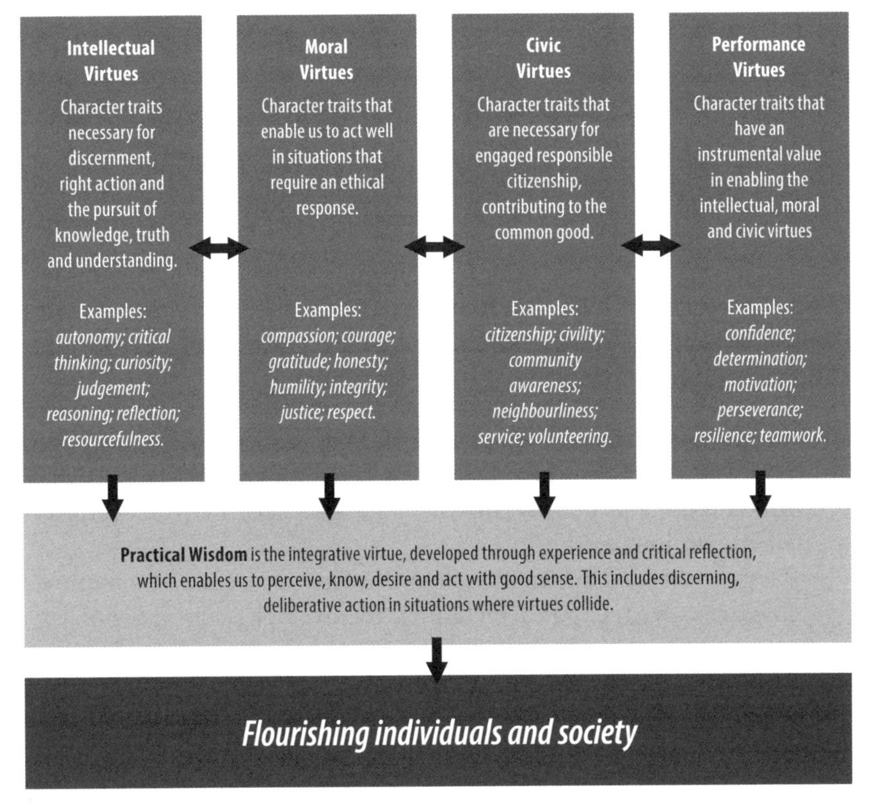

It goes on to include 'A Neo-Aristotelian Model of Moral Development' (Figure 3), which depicts possible pathways to 'becoming virtuous' through the Aristotelian lens of habituation, foregrounding the importance of early family upbringing.

Figure 3: The Jubilee Centre neo-Aristotelian model of moral development

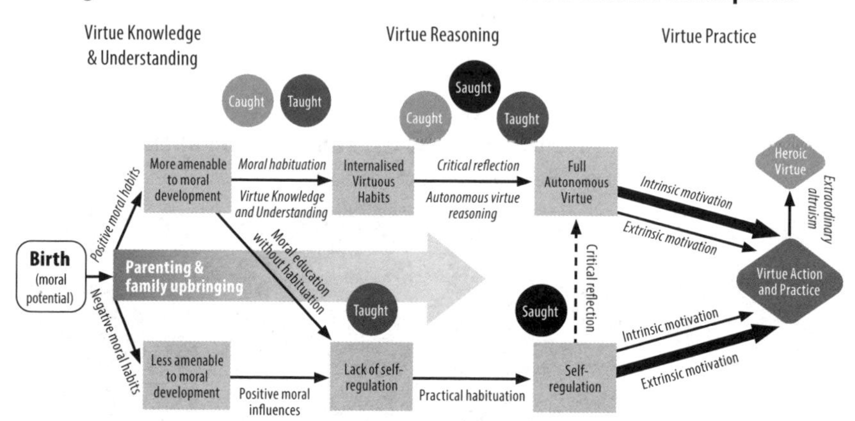

England's Department for Education, heavily influenced by the Jubilee Centre approach, has identified four important aspects of character, which they believe can inform the way schools shape their wider provision for children and young people:

- The ability to remain motivated by long-term goals, to see a link between effort in the present and pay-off in the longer-term, overcoming and persevering through, and learning from, setbacks when encountered.
- The learning and habituation of positive moral attributes, sometimes known as 'virtues', and including, for example, courage, honesty, generosity, integrity, humility, and a sense of justice, alongside others.
- The acquisition of social confidence and the ability to make points or argumentsclearly and constructively, listen attentively to the views of others, behave with courtesy and good manners and speak persuasively to an audience.

- An appreciation of the importance of long-term commitments which frame the successful and fulfilled life; for example to spouse, partner, role or vocation, the local community, to faith, or world view.[17]

Research does indeed suggest that there are enabling character traits which can improve educational attainment, engagement with school, and attendance. A 2013 literature review for the Education Endowment Foundation and the Cabinet Office carried out by Gutman and Schoon found that:

- High self-efficacy, or self-belief, is associated with better performance, more persistence and greater interest in work.
- Highly motivated children (linked to tenacity), driven internally and not by extrinsic rewards, show greater levels of persistence and achievement.
- Good self-control (or self-regulation, the ability to delay gratification) is associated with greater attainment levels.
- Having good coping skills (part of being able to bounce back) is associated with greater well-being.

However, Jerome and Kisby (2019) argue character education, as conceived here by central government, is about seizing control of how a school promotes values. They make the point that it treats the good person and the good citizen as synonymous, and they highlight the work of the philosopher John Rawls in trying to shift the question of 'How should I live?' to 'How can we live together in society given that there are different answers to the question how should I live'.

The focus of character education is, for them, fixed on personal rather than public ethics, and with addressing moral or political issues at the level of the individual rather than at any other level. This, they argue, is problematic. It is a weak way of understanding the world and places sole responsibility on individuals for their position in society. As Kohn (1997) has suggested it is about trying 'fix the kids' rather than advocating

17. Department for Education (2019), *Character Education Framework*. Available at: https://www.gov.uk/government/publications/character-education-framework.

structural changes to the broader social environment in which they find themselves.

It would be fair to point out that the Jubilee Centre framework above (Figure 2) goes some way to address this concern by recognising the place of civic virtues, though perhaps also these still require a wider and more active and political component. That is why we believe it is helpful and necessary to give equal weight to the notion of agency as our third component of deep learning for future sustainability.

Agency

We have chosen the word agency deliberately as distinct from perhaps apparently similar concepts such as voice or participation. Agency is about equipping young people to understand and shape their futures, both individually and collectively. It is about working with intentionality and deliberately accepting responsibility in making choices. Of course, this assumes that human beings are self-organising, proactive, self-managing and reflective, and that their behaviour is intentional — focused on desired outcomes. Developing agency is therefore very much focused on cultural capital, being comfortable with making choices, and learning from the process.

However, agency, and more specifically student or learner agency, can mean different things in different cultures. For example, in Japan, agency is commonly used in the context of collectivity, where maintaining harmony within communities is more important than an individual's opinion. In China, the concept of agency refers to the traditional values of prioritising harmony within groups and the individual's obligation to contribute to the country's growth. In South Africa, the interpretation of student agency is grounded in the notion of *Ubuntu*, that 'a person is a person through other people'.

The OECD *Learning Compass 2030* views student agency as rooted in the principle that students have the ability and the will to positively influence their own lives and the world around them. Student agency is thus defined as the capacity to set a goal, reflect, and act responsibly to effect change. It is about:

> acting rather than being acted upon; shaping rather than being shaped; and making responsible decisions and choices rather than accepting those determined by others.
>
> (OECD, 2019, p. 4)

Importantly, agency is not presented here as a synonym for student autonomy. The document is explicit that students need support from adults in order to exercise their agency and realise their potential. Agency involves recognising interdependence as well as independence.

OECD qualifies this definition further with a number of helpful additions. Among these they argue that student agency is not a personality trait; it is something malleable and learnable. Furthermore, agency can be exercised in nearly every context: moral, social, economic, and creative. For example, students need to use moral agency to help them make decisions that recognise the rights and needs of others. A well-developed sense of agency can help individuals achieve long-term goals and overcome adversity. However, students also need foundational cognitive, social, and emotional skills so that they can apply agency to their own — and society's — benefit. While a sense of agency can help students overcome adversity, disadvantaged students need carefully designed support to build foundation skills, such as literacy and numeracy, as well as social and emotional skills.

Developing agency is both a learning goal and a learning process. In education systems that encourage student agency, learning involves not only instruction and evaluation but also co-construction. Co-agency is when teachers and students become co-creators in the teaching — and — learning process. The concept of co-agency recognises that students, teachers, parents, and communities work together to help students progress towards their shared goals. Teachers play a key role in designing a learning environment that values agency, but students are also agents in their learning and play an active role in deciding what and how they will learn. Pupils then tend to show greater motivation to learn and are more likely to define objectives for their learning.

In the traditional teaching model, teachers are expected to deliver knowledge through instruction and evaluation. In a system that encourages student agency, learning involves not only instruction and evaluation but also co-construction. For teachers to be effective co-agents, they need 'the capacity to act purposefully and constructively to direct their professional growth and contribute to the growth of their students and colleagues' (OECD 2019b, p. 8). In order to achieve this, teachers need support, including in initial teacher education and professional development, in designing learning environments that support student agency.

In 2018, the OECD Student Focus Group — students from 10 countries who had volunteered to help steer the development of the *Learning Compass 2030*, and were selected by their respective countries to do so — created the 'sun model of co-agency'. It draws on the ladder view of participation developed by Hart (1992), but importantly the students changed the visualisation from a ladder to a sun (see Figure 4), as they determined that agency is better represented by a circular image than a linear one.

They also wanted to show that in every degree of co-agency, students work with adults. The exception is the newly added degree of 'silence' (or 0), where neither young people nor adults believe that young people can contribute, and young people remain silent while adults initiate all activities and make all decisions. In contrast, in the first three degrees of co-agency ('manipulation', 'decoration', and 'tokenism'), students believe that they could contribute to decision making, but they are not given the opportunity to do so. The stronger the degree of co-agency, the better the outcomes for the well-being of both students and adults.

Figure 4: The OECD sun model of co-agency

The light is brightest when we shine together

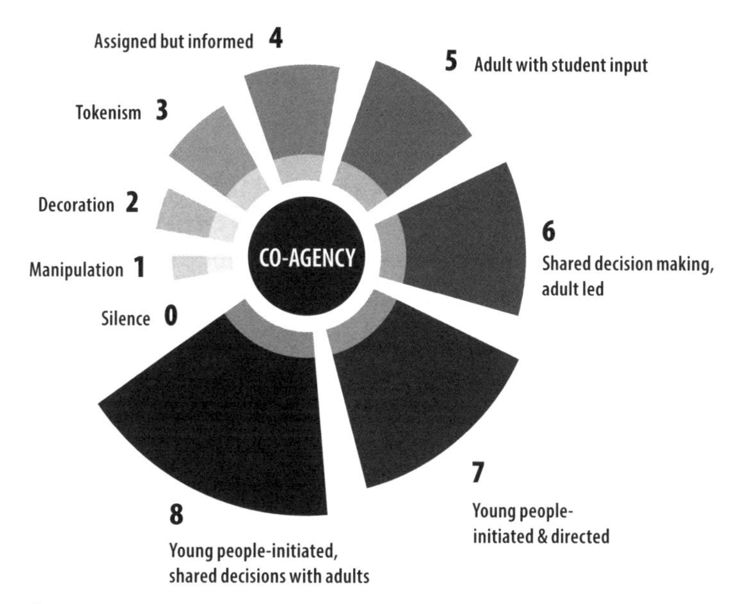

Table 1. Degrees of co-agency

0. Silence	Neither young people nor adults believe that young people can contribute, and young people remain silent while adults take and lead all initiatives and make all decisions.
1. Manipulation	Adults use young people to support causes, pretending the initiative is from young people.
2. Decoration	Adults use young people to help or bolster a cause.
3. Tokenism	Adults appear to give young people a choice, but there is little or no choice about the substance and way of participation.
4. Assigned but informed	Young people are assigned a specific role and informed about how and why they are involved, but do not take part in leading or taking decisions for the project or their place in it.
5. Adult led with student input	Young people are consulted on the projects designed, and informed about outcomes, while adults lead them and make the decisions.
6. Shared decision making, adult led	Young people are a part of the decision-making process of a project led and initiated by adults.
7. Young people-initiated and directed	Young people initiate and direct a project with support of adults. Adults are consulted and may guide/advise in decision making, but all decisions are ultimately taken by young people.
8. Young people-initiated, shared decisions with adults	Young people initiate a project and the decision making is shared between young people and adults. Leading and running the project is an equal partnership between young people and adults.

This sun model is an interesting and more organic representation of participation and agency, moving away from the more hierarchical and rigid concept of a ladder. There are perhaps additional perspectives to include that would require a more three-dimensional model. These would involve balancing individual and collective agency. Collective agency refers to the idea of individual agents acting together for a community, a movement or a global society. In contrast with co-agency, collective agency is exercised on a larger scale and includes shared responsibility, a sense of belonging, identity, purpose, and achievement. Many complex challenges, including climate change, demand collective responses. This means that individuals put their differences and tensions aside and come together to achieve a common goal.

A further dimension would relate to agency within the school and beyond the school. School is not the only place where children learn. Educating children is a responsibility properly shared among parents, teachers, and the wider community. When the community is also involved in education, children can learn about the opportunities for their future and also how to be engaged, responsible citizens, while the community can learn about the needs, concerns, and views of its younger members.

Towards a Doughnut Model of Education

In chapter 1 we set out the urgent challenges facing humankind and resulting need for real change in the way that we and future generations live. Schools have a significant role in helping to make that achievable. In chapter 2 we described the systemic weaknesses within the education system that are hindering this quest for a just and sustainable education for all. We have argued that schools have become, often in response to wider pressures placed on them, too focused on shallow learning. The challenge now for school leaders is to shift thinking and practice towards deeper learning geared for future sustainability.

We try to capture the shifts we are describing in our own version of a doughnut (Figure 5), moving from the systemic barriers and shallow water at the centre towards the deeper learning necessary for a just and sustainable education for all. To do that will involve addressing the three systemic weaknesses identified in chapter 1, but also, utilising the three drivers of deep learning described in chapter 2 — understanding, character and agency. And an education fit for the future, a Doughnut Education, needs to focus on all three.

For schools to face the future honestly they have to be confident enough to make significant steps in this direction, even within the present system constraints in which they operate. We provide detailed examples of change happening in three schools in chapter 8 and seek to show how the impetus for change can be developed more widely in chapters 9 and 10.

Figure 5: Towards a model of doughnut education — deep learning for future sustainability

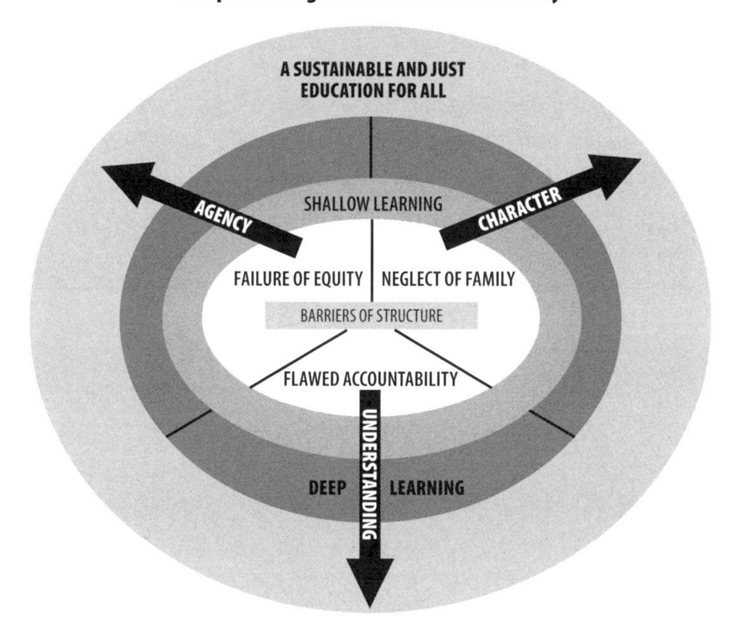

Of course, at a system level a similar move is required to support this shift. Across the school system a focus on shallow learning is closely associated with the three barriers to learning identified in chapter 2. It leads to a flawed accountability system, such as we have in England. It results in a neglect of family and community, and it leads to a lack of equity for learners, with too many left behind, not because of their circumstances but because of the systemic failure to recognise and respond appropriately to them. These structural barriers need to be addressed if we are to create a sustainable and just education for all. However, the key to such a future lies not just in a renewed systemic focus but, more importantly and urgently, in tangible action at a school level. It requires school leaders to now focus with clarity and purpose on deepening learning, which is powered by those three key drivers of understanding, character, and agency, for all students.

Opportunity for self-reflection and collaborative review

- *Reflect on the shallow-deep, three driver model of Doughnut Education. Does your own experience as a learner confirm or question this model?*
- *Reflect on your own experience of deep learning — what are the key variables that enable learning for understanding, character, and agency?*
- *What are the barriers to securing deep learning at school level? What can be done through collaborative working?*

PART TWO

WHAT LEARNING?

THOUGHT PIECE: Marcelo Staricoff — Hertford Infant and Nursery School

Discovering the joy of learning

When I was appointed to my first headship at Hertford Infant and Nursery School in January 2009, I was very keen to develop a whole-school approach to teaching and learning based on what I now to refer to as 'The Joy of Not Knowing' or JONK™ approach (Staricoff, 2021).[18] I wanted to see if we could exploit the pedagogical principles and philosophy of the Early Years throughout the school.

The Joy of Not Knowing approach focuses on explicitly teaching children the value and importance of realising that in order to learn something new they must not know it first, and on then setting up a whole school infrastructure that equips learners with all the values, dispositions, skills and strategies to enable them to develop an intrinsic motivation and enthusiasm to want to learn, evolving as successful individuals, lifelong learners and global citizens with a deep and lifelong love of learning. Teaching learners how to enjoy not knowing lies at the heart of this.

When we started to move towards the JONK philosophy, the school's combined measure of attainment, which was then measured as the Average Point Score (APS) was 14.6. In consecutive years this increased to 15.6, 15.9, 16.2, and 16.6. In 2013, the school achieved a score of 17.0+ for the first time — 17.3 in reading. As a significant proportion of the intake traditionally join the school below national expectations, these standards demonstrated to us that the children were making excellent progress and that the school was adding significant value to their lives.

18. Staricoff, M. (2021), *The Joy of Not Knowing.* See also: https://www.jonklearning.co.uk/.

Our approach places great emphasis on the partnership with families and links to the community. The school became over-subscribed and, four years into the process, the school welcomed a new cohort of Reception children entirely made up of first choice preferences for the first time in its history. Attendance also increased from 91.4% to 94.1% in these four years.

When the school was inspected in the third year of the process, it was judged to be outstanding overall in each of the four areas, again for the first time ever. Inspectors spoke very positively not just of the rising standards but also of the children's engagement in, and enthusiasm for, learning, and of their high level of self-esteem, which for me are the key components of what we do. Even more fascinating was how the children perceived and understood the concept and how they would very happily inform all the prospective families that at Hertford 'we love not knowing!'. What we realised is that the approach was enabling children to know how to know what they were curious to know that they knew they didn't know!

The Hertford JONK Model evolved gradually by introducing initiatives and establishing whole school cultures 'one layer at a time'. I believe that its success is mostly due to giving ourselves plenty of time for each layer to be fully embedded before introducing next steps, working in multi-professional teams and working as a whole school.

In part one we have argued that the learning which young people need to gain from schools to equip them for a very precarious future involves a shift of emphasis from shallow to deep learning. Such deep learning for future sustainability is characterised by three underpinning key drivers: understanding, character, and agency.

In part two we now look in much more detail at this notion of deep learning for future sustainability, its components, and what we already know about how it can be developed. For we do not have to start from scratch, as this thought piece indicates.

We have always been fascinated by the ability to present learning to children in a way that is perceived by them as being fun and playful, while still maintaining all the required academic content, rigour, depth, and progression. Perhaps the closest one comes to this approach in the English education system is in the pedagogy that underpins the Early Years Foundation Stage curriculum. We could do a lot worse than draw on that spirit to guide our enquiry.

CHAPTER 4

CORE PRINCIPLES OF DEEP LEARNING FOR A SUSTAINABLE FUTURE

> *We have come so far because we are the cleverest creatures to have ever lived on Earth. But if we are to continue to exist, we will require more than intelligence. We will require wisdom ... we have one more thing — an ability, perhaps unique among living creatures on the planet — to imagine a future and work towards achieving it.*
>
> David Attenborough, 2020

One of the most sophisticated discussions of learning in modern times is the work of the philosopher and educationalist John Dewey, whose professional life was centred on the interaction of theory and practice through his experience of teaching in a one-classroom rural school, and in leading social and political movements focused on the development of democratic communities. In his work on education, he offers philosophical and psychological insights into the theory and practice of effective education. As part of this work, Dewey provides a concise yet complete definition of successful learning:

> We state emphatically that, upon its intellectual side, education consists in the formation of wide-awake, careful, thorough habits of thinking.
>
> (Dewey, 1933, pp. 78–79)

Dewey goes on to provide one of the key definitions informing our discussion:

> Of course, intellectual learning includes the amassing and retention of information. But information is an undigested burden unless it is understood. It is knowledge only as its material is comprehended. And understanding with comprehension means that the various parts of the information acquired are grasped in their relations to one another — a result that is attained only when acquisition is accompanied by constant reflection upon the meaning of what is studied.

Dewey's identification of the elements involved in learning for understanding was extended by Howard Gardner:

> An individual understands a concept, skill, theory, or domain of knowledge to the extent that he or she can apply it. This formulation entails an acid test for understanding: posing to students a topic or theme or demonstration that they have never before encountered and determining what sense they can make of those phenomena. An individual who possesses relevant understanding will be able to draw on appropriate concepts.
>
> (Gardner, 1999, p. 119)

In these definitions Dewey and Gardner identify and emphasise what can be summarised as the essential components of learning for understanding. This involves:

- Recognising the process of amassing and retaining information.
- Differentiating information and knowledge.
- Focusing on understanding and comprehension as the basis for understanding.
- Grasping the relationship between examples, concepts, and theories.
- Seeing reflection as the key process in achieving understanding.
- Being able to apply knowledge in practice.

Dewey and Gardner provide us with a model of learning that applies to almost every dimension of human activity — it is essentially the movement from knowing 'what?' to knowing 'how?' and 'why?'. Much of our experience of schooling is centred on knowing 'what?'. Of course, the chemist needs to know the Periodic Table, the musician needs to be able to read music, and the mathematician to use the range of arithmetical functions with accuracy and confidence. Equally, the historian has to have a grasp of chronology. But dates are not history, any more than lists of rivers and mountains are geography.

Unfortunately, because deep learning is a complex process for the teacher and the learner, it is difficult to codify and classify, and so difficult to assess. It is much easier to deliver content than to support the emergence of understanding. Equally, it is much easier to assess the retention of information than the development of understanding.

A very significant contribution to this debate lies in the work of Kathryn Asbury and Robert Plomin, which combines rigorous science with practical implications for schools:

> We suggest a model of education that recognises the important role of genetics. Rather than a passive model of schooling as instruction (*instruere*,'to build in'), we propose an active model of education (*educare*,'to bring out') in which children create their own educational experiences in part on the basis of their genetic propensities, which supports the trend towards personalised learning.
>
> (Asbury & Plomin, 2014, p. 158)

As will become increasingly evident, our focus throughout this book is on bringing out rather than building in. Therefore, we will refer to 'learning-centred leadership' rather than 'instructional leadership'. These concepts are almost interchangeable in practice, but following Asbury and Plomin, we avoid referring to instructional strategies in order to focus on learning based on the evidence of actual practice. In the common usage, instruction is redolent of teacher control and a subordinate role for the learner, who is in a dependency relationship — a position that must inevitably compromise the potential for classrooms and schools to become learner-centred.

Insights into the fundamental differences between wisdom, knowledge, and information are not new. In his play *The Rock* (1934), the poet and playwright T.S. Eliot wrote:

> Where is the Life we have lost in living?
>
> Where is the wisdom we have lost in knowledge?
>
> Where is the knowledge we have lost in information?

In an educational context Elif Shafak (2020, p. 81) articulates a very similar sentiment:

> We live in an age where there is too much information, less knowledge and even less wisdom. That ratio needs to be reversed. We definitely need less information, more knowledge, and much more wisdom.

She goes on to stress the importance of reading and explores how emotional intelligence and empathy expand wisdom through storytelling.

Russell Ackoff (1989, pp. 3–9) has offered a pyramid model (Figure 6) based on four layers to describe the progression from shallow to deep knowledge — data, information, knowledge, wisdom.

Figure 6: Ackoff's pyramid of knowledge

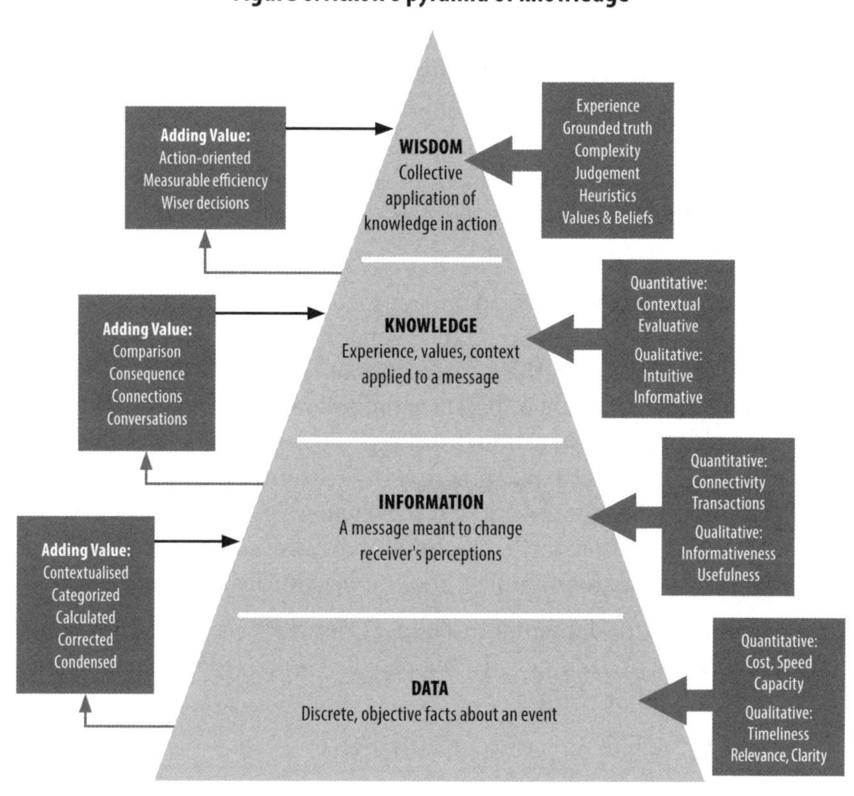

While this may justifiably be criticised for being too linear as a model, it is one small example of a framework. How might such a model, for example, inform leadership and management practice in a school? Consider the process by which schools draw conclusions from the statistical information they collect about their students:

- Schools collect lots of *data* about students assessment and attendance. If appropriately collected, it provides objective facts, but these have only limited value.
- Translating data into *information* requires classification, comparison and links with other relevant sets of data either historically or in terms of peer groupings — for example, comparing school pupil premium data with national figures and similar schools.
- Translating information into *knowledge* involves testing for validity and reliability, comparing with other sources of evidence and personal experience, and being able to explain, justify and engage in dialogue; for example, analysing pupil premium students in terms of attendance, special educational needs, exclusion, and pupils speaking English as an additional language.
- Yet even the most fair-minded knowledge base might still lack the *wisdom* of a special needs coordinator with years of experience, a real understanding of safeguarding, and sensitivity to the family situation of their students.

Schneider and Stern argue for multiple forms of knowledge, such as abstract concepts, how to solve problems, how to master complex and dynamic situations, learning strategies, and regulating one's emotions. They also go on to point out that a person may have knowledge but not be able to apply it to solve real-life problems.

> It is a commonplace when somebody refers to 'knowledge' that they mean only knowledge of facts. In that view, knowledge is something that has to be acquired in addition to other favourable learning outcomes such as conceptual understanding adaptive confidence or literacy in a domain. In contrast, modern day cognitive science shows that even these complex competences arise from well-organised knowledge structures.
>
> (Schneider & Stern, 2010, p. 71)

Before going further into the nature of deep learning as a concept, it will be useful to differentiate between the various usages of the word 'learning'. Similarly to 'knowledge', 'learning' is a highly ambiguous and contested concept. In broad terms learning is used both as a noun and as a verb — learning as product and learning as process. Common language might include the following usages and synonyms:

1. A quantitative increase in information. *Please learn these spellings for a test tomorrow.*
2. Learning as the outcome of being taught. *When we finish this section, you will have learned this part of the curriculum.*
3. Learning as memorising. *You need to learn the seven times table.*
4. Learning as developing skills and techniques. *I would advise you to practice reversing your car.*
5. Learning as developing understanding, seeing relationships, and being aware of the cognitive processes involved. *Coaching that is based in challenge and reflection is one of the best ways of developing mastery.*
6. Learning as creating new realities, personal change, developing wisdom, and re-creating knowledge. The dictum from Socrates that 'The unexamined life is not worth living' reminds us that learning involves change.
7. The accumulated wisdom and experiences of the years. *She is a teacher of deep learning and professional wisdom.*

The first three of these usages may be defined as managing and memorising information. We might describe this process as being essentially shallow. The fourth and fifth categories involve usages that are different and so might apply to deep learning, in that knowledge is being created and understood through the use of higher order cognitive skills (e.g. analysis, synthesis, and application). But there is also more to deep learning in that it extends to become personal to the learner. The sixth and seventh usages are best described as intellectual and cultural capital — the accumulated knowledge of the years that serve as the foundations of many different aspects of life in society.

If we are to work towards authentic engagement with learning as 'bringing out', then we have to recognise the importance of the proposition advanced by Kelly:

> The mind is essentially a function of the brain: the brain is the organ; the mind is the pattern of activity within it. Understanding learning will mean understanding the process of making minds.
>
> (Kelly, 2008, p. 143)

It is this process of 'making minds' that is at the heart of this book and also holds the key to the future.

Capturing the modes of learning

Shallow learning equips you to appear on Mastermind or University Challenge, and to play Trivial Pursuit without totally compromising your dignity. Deep learning, however, means that you change in a significant way — being able to drive a car, play a musical instrument, or speak a foreign language. Although this book is focused on deep learning there is obviously a need to explore the relationship with shallow or surface learning. For a significant element in the development of deep learning strategies is understanding how the building blocks of information are arranged in order to create knowledge.

One very real problem is the tendency in some quarters to see shallow learning that is successful in terms of its quality and quantity as being synonymous with deep learning. The successful accumulation of facts, lists of spellings, quotations from literature, or dates in history, are all components of learning that, when combined with appropriate and relevant learning skills and strategies, can lead to the creation of knowledge. However, accurate replication is no substitute for the ability to question, challenge, and interpret.

> Important to curriculum design is the recognition that students develop meaningful understanding through prior knowledge transfer, epistemic reasoning and meta-cognitive skills rather than by accumulating facts in an ever-growing variety of topics. Deep learning processes requiring teaching strategies featuring cognitive

> activation, providing space for self and collaborative reflection, and offering well-designed scaffolding.
>
> (OECD, 2020, p. 26)

Shallow learning focuses on the memorisation and replication of information, with largely uncritical acceptance of data and facts, seeing information as unrelated and isolated topics. Learners are passive. The emphasis is on coverage of content. Assessment is summative and assessed content is probably quickly forgotten. The teacher controls shallow learning with the learner compliant and dependent. Shallow learning is essentially transmissive and assessable in terms of right and wrong answers. The essence of shallow learning is 'getting the right answer'.

It is this compliance and dependence that inhibits personal potential and development — in the worst-case scenario it results in unthinking and unquestioning acquiescence. Shallow learning becomes important and significant when it is seen not as an end in itself, but rather in laying the foundations that may enable deep learning to take place. Practice is an important exemplar of this — the greatest musicians, athletes, and dancers practice every day in order to have the confidence to perform at the highest level.

Deep learning focuses on the creation of knowledge through the demonstration of understanding, the analysis and synthesis of facts to create conceptual models and frameworks, the integration of prior learning, and cross-referencing to other themes and subjects. Learning is active and based in relationships. Emphasis is placed on depth. Assessment is formative and negotiated, and content is remembered and codified. Deep learning is controlled by the learner, who understands their own learning process, with the teacher acting as facilitator, mentor, and co-constructor of knowledge.

The goal is the point where knowledge becomes wisdom, in other words intuitive and fundamental to the identity of the person learning. It involves the capacity to create new meaning in changing situations and contexts, developing a holistic awareness of the relationship between themes, subjects, principles, and practice

Such learning is not purely academic, and certainly not confined to an intellectual elite. Nor is it necessarily linked to age or experience. This is how Atul Gawande describes a stage in the development of a surgeon:

> But then there are other times when everything goes perfectly. You don't think. You don't concentrate. Every move unfolds effortlessly ... At such moments it is more than easy; it is beautiful.
>
> (Gawande, 2003, p. 22)

It does seem strange to equate flow with a basic surgical procedure but that is exactly the point — get the balance of challenge and skills right and full engagement is possible, irrespective of role or status. Deep learning has many manifestations, from learning to talk in childhood to the artistry of the concert pianist; from the skills and compassion of the nurse to the great scientific discovery; from the skill of the joiner to the creativity of the painter.

Shallow learning is playing the notes on the piano; deep learning creates the melody and goes on to enable interpretation. Shallow learning gives access to vocabulary and the rules of grammar; deep learning allows conversations and leads to engagement with poetry, ideas, and thinking. Such learning is the characteristic of the Formula One motor racing driver, the mentor, the highly successful learner, and the athlete. Such learning moves us from religious observance to spirituality, from knowledge to wisdom. Such learning is distilled in Sternberg's definition of wisdom:

> ... an individual is wise to the extent he or she uses successful intelligence and experience as moderated by values to (a) seek to teach a common good for all stakeholders, (b) by balancing intrapersonal (one's own), interpersonal (others'), and extrapersonal (organisational/institutional/spiritual) interests, (c) over the short and long term, to (d) adapt to, shape, and select environments.
>
> (Sternberg, 2005, p. 358)

Deep learning can also be expressed through the higher order personal qualities such as empathy, compassion, and trust. Deep learning helps to explain the discovery of DNA by Watson, Crick, and (especially) Franklin, the novels of George Eliot, and the music of Ravel. It equally explains the craft of the joiner and the creativity of the game designer. The intuitive dimension of deep learning is fundamentally important in how we make our judgements and develop confidence in our decision-making.

The model shown in Figure 7 is designed to be read as a continuum from shallow to deep learning. There can never be neat and definitive boundaries between these categories so the relationship between them is best understood as incremental with varying degrees of significance for each component of the model.

The movement from shallow to deep learning can be best characterised as the growth of personal understanding, of ownership, and movement away from dependency. As a child learns to read and write, they gradually grow in confidence and control, and their increasing understanding is manifested in personal autonomy. At the heart of moral and spiritual development is the process of internalisation — the movement from generic, public information to specific, personal understanding, in other words, becoming a person.

The essential stages in moving from information to knowledge, from generic instruction to personal growth, can be summarised as:

- The presentation of relevant information through lectures, reading, etc.
- Modelling of that information through discussion, debate, exercises, simulations, and experiments.
- Application of the emerging understanding into real-life situations in which theories and hypotheses are tested against experience.
- Feedback, review, and reflection on the implications of the inaction between theory and practice.
- Support in improving practice, application in new contexts, building and extending confidence.

Figure 7: Modes of learning (after West-Burnham & Coates, 2005)

	Shallow (What?)	**(How?)**	**Deep Learning (Why?)**
Means	Rote - Memorisation Practice	Challenge - Fluid Intelligence	Intuition - Crystallised Intelligence
Outcomes	Information	Knowledge	Wisdom
Evidence of success	Replication	Understanding	Meaning
Motivation	Extrinsic	Intrinsic	Flow
Attitudes	Learned Helplessness	Interpretation	Creativity
Relationships	Dependence	Interdependence	Independence
	(Single loop)	**(Double loop)**	**(Triple loop)**

There is not necessarily a causal relationship from shallow to deep. There are many examples of people who go directly to deep — some never pass shallow. It is the metacognitive dimension of practice that leads to success.

> Every good craftsman conducts a dialogue between concrete practices and thinking: this dialogue evolves into sustaining habits, and these habits establish a rhythm between problem solving and problem finding. The relationship between hand and head appears in domains seemingly as different as bricklaying, cooking, designing a playground or playing the cello.
>
> (Sennett, 2008, p. 9)

We have to be very careful when talking of geniuses, prodigies, and savants. They are, by definition, exceptional. Thus, the young Mozart (and even more remarkably the young Mendelssohn) displayed both creative genius and technical mastery — notably in orchestration. There are numerous examples of child prodigies in chess, music, and mathematics. Interestingly, there are fewer examples in the literary domains. This may reflect cultural patterns or different aspects of cognitive development. Precocious ability seems to be more likely in those disciplines using symbolic notation.

Equally, depth is not necessarily equally available for all aspects of a person's learning — thus the same person may be shallow with regard to ICT, but deep in their understanding of learning and teaching or in their interpersonal relationships. It is possible to be shallow or deep in each of Gardner's multiple intelligences. The chess grand master may lack interpersonal intelligence; the person with high linguistic intelligence may lack spatial and kinaesthetic abilities.

Just as important as defining the effective learner is defining the characteristics of the effective teacher — or, perhaps, the facilitator of deep learning. The effective teacher has a deep understanding of the neurological, cognitive, emotional, and social aspects of learning. They balance this knowledge with the ability to access subject information and the strategies to convert it into personal knowledge and share that understanding. They work through challenges, posing problems and setting questions, while ensuring they are appropriate to the individual learner and that the learner has the skills to respond to them. They create a sense of emotional security by building trust and confidence and working in an interdependent manner. They have a deep respect for the dignity, identity, and integrity of every learner.

So, the effective teacher works primarily as a facilitator and mentor. They are skilled in negotiating learning strategies, understanding the learner's motivation, and have a passionate belief in the potential of every learner. They recognise, reinforce, and celebrate achievement, ensuring that there are abundant opportunities for the learner to experience valid and appropriate success. They are highly sensitive to the student's social context. Above all, they model learning, reviewing their own practice with their mentors, deepening their understanding of the learning process and engaging in networks with other teachers.

Underlying assumptions about the learning process

This distinction between shallow and deep learning that we are trying to draw is based on eight underlying assumptions that we ought to make explicit if we are to be transparent about how we are approaching this discussion. Educational policies and strategies never work from a blank sheet. There are always explicit and implicit assumptions, beliefs, and competing values and priorities. These are the key assumptions that underpin our discussion:

1. **Education is essentially social justice in action.**
   Learning is a pivotal contribution to the achievement of equity.
2. **Learners are unique.**
   The complexity of our lives means that we all have personal learning biographies based on the distinctive pathways we have followed and the choices we have made or had imposed on us.
3. **Learning is a social activity.**
   Human interaction is the basis of most successful learning and, conversely, poor interaction can significantly inhibit learning.
4. **Learning is a neurological process**.
   There is no 'ghost in the machine'; learning is a brain-based electro-chemical process subject to genetic influences.
5. **Intelligence is not fixed.**
   Intelligence is plastic and can change over time so attempting to predict a young person's academic potential by testing is morally and scientifically wrong.
6. **The key role of the teacher is to facilitate and enable**.
   'Education is not about the filling of a pail but the lighting of a fire'.[19]
   And of course, the contents of the pail can put out the fire.

19. Strong, R. (2013), '"Education is not the filling of a pail, but the lighting of a fire": It's an inspiring quote, but did WB Yeats say it?', 15 October, *The Irish Times*. Accessed at: https://www.irishtimes.com/news/education/education-is-not-the-filling-of-a-pail-but-the-lighting-of-a-fire-it-s-an-inspiring-quote-but-did-wb-yeats-say-it-1.1560192.

7. **Learning can take place with anyone, anytime, and anywhere.** We are never not learning; we learn as much from mistakes as lessons. Learning is not restricted to schools.
8. **Successful learning is exemplified by the ability to apply that which has been learned.**

Table 3 is a conceptual map of these assumptions, but it is important to stress the very high degree of interdependence between the various elements. It might be described as a conceptual map of the nature of education, the way in which learning is understood as a process, and the origins of its various assumptions and beliefs.

Table 3: Key assumptions underpinning our concept of deep learning for future sustainability

Key proposition	Principle	Practice
Education is about social justice.	Securing equity.	Closing the gap.
Every learner is unique. Genetics (Plomin).	Personalisation. Supportive interventions.	Personal pathways, curriculum choice.
Learning is a social process (Vygotsky)	Social interaction. Coaching – Zone of Proximal Development.	Varying social settings Developing emotional literacy. Collaborative projects.
Learning is a genetic/neurological function. (Blakemore)	Cognitive development is not uniformly age-related.	Application of neurological principles e.g. challenge, memory.
Intelligence can be learnt. (Adey, Gardner, EEF)	Cognitive strategies. Learning to think.	Metacognition. Challenge and problem solving.
The focus is on learners learning, not teachers teaching.	Managing time, place and relationships.	Learning in the community.
Learning, progress, and achievement require a growth mindset. (Dweck)	Appropriate feedback and application.	The teacher as mentor/coach/ facilitator.
Learning can take place anytime, anywhere with anyone.	Family-based learning	Self-directed learning.
Learning is assessed through understanding.	Negotiated outcomes. Formative assessment.	Assessment as learning. Pedagogy based on learning for understanding.

Conclusion

Engaging with learning, as opposed to simply delivering information, is a complex process for the teacher and the learner; it is difficult to codify and classify and can be difficult to assess. It is much easier to deliver content than to support the emergence of understanding. Processing information is essential to any model of human learning, but:

> ... it can serve practical and cognitive needs and provide a basis for further learning. But it does not in any fundamental way alter our outlook on the world. It does not make us better people. Every once in a while, something does break through. We encounter a powerful idea or read a powerful book or hear a powerful piece of music that changes us, that radiates through our whole person.
>
> (Leithwood et al., 2006, p. 15)

This quotation also underpins much of our thinking in this book — recognising that learning as a process can have fundamentally differing outcomes. To that end, it encompasses understanding, character, and agency.

There is a clear connection between the approach adopted to teaching and the nature of the outcome in terms of successful learning. In many respects the 'medium is the message', *how* we learn determines *what* we learn. A focus on rote learning will produce very different outcomes and habituated learning strategies compared with a focus on problem-solving.

There appear to be a range of strategies that support the development of deep learning, which we will explore further in later chapters. In no particular order of priority, these might include:

- A clear understanding of learning preferences, aptitudes, dispositions and motivation, supported by regular review and the development of strategies to enhance and sustain personal learning effectiveness.
- Access to a portfolio of cognitive strategies — analysis, synthesis, causality and cognitive skills, e.g. memorising.
- Teaching which is based on challenge, problem-solving, and relevant decision-making.
- The use of coaching and mentoring and the facilitation of small group and team-based strategies.
- The development of sophisticated interpersonal relationships, with high emphasis on the social dimensions of learning, and the development of emotional literacy across the school.

- The use of personalised learning pathways with negotiated learning outcomes and assessment for learning strategies used to ensure relevance and potential application.
- A focus on the 'whole' learner, recognising the role of the family and community in supporting access to effective learning.
- Systematic review and reflection.

Deep learning for future sustainability is about academic success, but it is also about developing the confidence to make choices and to become 'consciously competent'. It is about empowering learners so that they can form opinions based on evidence, analysis, critique, and alternative perspectives, and so create knowledge and act on it, rather than be dependent on the perspectives of others. It is about being evidence-informed when appropriate but, equally, intuitive as necessary.

Deep learning for future sustainability is equally about emotional literacy and personal authenticity. Crucially such learning has the potential, in Schleicher's memorable phrase, to help develop 'first-class humans rather than second-class robots' (Schleicher, 2018 a).

Opportunity for self-reflection and collaborative review

- *What are the key assumptions underpinning your view of the nature of the learning process? How does this inform and influence your leadership role?*
- *To what extent does your school have a shared and consistent view of learning that informs practice in classrooms across the whole school?*
- *How far do pupils contribute to the development of a shared learning vocabulary? To what extent are all pupils engaged in a regular dialogue about their development as self-managing learners?*
- *What are the implications of an education system where curriculum and pedagogy are based on shallow learning? What needs to change in order to secure deep learning?*

CHAPTER 5

IT STARTS WITH US!

> *To survive and flourish in such a world you will need a lot of mental flexibility and great reserves of emotional balance. You will repeatedly have to let go of what you know best and feel at home with the unknown ... teachers themselves usually lack the mental flexibility that the twenty-first century demands, for they themselves are the products of the old educational system.*
>
> Yuval Noah Harari (2018, p. 265)

Before going further, we ought to highlight the one other fundamental assumption which really matters for a school which is truly trying to face the future. Thus far we have focused primarily on pupils as the learners. But we do not believe it is possible to address understanding, character, or agency without recognising that deep learning for future sustainability must extend to all who are connected with the school, not just those who are formally designated pupils. Teachers who have not had the opportunity to become deep learners themselves will find it much more difficult to act as guides to their students. Likewise, it is not possible to develop agency in pupils if staff lack agency. It is not possible to develop character in pupils if staff are not also role models for them. If families are not also playing a part in promoting understanding, character, and agency, then the task will also be much, much harder for schools.

So, we are led inexorably not just into the classroom but also into learning beyond the school. And if we are to construct a different just and sustainable future for all, then families and communities must not only necessarily be involved in imagining what this might mean for the education of their children, but become active partners in that ongoing conversation. The task of leadership then, is one of building a culture of deep learning across the whole school which also radiates beyond its walls. It means becoming a genuine learning community.

However, such a learning community begins with the educators. For it is they who are best placed to model deep learning to others and best equipped to understand how it can be fostered. A central argument of this book is that what we now know about how humans learn best needs to be applied more radically in schools if young people are to be to thrive and survive in a fundamentally different future world. This approach is necessarily embedded in evidence-informed approaches to learning and teaching, and in the debate around what constitutes knowledge and the nature of valid and reliable evidence. This is the professional dimension of deep learning for educators.

Why school-based and evidence-informed research matters

In principle, all professional practice is a constant dialogue between valid, reliable, research-informed practice and approaches based on common sense, personal experience, or personal beliefs. However, professional practice in education in the Anglophone world seems to be cautious about research, trusting instead in successful professional experience, pragmatic responses to change, or environmental and cultural factors. Many teachers would not accept the same approaches from their doctor.

The relationship between personal practice and public theory is a complex one given the lack of consensus around the various conceptual frameworks that are available. For example, there is a lack of consistency in common usage of the terms evidence-based and evidence-informed. For the purposes of this discussion, we argue they differ as follows:

> **Evidence-based:** strict adherence to the conceptual framework, methodology, and findings of a piece of published research. In other words, replicating the original research and giving it authoritative status to the extent of precluding alternative findings or interpretations.

> **Evidence-informed:** employing an openly eclectic approach that encourages a culture of investigation and enquiry where assumptions and outcomes are open to analysis, critique, and challenge. Thus, a piece of research may be questioned by alternative conceptual models, differing accounts of practice or personal experience based on professional investigation and review.

Most forms of professional activity involve choices. The ability to make the appropriate choice is one of the key criteria for professional expertise and authority. One of the most significant elements of deep learning is its combination of the confidence to make decisions and the knowledge to make optimum judgements. Our ability to make the most effective decision is directly related to the knowledge that we have about the topic under review and the skills and strategies that we use to interrogate that knowledge and its contextual applications to bring about the optimum outcome.

Why should a very busy teacher or school leader engage in research? Perhaps for the same reason they hope that their GP, dentist, and optician do — to improve their professional practice through a process of review, analysis, and knowledge growth. And of course, in some countries this happens:

> In some parts of the world, it is impossible to climb the career ladder of teaching without understanding how research can improve practice, and publishing articles in teaching journals. Teachers in Shanghai and Singapore participate in regular 'Journal Clubs', where they discuss a new piece of research, and its strengths and weaknesses, before considering whether they would apply its findings in their own practice. If the answer is no, they share the shortcomings in the study design that they've identified, and then describe any better research that they think should be done, on the same question.
>
> (Goldacre, 2013, p. 17)

But too often in English education:

> ... many studies have little impact. They are small-scale and serve to ensure an individual's or group's profile within a research community which largely debates its own research activity, usually without any

> ground-breaking findings which could influence practice on a large scale ... If an academic writes a book aimed at enlightening teachers or students, there is no credit in it ... so what's the point in writing it? Teachers don't tend to read academic journals. There they sit, on the shelf, read only by other academics.
>
> (Waters, 2013, p. 229)

The antidote to Waters' pessimism is the development of a school culture that embeds the theory and practice of research into every dimension of professional activity. An evidence-informed research culture might incorporate the following principles:

- The most effective strategy to improve the quality of teaching and learning is for teachers to become active learners through investigating and improving their own practice.
- Given education is a complex and contested area of activity, it is essential that strategies are explicitly evidence-informed.
- Teachers and leaders need to be able to demonstrate that they understand the conceptual basis of their own practice and are engaged in systematic review and analysis of that practice.
- They can critique the claims of other researchers in their chosen field and those who seek to base policy on research.
- Work-based research is seen as a potentially high-impact development and improvement strategy.
- School leaders and all those involved in the learning of pupils need to model what it means to be a learner and be effective learners themselves.

Evidence-informed practice and the nature of knowledge

There are numerous manifestations of human knowledge. These range from the most scrupulous double-blind experiments to socially realistic novels, from scientific discourse to the sharing of wisdom, not to mention professional and personal experience. It is important to be clear that there are many different forms of knowledge which we use, often subliminally, in our everyday life. Knowing that God exists, that there are black swans in Australia, that the Sun will explode in 5.5 billion years, and that your partner loves you all derive their integrity from different epistemological models, or forms of knowledge.

When we are considering how we might create the optimum learning environment for young people, it rapidly becomes obvious that there are multiple competing rationalities, all seeking to become the pervading orthodoxy.

In the context of research, especially that to do with teaching and learning, it is vital that the researcher is confident and clear about the type of knowledge they will be creating. In other words, researchers need to understand the methodological basis of their research to a) identify the most appropriate methods and b) create confidence in the integrity and trustworthiness of their findings. The same can be said of leaders, teachers, and learners.

One way of understanding these epistemological issues is to relate the spectra shown in Figure 8 to all aspects of educational practice:

Figure 8: Mapping epistemological differences

Positivist	________	**Interpretivist**
Objective	________	**Subjective**
Quantitative	________	**Qualitative**
Empiricism	________	**Relativism**
Normative	________	**Negotiated**
Realism	________	**Nominalism**
Experimentation	________	**Observation**

This figure is not a representation of binary opposites. Rather we view each polarity as a continuum in terms of degrees of difference. Deep learning draws on both positivist and interpretivist approaches. How these inform each other and interact is an essential component of any methodological discussion. From the design of project-based learning in the primary school, to Lesson Study, to higher degree dissertations, deep learning is as concerned with the how and why as the what. Engaging with issues around types of knowledge is at least as significant as codifying subject information.

Positivist approaches tend to work on the following assumptions:

- Research is based on quantification and statistical methodology.
- Reality can be discovered through scientific methods. It is objective and rational.
- The influence and significance of the researcher is minimised by the use of standardised protocols, i.e. the scientific method.
- Hypotheses are subjected to empirical verification and conditional acceptance or rejection.
- Only observable and measurable phenomena can be regarded as knowledge.

Goldacre (2013) argues for randomised trials as a powerful way of moving from personality-driven practice into one that is evidence based. In fact, he argues that such trials are the sine qua non of high-quality research, notably in medicine, but also in education.

> Where they are feasible, randomised trials are generally the most reliable tool we have for finding out which of two interventions works best. We simply take a group of children, or schools (or patients, or people); we split them into two groups at random; we give one intervention to one group, and the other intervention to the other group; then we measure how each group is doing, to see if one intervention achieved its supposed outcome any better.
>
> (Goldacre, 2013, p. 8)

Interpretive and qualitative approaches tend, in contrast, to work on the following broad principles:

- Research is a qualitative process that explores alternative versions of reality.
- Reality is subjective and negotiable, and multiple alternative perspectives are recognised and respected.
- The influence and significance of the researcher is recognised and incorporated into the outcomes of the research.
- The core purpose is to identify, analyse, understand and explain human behaviour, thus biography, narrative, and personal voice are valid.

- Research is seen as an iterative process with knowledge being seen as contingent on time and place and variables such as gender, race, class, culture, and politics are all potentially significant.

For many aspects of deep learning, a qualitative approach is probably more appropriate: given the personal and subjective nature of understanding, character, and agency. Historically, though, the social sciences have tended to defer to scientific method — often in a defensive mode, aspiring to the same sort of knowledge as, for example, physics.

Ethnographic studies owe more to biology and anthropology, generally working in a conceptual framework of 'naturalism':

> Naturalism proposes that, as far as possible, the social world should be studied in its natural state, undisturbed by the researcher. Hence 'natural' not 'artificial' settings, like experiments or formal interviews, should be the primary source of data.
>
> (Hammersley & Atkinson, 1989, p. 7)

In essence this approach requires respect and sensitivity towards the social world being investigated — ethnography is not far removed from the means that we all use in everyday life to make sense of our surroundings. The difference is that the ethnographer is systematic and rigorous in the collection and analysis of evidence.

The complexity and nature of research may sometimes require that the investigator is a 'participant observer', in other words becoming a significant variable in the research itself by virtue of role, relative status, and perceived expertise, as well as their contextual authority. Feminist models additionally and properly raise issues around the power of the researcher and its potential to significantly influence relationships and so perceptions. The researcher may also develop a degree of commitment to the sample group which can lead to internalisation of the topics being studied and, in extreme cases, identification with the sample.

In terms of the integrity of the research this is not a problem when acknowledged explicitly and the implications of this relationship are identified. In essence, the participant observer becomes more of a participant and less of an observer. While this may challenge many views of effective research, it also opens the door to co-construction and increases the potential for application and so meaningful change. Deep learning requires this kind of deep relationship.

Components of evidence-informed practice

What follows is an exploration of the range of strategies that are available to support evidence-informed practice. A properly evidence-informed approach will engage with all four of the elements in Figure 9.

Figure 9: Evidence-informed practice

Personal and anecdotal experience

There is a very narrow borderline between deep learning and expertise and prejudiced and subjective experience derived from a limited range of largely anecdotal sources. At the same time, it is important to recognise and respect on the one hand the importance of the authentic professional voice, and on the other the 'right to be heard' of pupils, their parents, and other stakeholders in the school.

In the 1990s and 2000s, there was a spate of publishing of what might best be described as professional autobiographies by a range of headteachers. In most cases they were not so much apologia as open and sometimes painfully honest reflections and analyses of their author's leadership. In many respects they were personal narratives that were subjective and anecdotal — but that was precisely their strength, they provided leadership stories. Narratives about leadership have a long and distinguished history, although comparing stories of headship in the 20 century with Homer's Odyssey might be pushing credibility too far. However, like most myths, these recent examples of successful practice serve as way of keeping a tradition alive and acting as a model of learning for successive generations.

Feminist research methodology places great emphasis on the value of the personal voice and there is a very strong case for securing personal and professional life stories. Equally there is a very strong case for extending the same value and significance to student voices, not to forget those of all staff and parents. Deep learning is often seen as being synonymous with intuition, personal authenticity, and credibility. Deep learners tend to work through synthesis and by reconciling theory and practice. Professional wisdom is found in the experienced nurse and the hospital consultant, but also in the hospital porter and the ward cleaner. In schools, in many different ways, this wisdom is present in students and younger children.

In the evidence-informed school, hearing as many different perspectives as possible is fundamental to any decision or judgement. Equally, treating alternative voices with respect is a classic demonstration of values in practice, notably openness, transparency, and accountability.

School-focused research

Research to inform deep learning is potentially at its most effective if it is personal rather than abstract, shared rather than individualistic, and focused on personal change and growth. There is a danger that professional development is seen in transactional terms and not as a necessary corollary of what it means to be professional educator.

School-focused research in England has a chequered history compared to several high performing school systems — notably those of Finland, Singapore, Japan, and parts of China. Research is not seen as a norm in England, nor as a professional obligation. Rather, it is often just part of a personal development project that is independent of school. David Hargreaves has developed an alternative approach based on Joint Practice Development (JPD), which was in turn informed by Lesson Study — a form of action research driven by teachers focusing on their classroom practice and working collaboratively.[20] However, the extent to which JPD and related practice is embedded into school cultures is as yet unclear. School-focused research has the potential to inform:

- The development of effective pedagogy through analysis of classroom practice.
- The development of research skills for students.
- The introduction of philosophy-based techniques and strategies, e.g. P4C.[21]
- Developing presentational techniques.

One less frequently referenced aspect of educational practice in Finland is its emphasis on research-informed practice, exemplified in the pivotal concept of research-informed teacher education.

> Each student (teacher) ... builds an understanding of the systemic, interdisciplinary nature of educational practice. Finnish students also acquire the skills of designing, conducting, and presenting original research on practical or theoretical aspects of education.
>
> (Sahlberg, 2015, p. 116)

Three principles guide research-informed teacher education in Finland:

1. Teachers need a deep knowledge of advances in research in the subjects they teach — they also need to be familiar with the research on teaching and learning.
2. The professional practice of teachers must be evidence-based, using an analytical and open-minded approach, and drawing on a range of sources of evidence as well as a critical perspective on their own practice.

20. Education Endowment Foundation (2017), 'Lesson Study: A collaborative professional development programme that originated in Japan'. Available at: https://educationendowmentfoundation.org.uk/projects-and-evaluation/projects/lesson-study; Hargreaves, D. H. (2012), *A self-improving school system: towards maturity*, Nottingham, National College for School Leadership. Available at: https://dera.ioe.ac.uk/15804/1/a-self-improving-school-system-towards-maturity.pdf.

21. See Philosophy for Children. Available at: https://p4c.com/.

3. Teacher education should, of itself, be studied and investigated.

In her analysis of the factors that explain Finland's consistently high levels of educational performance, Lucy Crehan quotes a Finnish teacher:

> … you have to read books, study documents, and discuss research with colleagues in order to be a good teacher: 'I don't feel like I can do my job properly if I don't study every now and then'.
>
> (Crehan, 2016, p. 51)

One of the most substantial evidence-informed resources is the Education Endowment Foundation (EEF) *Toolkit*.[22] The *Toolkit* was first published in 2012 to support the implementation of the pupil premium. It was an immediate success, with half of school leaders referring to it in their decision-making about the spending of their pupil premium funding. Its success and credibility were the result of its accessibility, clarity, focus and support in terms of application and implications — the guide includes information about the cost-benefit potential of each strategy it describes, a judgement as to its relative impact, and the trustworthiness of the research cited.

The *Toolkit* is a model for maximising the direct application of research in the classroom. The College of Teachers journal *Impact* is developing similar approaches for the dissemination of high-quality school-based research.

Academic research

This area covers a wide spectrum of evidence informed activity from ethnographic studies, through the range of qualitative research, contributions synthesising research, as well as what might be described as social philosophy and work based on developing conceptual models.

Work in this category is generally defined in terms of scholarship, and generally meets all or most of the following criteria:

- Is of postgraduate/ professional level — e.g. at master's degree or doctoral level.

---

22. Education Endowment Foundation, *Teaching and Learning Toolkit*. Available at: https://educationendowmentfoundation.org.uk/evidence-summaries/teaching-learning-toolkit.

- Draws on a wide range of appropriate methodology.
- Develops evidence that is trustworthy, valid, and reliable.
- Recognises epistemological issues and the integrity of the chosen methodology.
- Meets the appropriate higher education research ethics standards.
- Is made available and shared across the profession.

According to Richard Pring, the relationship between academic research and professional practice can be problematic for a number of reasons. Firstly, academic research is valued to the extent it is published in journals that work to their own criteria. Secondly, there is pressure to publish within often inappropriate time scales. Thirdly, research might be compromised by the use of rewards to encourage publication. And:

> Fourth, most significantly for educational research, much less importance is likely to be given to the more practically focused research (the action research of the teachers) which cements the relationship between universities and schools but which, by its very nature (locally focused and not highly theoretical) is unlikely to be graded as of 'international significance'.
>
> (Pring, 2015, p. 169)

Scientific research

This element of the research community is often found, especially in education, in a very different location to the other components. Scientific research works to the same criteria as academic research but, from the scientific researcher's perspective, it is far more rigorous and objective, with high levels of confidence in the integrity of the outcomes. Scientific research almost always involves a high degree of quantification and rigorous statistical methodology. This research culture is found in a range of contexts, notably medical research charities, commercial pharmaceutical companies, and entrepreneurial laboratories.

What these have in common is what might be described as laboratory conditions — the ability to control *all* the variables influencing the study. Unfortunately, such control over conditions are difficult to achieve in education and rarely, if ever, available in schools. But this approach can have a place. For example, a charity working with schools in Kenya was faced with the challenge to improve school attendance. Various strategies were tried, new textbooks, extra teachers, and the use of flipcharts. However, the radical departure was the introduction of randomised controlled trials; rigorous analysis of data collected from schools and including a control group. None of the original strategies had made any difference. The new approach, however, offered a spark of creative insight and suggested adopting de-worming — a simple, cheap treatment to remove intestinal worms that made children ill. De-worming reduced absenteeism by 25%, and children who had been treated spent an extra two weeks in school.[23]

Applying evidence in context.

Teachers face a complex decision-making process when applying scientific research and methods. Such professional decision-making is a complex process involving the interaction of various sources of evidence that have varying degrees of confidence. This has parallels to the practice of medicine. Medicine is largely a matter of diagnosis based on evidence, followed by the identification of the most appropriate intervention strategies. Misdiagnosis or a failure to identify the appropriate intervention can result in tragedy. For example, a clinical diagnosis will usually be based on a wide range of data from measurements (e.g. blood pressure) to observation (e.g. a CAT Scan) to responses from the patient. The combination of these factors hopefully results in a successful and accurate diagnosis and so treatment. A further key element to the diagnostic process is the knowledge, expertise, and often intuition of the professional.

The spectrum of professional evidence-informed decision-making then embraces the full range of categories of evidence, from the hard science of DNA testing, that is virtually incontrovertible, and the scientifically rigorous randomised trial to the intuitive, anecdotal, hearsay, and gossip. It is important to respect experience, wisdom, and insight and achieve a balance of approaches appropriate to the topic under review. At the same

23. For more background, see 'Kenya's School Based Deworming Program', *Millions Saved* (2016). Accessed at: http://millionssaved.cgdev.org/case-studies/kenyas-school-based-deworming-program.

time, it is important not to defer to the tyranny of experience or the attraction of the anecdotal. As Goldacre describes,

> ... just a few decades ago, best medical practice was driven by things like eminence, charisma, and personal experience. We needed the help of statisticians, epidemiologists, information librarians, and experts in trial design to move forwards. Many doctors — especially the most senior ones — fought hard against this, regarding 'evidence-based medicine' as a challenge to their authority.
>
> (Goldacre, 2013, p. 4)

Developing an understanding of deep learning through research is an area of professional activity that is highly subjective and open to multiple interpretations. It is likely to display a range of features:

- The researcher must be able to acknowledge her own experiences and expertise in the area.
- The researcher has a range of different types of social relationship with the sample group, e.g. professional interaction, accountability-based relationships, and collaborative relationships. These often involve hierarchies.
- There can be no definitive or objective truth available as an outcome of such research. In researching human emotions, subjective judgements, and self-perception, the researcher has to be aware of the rationalistic fallacy.[24]
- Research into factors that have a direct impact on the quality of children's learning has to recognise that what works at one time in one place may not have the same effect in a different context, or even the in same place at a different time or with different learners. This is of course not dissimilar to the general practice of medicine.
- Qualitative research inevitably involves change in the researcher — through an iterative process in which the researcher learns and develops as the research proceeds.

24. For more information on the fallacy, see for example https://www.informationphilosopher.com/freedom/rational_fallacy.html.

Trustworthiness in research and professional practice

It could be argued that research in education is essentially a moral activity in two key respects. The first is the issue of informed consent. Pupils, teachers, and parents are not specimens, nor the school a Petrie dish. People have a right to know that they are contributing to research with an explicit educational purpose.

Where research in schools is carried out, it needs then to follow several key ethical principles:

- Approval for the research should be subject to peer review and approved by senior staff.
- Everyone involved should know that they are taking part in a research project and should be invited to choose to opt in — the principle of informed consent.
- Confidentiality must be the norm.
- The nature, purpose, and potential applications of the research should be made clear.
- No individual's learning or potential should be compromised by virtue of participating.
- Any benefits discovered during the research should be made available to all participants.

Secondly, there is a case for arguing that research based in schools should be directly related to school improvement, closing the gap, and contributing to social justice for the most disadvantaged and vulnerable.

Central to any research-informed strategy is the issue of the trustworthiness of the research process and so the validity and reliability of the findings and conclusion. Validity and reliability are concepts essentially derived from quantitative models of research in that they are manifestations of certain aspects of scientific method, in particular the extent to which a piece of research is consistent over time (reliability) and is transferable between different contexts (validity). Thus, a set of bathroom scales are trustworthy, and so useful, to the extent that they are consistent over time (reliable) and their performance is consistent with other scales (valid). Ones response to the results of weighing oneself should be based on confidence in the accuracy and integrity of the scales.

Consider the following case. Unplanned teenage pregnancy can have highly negative impact on a young person's well-being and academic success and lead to wider social issues. One strategy to minimise the possibility of unplanned teenage pregnancy is the use of baby simulators at a cost of between £150 and £350 per doll. This is not so much aversion therapy as developing the confidence in girls and young women to make an informed and appropriate choice. Baby simulators have been used in 89 countries as part of a strategy to reduce teenage pregnancy. The dolls provide a cautionary experience in that they cry, 'urinate', and require 'feeding' 24 hours a day. When the government of Western Australia asked, prior to their introduction, if there is any evidence that the dolls actually lead to a fall in pregnancy rates, the answer was that there was no published evaluation.

A subsequent study of 2800 girls in 57 schools has found that girls who have cared for a doll may indeed have higher rates of pregnancy and abortion. The dolls do not actually work in terms of their intended outcome (though they may of course have had significant other impacts for the girls involved). Put another way the dolls are not *valid* pregnancy prevention strategy. The studies that claimed success for the product were not *reliable*, being largely based on short-term responses rather than longitudinal studies based on randomised samples. In other words, a halo, or Hawthorne, effect had occurred.[25]

Guba and Lincoln (2005) posit that the trustworthiness of a research study is important to evaluating its worth. Trustworthiness involves establishing:

- Credibility: confidence in the 'truth' of the findings.
- Transferability: showing that the findings have applicability in other contexts.
- Dependability: showing that the findings are consistent and could be repeated.
- Confirmability: a degree of neutrality or the extent to which the

25. For more detail, see Brinkman, S. A., et al. (2016). 'Efficacy of infant simulator programmes to prevent teenage pregnancy: a school-based cluster randomised controlled trial in Western Australia', *The Lancet*, 388/10057, pp. 2264-2271.

findings of a study are shaped by the respondents and not researcher bias, motivation, or interest.

A possible way of understanding trustworthiness is to think in terms of evidence in the context of a criminal trial. The guilt or innocence of the accused is largely determined by the credibility and relevance of the evidence offered by the prosecution and defence. Some forms of evidence are trusted more than others, for example, the testimony of an expert witness or DNA-based evidence. Other forms are seen as less reliable, such as hearsay testimony or anecdotal evidence. Once the relevant evidence has been presented it is the duty of the jury to decide which case has the clearest integrity. In exactly the same way, teachers and school leaders have a professional duty to consider the evidence for the key decisions they have to make.

Why bother?

Our discussion of the need for staff in schools to participate in and foster a culture of deep learning, has focused particularly on their ability to understand, apply, and learn from research, in a way that is evidence-informed but respects the contribution of all four of the elements discussed above.

For anyone who doubts the practical relevance of this or wonders what it might look like in practice, we offer two examples where we have tried to bring those elements together in order to understand the contribution of two major concepts of huge significance for educators: *intelligence* and *cognitive neuroscience.*

Practical example 1: An intelligent understanding of intelligence

Few topics in education have generated as much debate and controversy as the nature of intelligence. As with learning, intelligence remains a contested area. Indeed, the two concepts have a range of issues in parallel, notably the lack of an agreed definition and consensus as to how they might best inform educational practice. There is therefore a heated, indeed almost theological, debate with true believers and heretics gathered around the two opposing camps of 'general intelligence' and 'multiple intelligences'.

The prevailing orthodoxy about intelligence centres on general intelligence or *g* — most commonly encountered in IQ testing. IQ tests assess for 'fluid intelligence'; your cognitive functions that are dedicated towards short term/working memory, processing speed, verbal comprehension, and perceptual reasoning.

However, they do not assess for 'crystallised intelligence' — essentially knowledge, for the purposes of this discussion. A key feature of the case for learning for understanding is to move away from the focus on fluid intelligence and stress the importance of developing a unified and coherent approach that integrates fluid and crystallised intelligence — i.e. shallow and deep learning.

Sennett (2008, p. 282) identifies the following assumptions inherent in IQ tests:

- Intelligence can be measured by correct answers to questions.
- The answers will separate groups of people into a bell-shaped curve.
- The tests identify a person's biological potential rather than cultural formation.

The supporters of *g* and IQ testing argue that it provides an objective, scientific basis for making crucial decisions about children's learning. The English education system was in thrall to intelligence testing for much of the first half of the 20th century, with the result that a significant proportion of young people were systemically disadvantaged. During the second half of the 20th century, there was increasing anxiety about the intellectual veracity of testing, as well as a growing awareness that it is over-simplistic and fails to recognise the complexity and interdependency of the components of education.

The growth of comprehensive schools, and the number of students in those schools who went on to university having been told at the age of 11 that they were unsuited to an academic education, increased the disquiet at the continued use of the 11+ exam. This exam itself raises contentious issues:

- It covers a very limited range of human experience and activity.
- It provides no indication of the potential for agency and engagement.
- It assumes intelligence is fixed not learnable.

- It is subject to cultural influences, such as social class.
- Its measurements may not always be reliable.

In many ways IQ and its related testing regimes were being questioned in terms of their validity and reliability. The concern was that they did not justify the significance and confidence placed in them. There is absolutely no guarantee that a high IQ score means that a person will be a better doctor, composer, leader, or virtually any other human activity. In fact, quite the reverse may be true: 'We all know very clever people who are conspicuously lacking in horse sense' (Claxton & Lucas, 2009, p. 33).

Syed (2019) provides a graphic example of the dangers of IQ-based thinking: the crucial issue of variation. The US Air Force were experiencing a very high number of accidents with a particular aircraft. An insight led to analysis of the dimensions of the pilots and the cockpits they occupied when flying. The result of the survey demonstrated that while the cockpit was designed around the average pilot, most pilots (inevitably by mathematics) did not meet that exact average. There were so many variables influencing the interaction between the pilots and the controls that the normal distribution curve of the physiognomy of aircrew did not apply.

> The standardised cockpit of the US Air Force was not just a hazard, it is also a metaphor. It is just one example of the standardisation of our world. We have standardised education, standardised working arrangements, standardised policies, standardised medicine even standardised psychological theories. All in their different ways fail to take into account human diversity. They treat all people as manifestations of a mythical average rather than as individuals.
>
> (Syed, 2019, p. 216)

This rigidity is also the problem with IQ. It permits no variation — you are your score. Surely what is needed is a theoretical framework that recognises the complexity of human intelligence, the range of potential expressions of learning, and the interaction between them.

The narrowest definitions of intelligence based on IQ testing are clearly problematic from a range of perspectives; what is needed is a definition of intelligence based on general intelligence that actually relates to learning.

> Intelligence is a very general mental capacity, that among other things, involves the ability to reason, plan, solve problems, think abstractedly, comprehend complex ideas, learn quickly and learn from experience. It is not merely book learning, a narrow academic skill or test-taking smarts. Rather it reflects a broader and deeper capability for comprehending our surroundings — 'catching on', 'making sense' of things, or 'figuring out' what to do.
>
> (Deary, 2001, p. 17)

Sternberg (1985) proposed a model of intelligence that focuses on the interaction and interdependence of three factors: analysis, creativity, and application. It is the interaction between these three elements that constitutes the intelligence that enables us to make the choices, and to reconcile our needs with what we are able to do.

Sternberg's model is particularly apt in novel or complex situations where there are few or no precedents to draw on. Equally, this triarchic model (Figure 10) saves us from 'paralysis by analysis' by stressing the importance of practice and what is described as 'real-world' intelligence, that is the ability to flourish and to be successful outside of the normal or standard parameters of social action.

Analytical intelligence is involved when the components of intelligence are applied to evaluate, judge, or compare and contrast. It is typically involved in dealing with relatively familiar kinds of problems where the judgments to be made are of an abstract nature.

Figure 10: Sternberg's triarchic model of intelligence

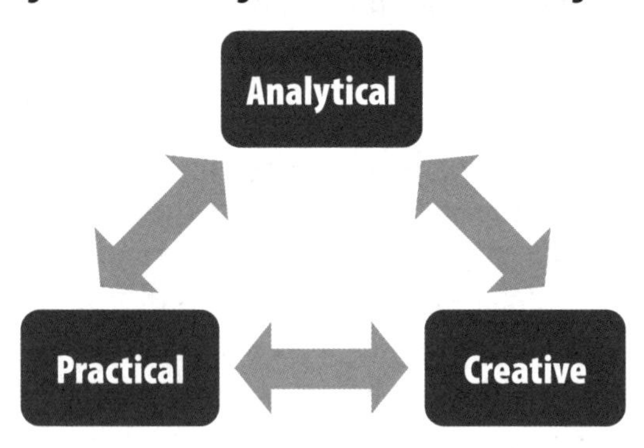

Creativity is relatively, although not wholly, domain specific. In other words, people are frequently creative in a particular domain, but this is not necessarily transferable. They also found that correlations with conventional ability tests were modest to moderate, demonstrating that tests of creative intelligence measure skills that are largely different from those measured by conventional intelligence tests.

Practical intelligence involves individuals applying their abilities to the kinds of problems that confront them in daily life, such as on the job or in the home. Much of the work of Sternberg and his colleagues on practical intelligence has centred on the concept of tacit knowledge. They have defined this construct as that which one needs to know in order to work effectively in an environment, but which is often not even verbalised never mind explicitly taught.

Sternberg argues:

> … that intelligence is not, at root, for reasoning and arguing; it is for getting things done that matter, in specific situations. Intelligence is the process that enables us, in the heat of the moment, to reconcile what we would like or need to do with what we can do, especially when normal routines and habits do not apply. Intelligence is what integrates our concerns, our capabilities and the opportunities that are open to us.
>
> (Sternberg, 1985, quoted in Claxton and Lucas, 2012, p. 32)

A fundamental difference between shallow and deep learning is the ability and propensity to act in order to achieve a desired outcome. We have termed this 'agency'. To paraphrase Marx, proponents of IQ have hitherto only interpreted intelligence in various ways — the point is to apply it in the world.

Perhaps the best known and most contentious attempt to develop a coherent model of human intellectual potential is Howard Gardner's work on Multiple Intelligences.

Gardner has expanded his original seven intelligences to nine with the addition of naturalist and existential categories (he has resisted the idea of spiritual intelligence because of the difficulties codifying quantitative and rigorous data). These are:

- Words (linguistic intelligence).
- Numbers or logic (logical-mathematical intelligence).
- Pictures (spatial intelligence).
- Music (musical intelligence).
- Self-reflection (intrapersonal intelligence).
- Physical activity (bodily-kinaesthetic intelligence).
- Social experiences (interpersonal intelligence).
- Experience of the natural world (naturalist intelligence).
- Reflecting on the nature of humanity (existential intelligence).

Although still debated, Gardner's contribution to the debate about intelligence and learning provides a highly detailed and sophisticated model that meets many of the concerns within more academically focused examples. Equally, his work can be quite arbitrarily dismissed because it does not conform to the rules of science (in the sense of being derived from experimentation and meeting criteria of validity and reliability) — which itself raises the interesting issues about the limitations of scientific method. Given the complexity of cognitive and neurological functioning it would surely be surprising if intelligence could simply be reduced to a distribution curve with precise statistical values. What is truly concerning is the amount of academic energy expended in pursuit of intellectual orthodoxy, and the passionate commitment to securing one best and only way, when it is just as possible that there might be several valid alternative perspectives.

The strengths of the Gardner's multiple intelligence framework are:

- Recognition and respect for human difference.
- Accounting for the potential to excel in different fields rather than judging by one set of narrowly focused criteria.
- Recognition that ability and potential wax and wane.
- Respect for human agency.

The potential to embed deep learning in the learning and teaching repertoire is significantly enhanced by an informed understanding of multiple intelligences. It provides opportunities for learning to be accommodated across a wide range of themes and disciplines and to do so in response to the needs and interests of learners.

We are unlikely to resolve long standing debates around the nature of intelligence here. However, by recognising and describing the interaction of a number of key variables from these debates we can create a synthesis that has the potential to inform strategies relating to effective learning. The major issue with Gardner's model of multiple intelligences is his use of the term 'intelligence'. He has acknowledged this issue of terminology while continuing to vigorously defend the intellectual integrity of his model. According to Willingham (2009, p. 161), Gardner:

> ... argues that some abilities — namely logical-mathematical and linguistic — have been accorded greater status that they deserve. Why should those abilities get the special designation 'intelligence' whereas others get the apparently less glamorous title 'talent'? ... Gardner himself has commented more than once that if he had referred to seven talents instead, the theory would not have received much attention.

The most serious critique of Gardner's work is that it is not scientific. In other words, it does not meet the basic criterion of scientific veracity — a theory must be falsifiable. The basis for falsifiability is proof derived (or not) from experimentation and the meeting of rigid criteria over validity and reliability. However, the fact that something is not falsifiable does not inhibit its potential contribution to the creation of knowledge — if it is seen as a different type of knowledge with all that this shift implies in terms of trustworthiness and applicability.

What Gardner is describing is not intended to replace or be an alternative to general intelligence, or *g*, but rather to provide framework for recognising, analysing, and so understanding the rich diversity of human potential. Whether we choose to talk in terms of intelligences or talents/abilities, Gardner offers a conceptual framework on which to base analysis and review. His model can help us develop conceptual maps and models, build hypotheses, and develop a rich vocabulary to inform dialogue between teachers and learners, between teachers and other teachers, as well as learners and their peers. That dialogue is one of the key foundations of developing a culture focused on deep learning.

So, from the perspective of enabling learning focused on the individual, current thinking about intelligence offers the teacher two powerful propositions. Firstly, intelligence is not one monolithic category, but is rather best seen as a general intellectual capacity, amenable to change and growth over time, and responsive to interventions. Secondly, there is a variety of parallel aptitudes and predispositions that describe human potential and educability, and these are underpinned by different techniques and strategies. For example, it is entirely plausible that two people with similar levels of general intelligence will perform very differently in terms of literacy, numeracy, music, or sports.

Practical example 2 — The contribution of cognitive neuroscience

> One of the contributions to education that neuroscience is capable of making is illuminating the nature of learning itself. It is unlikely that there is one single all-purpose type of learning for everything. In terms of brain structures involved learning mathematics differs from learning to read, which differs from learning to play the piano. Each memory system relies on a different brain system and develops at a slightly different time.
>
> (Blakemore & Frith, 2005, p. 139)

The impact of genetics is everywhere in our world. Hopefully you had some breakfast this morning, cereal followed by some toast perhaps — all the product of genetic manipulation, mainly by farmers. Modern wheat, oats, milk and eggs are the outcome of selective breeding over generations. Farmers have been modifying wheat for over 7000 years. Selective breeding combines use of existing, naturally present, gene variants in a species and the natural process of breeding. Genetic engineering involves a direct change to an organism›s genome in the laboratory. Understandably, we need to apply appropriate caution when shifting from discussing eggs and cereals to people — perhaps especially in the context of education, which played a central part in the discredited pseudo-science of eugenics that gained popularity and traction in the early twentieth century. Even today there are widespread myths about the brain and learning that must be addressed when considering neuroscience and its implications for learning.

The classic antagonism of *nature versus nurture* is now more often understood as *nature via nurture*. But there are fundamental and deeply held alternative perspectives. For example, James (2016) places a strong emphasis on the contexts of social deprivation:

> Locating the issue in the genes and brain of the child displaces the focus away from the family that created it and the society which created that family. The fact that about one quarter of British children leave school without five grade A-Cs at GCSE has nothing to do with genes and everything to do with the high proportion raised in low-income families.
>
> (James, 2016, p. 165)

By contrast, Plomin argues for the diametrically opposite position:

> Genetics accounts for 50 per cent of psychological differences, not just for mental health and school achievement, but for all psychological traits, from personality to mental abilities. I am not aware of a single psychological trait that shows no genetic influence.
>
> (Plomin, 2018, p. viii)

As is so often the case, the most plausible answer lies not in one position being vindicated over the other but rather in an integrated approach:

> The most logical conclusion … is that while some combination of genes and environments can strongly influence *g* (general intelligence, this combination will rarely be passed intact from parents to their children … Intelligence, in short, is *heritable*, (i.e. influenced by genes), but not easily *inheritable* (i.e. moved down intact from one generation to the next).
>
> (Mukherjee, 2016, p. 346)

What are the implications of this emerging genetic and neurological theory for our currently dominant model of learning? In his study *Why don't students like school?* (2009) Daniel Willingham argues that teachers pay insufficient attention to the research available on cognitive aspects of learning:

> … knowledge of cognitive science can help teachers balance conflicting concerns. Classrooms are, after all, not just cognitive places. They are also emotional places, social places, motivational places and so on. These diverse elements prompt different concerns for the teacher, and they sometimes conflict …

> ... cognitive scientific principles do not prescribe how to teach, but they can help you predict how much your students are likely to learn.
> (Willingham, 2009, p. 213)

However, teachers' engagement with cognitive aspects of learning should be evidence-informed rather than based on hearsay. Here are some examples of popular neuromyths:

- We are good multitaskers.
- We only use 10% of our brains.
- The left half of the brain is analytical, and the right half is creative.
- You can train your brain with brain gym and brain games.
- Men have a different kind of brain than women.
- We can learn while we are asleep.
- Babies become cleverer if they listen to classical music.
- We think most clearly when we are under pressure.

(De Bruyckere, 2015, p. 6)

The problem with these beliefs is that they are not scientific — they do not meet the core criteria of validity and reliability and therefore lack trustworthiness. There are, of course, advocates for each of these myths in the same way that some people believe that the sun rotates around the earth or that the earth is flat. There are many explanations for the persistence of such myths. The most persistent probably meet a need to explain a habitual problem, or offer well-intended but misguided interpretation and application of facts. For example, it is the case that dehydration leads to memory loss — however it takes 3 days before an absence of fluids becomes serious, not the time between the start of school and morning break. The most sensible justification for access to water is surely that it is a basic human right and a matter of personal well-being — not something that involves permission seeking and giving.

What is dangerous is when a spurious or unsound model develops an unwarranted credibility. The recent fad for 'learning styles' is a case in point. Coffield summarises his view of learning styles as 'unreliable, invalid and impractical':

> Teachers would be well advised to concentrate on formative assessment rather than on learning styles because the evidence shows that it can't

> produce significant and often substantial learning gains. In other words, providing rich dollops of feedback to students to students has been shown to have much greater impact than labelling them 'left brainers' or 'right brainers,' terms for which there is no biological justification.
>
> (Coffield, 2012, p. 226)

Blakemore (2018, pp. 190–91) provides a powerful example of how neuroscience might positively influence educational practice in schools. Her argument is derived from the following five propositions:

1. People who engage in a complex task and perform well on that task on the following day do so because their brain continued processing that task while they were asleep.
2. Our ability to carry out complex tasks depends on the time of day.
3. Teenagers do not have enough sleep — i.e. nine hours per night. Their circadian rhythms change at puberty, so they are less sleepy in the evening and sleepier in the morning.
4. Post-puberty melatonin is produced later at night, so sleepiness occurs later.
5. The current pattern of schooling deprives teenagers of their sleep and 'sleep deprivation inhibits learning and lowers mood'.

Anyone who has travelled by public transport in the early morning in London will be aware of the number of young people commuting across the city having left home before 7.00 am in order to meet their school's view of the structure of the educational day. At the same time, children in rural areas are getting up in order to walk to the bus stop to get to school at a time that bears no relationship to what the young person's brain is saying is an appropriate activity for that time of day. Add in waiting for a bus in the pouring rain and a late arrival at school and you can confirm that this is going to be a bad day. The current scheduling of schools is in many respects not fit for purpose.

Would it lead to a collapse of public order and decency if the school day started at 10.00 am and finished at 4.30 pm for some students in some schools? For example, perhaps Years 7,8, and 9 (i.e. teenagers) could be scheduled for later in the morning? However, possible reforms to school organisation informed by neuroscience go far beyond scheduling. Is there any real justification for exams at age 16 and 18, not to mention testing at 11? What about the arbitrary transfer of pupils from primary to secondary at 11, as opposed to at 14 as is the case in many high-performance education systems? These are all examples of habituated, historical practices rather than contemporary evidence-informed policies.

Caine and Caine (1994, pp. 88–95) claim to have deduced twelve principles from neuroscience that hold strong implications for education and can be linked to specific educational practices:

1. The brain is a complex adaptive system.
2. The brain is a social brain.
3. The search for meaning is innate.
4. The search for meaning occurs through patterning.
5. Emotions are critical to patterning.
6. The brain processes parts and wholes simultaneously.
7. Learning involves both focused attention and peripheral perception.
8. Learning always involves conscious and unconscious processes.
9. We have at least two different types of memory: a spatial memory system and a set of systems for rote learning.
10. We understand and remember best when facts and skills are embedded in natural, spatial memory.
11. Learning is enhanced by challenge and inhibited by threat.
12. Every brain is uniquely organised.

Consider what implications each of these propositions could have for your practice, and how much trust you place in each. On what combination of data, information, knowledge, and wisdom is that judgement based?

Conclusion

The establishment of a culture of deep learning begins with the leadership and staff of a school and the way they model deep learning in their own professional practice. It is from these seeds that the culture grows outwards to include pupils and their families.

If we are to achieve the level of change needed for our young people and ourselves to face the future in a just and sustainable way, then educators in schools are in the front line. Their understanding of learning holds the key. Deep learning for future sustainability involves openness and challenge, rigour and honesty. It recognises and respects different forms of knowledge and ways of knowing.

A powerful way forward that respects the alternative perspectives discussed in this chapter, provides a rigorous analysis, and offers a way forward in our developing understanding of deep learning is provided in five propositions put forward by Gillian Tett:

- We are all creatures of our own environment in an ecological, social, and cultural sense.
- There is no single natural cultural frame; human existence is a tale of diversity.
- We should immerse ourselves in the minds and lives of others.
- We must look at our own world with the lens of an outsider to see ourselves clearly.

Her final point is:

> ... we must actively listen to social silence, ponder the rituals and symbols that shape our routines, and consider our practices through the lens of anthropology ideas such as habitus, sense-making, liminality, incidental information exchange, pollution, reciprocity, and exchange.
>
> (Tett, 2021, p. 225)

These five propositions offer a deeply humanistic perspective that goes beyond simplistic narrative. They provide a powerful agenda for the move from shallow to deep learning through using an alternative perspective involving understanding, empathy, and inquiry.

Opportunity for self-reflection and collaborative review

- *How strong is the professional learning culture in your school? To what extent does it pervade all activities, for example meetings or purchasing decisions?*
- *What proportion of teaching and learning in your school is evidence-informed?*
- *Are research skills sessions available to all?*
- *What steps might you take to deepen the professional learning culture further?*

CHAPTER 6

RE-IMAGINING THE WHAT, HOW, AND WHERE OF LEARNING

We now accept the fact that learning is a lifelong process of keeping abreast of change. And the most pressing task is to teach people how to learn.

Peter Drucker

The simplest and most direct justification for developing a culture of innovation in education is encapsulated in two aphorisms that can be seen either as banal cliches or fundamental truths — 'if we do what we have always done we will get what we have always got' and 'we will not solve the problems of today by using the same thinking that created them'. There is a danger that the engagement with deep learning might become yet another initiative rather than creating fundamentally significant change.

Deep learning for future sustainability, as we have described it, depends on a radical re-conceptualisation of the nature of a curriculum, the role of teachers, and the prevailing orthodoxy with regard to assessment and school structures. If such innovation is to result in significant and sustainable change Matt Ridley (2020) argues it requires a culture that is 'collective and collaborative', 'organic', and 'authentic'.

> The main ingredient in the secret sauce that leads to innovation is freedom. Freedom to exchange, experiment, imagine, invest, and fail; freedom from expropriation or restriction by chiefs, priests and thieves; freedom on the part of consumers to reward the innovations they like and reject the ones they do not.
>
> (Ridley, 2020, p. 359)

Developing a culture of deep learning within the school and its communities, making use of a judicious combination of research evidence and professional judgement, and combining these with stakeholder engagement, makes it possible for leaders to envisage change and take innovative steps towards that vision, at a greater or lesser pace according to their context and confidence.

There are four areas where we think such a leader may look, in dialogue with all their stakeholders, as they begin to reimagine the 'what, how, and where' of learning for their school:

- Curriculum.
- Assessment.
- Personalisation.
- Pedagogy.

Let us look at each in turn.

Curriculum

If, for the sake of argument, we agree that one of the key functions of schools is to prepare young people for adult life — to be employable, to be committed citizens and lifelong learners, etc. — then we need to be aware of what that life might look like.

However, the shape of the future seems ever more uncertain, new trends and crises can appear quickly, and even at the time of writing:

- Many people across the world have died or are in isolation due to the Coronavirus pandemic.
- Significant parts of the UK are still recovering from the late winter floods.

- Victoria and New South Wales in Australia are counting the cost of the worst forest fires in many years.
- Civil war continues in the Yemen.
- Plagues of locusts cover parts of East Africa.
- 2019 was the hottest year on record.
- The potential of Artificial Intelligence (AI) is only just becoming clear.
- Life expectancy is higher than at any time in human history.
- The world is economically polarised — the north grows richer, the south poorer.
- More people have more access to more goods than ever before — 3.5 billion people own a smart phone.
- There has been no example of total war since 1945.
- World population was 7.9 billion in 2020.

In such a world, Harari suggests:

> ...the last thing a teacher needs to give her pupils is more information. They already have too much of it. Instead, people need the ability to make sense of information, to see the difference between what is important and what is unimportant, and above all to combine many bits of information into a broad view of the world.
>
> (Harari, 2018, p. 261)

To this we would add the capacity to act on that understanding in the common good.

A central preoccupation of this book lies in the interactions between learning and teaching, and information and knowledge. Any discussion of these relationships is bedevilled by a total lack of consensus as to authoritative definitions of these concepts and the complexity of their interactions. A further complication comes from the focus on the role of memory in learning, to the exclusion of other variables, as well as the emphasis placed on short- and long-term memory and the importance of recall. However, surely a curriculum is more than that which can be remembered? The primary purpose of a curriculum is to create knowledge not to transmit more complicated information.

It is perhaps worth returning to Bloom's taxonomy of educational learning objectives (Figure 11), as revised in 2001, which provides a challenge to the tyranny of memory in school curriculums by including categories beyond remembering.[26] The hierarchical approach used here can be debated — for example, it is difficult to see understanding being achieved without analysis — but, for Bloom, simply remembering is clearly subordinate. Understanding does not come from accumulating more remembering. Understanding, and the ability to act on or apply that, comes from the ability to conceptualise rather than memorise.

Figure 11: Bloom's Taxonomy

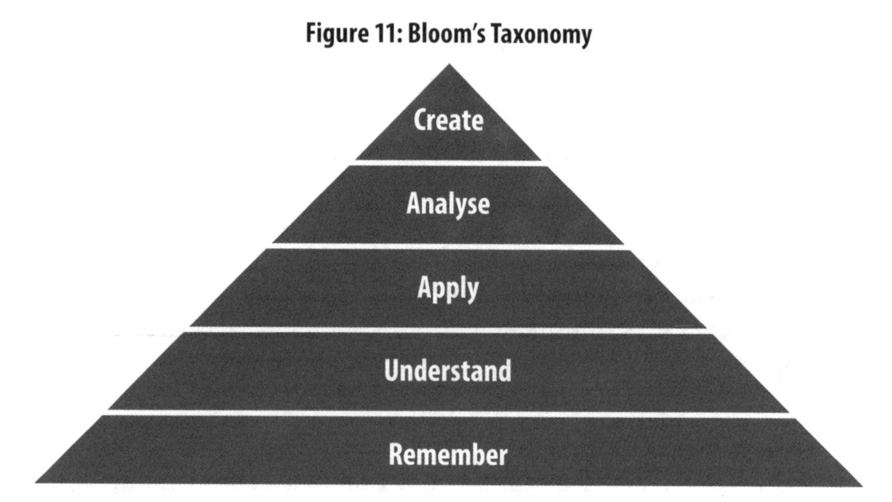

Learning the alphabet, spellings, vocabulary, times tables, names of geographical features, the laws of physics, and significant dates in history, all lend themselves to rote learning. Chanting as an aid to the memorisation of significant amounts of text is found in most faiths. What is worrying is when rote learning becomes an end in itself — as seems to have become increasingly common in England — but is not developed beyond simple memorisation:

> ... teachers in England ... reported a strongly constructivist view of teaching, but England was among the countries where students

26. On Bloom's taxonomy, first developed by Benjamin Bloom and his collaborators in 1956, see https://www.bloomstaxonomy.net/.

> reported the highest prevalence of memorisation strategies. The pattern is similar for many other English-speaking countries. In short, in some countries there is a significant gap between what teachers report to be desirable pedagogies and what actually happens in classrooms.
>
> (Schleicher, 2018 b, p. 67)

This is disturbing given that Schleicher goes on to argue that:

> Although memorisation seems to work for the easiest mathematics problems, its success as a learning strategy does not extend much beyond that.

In essence, the more complex a topic is, the less effective memorisation is as a learning tool. Indeed, this perspective is made explicit in the Ofsted Framework for School Inspection for 2019/2020. In a section headed 'Developing understanding, not memorising disconnected facts', it states:

> Learning can be defined as an alteration in long-term memory. If nothing has altered in long-term memory, nothing has been learned ... In order to develop understanding, pupils connect new knowledge with existing knowledge. Pupils also need to develop fluency and unconsciously apply their knowledge as skills. This must not be reduced to, or confused with, simply memorising facts. Inspectors will be alert to unnecessary or excessive attempts to simply prompt pupils to learn glossaries or long lists of disconnected facts.
>
> (Ofsted, 2019, p. 45)

Ofsted here presents learning as a process of moving from fluid intelligence (short-term memory) to crystallised intelligence (long-term memory), and from the accurate replication of facts to the demonstration of understanding.

While the suggested disconnect between the theory and practice of teaching is concerning, in proposing solutions it is important to move away from a combative approach and explore the potential for a middle ground that recognises the interdependence of process and content in developing a curriculum for deep learning. As Tim Oates observes:

> In public debate about the curriculum we have to move on from oppositions of:
>
> - Knowledge versus skills.
> - Learning inputs versus outcomes.
> - Theory versus application.
>
> These have been presented as gross polarities with the three on the left-hand side (knowledge, learning, and theory) being seen as 'traditional and outmoded' and the three on the right (skills, outcomes, and application, as 'progressive and modern'...)
>
> (Oates, 2018, p. 17)

We might question whether some of the polarity between 'traditional' and 'modern' has been unhelpfully reversed in recent years, but Oates's essential point remains — the polarity itself is false.

One way to understand the relationship between knowledge and skills is to think in terms of a double helix. One strand is the curriculum, the knowledge to be acquired, understood, and applied. The other is the skills and strategies necessary to create that knowledge — the cognitive curriculum. Linking the two strands are challenge and investigation — the learning process.

> Students learn more deeply when they can apply classroom knowledge to real world problems. Inquiry and design-based approaches are an important way to nurture communication, collaboration, creative and deep thinking. Attention to the processes as well as the content of learning is beneficial.
>
> (Barron & Darling-Hammond, 2010, p. 215)

Such thinking is very much reflected in the evidence-informed Future Learning model proposed by the Edge Foundation, which is grounded in three elements:

> **Real world learning**
> An approach to learning that provides students and teachers with opportunities to apply knowledge and skills through connections to the real world — from employer engagement in the classroom to externships in the workplace for teachers. These opportunities

break down the boundaries between school, college and real life, demonstrating relevance in order to build motivation.

Project-based learning (or expeditionary learning)
A pedagogical style that helps students develop knowledge, skills, and motivation through relevant, interactive learning experiences where they work on a driving question towards a tangible product. This creates opportunities to connect across traditional subject boundaries and build transferable skills such as teamwork and communication.

Community Connected Learning
A form of experiential learning where students collaborate to address societal challenges as part of their wider learning. Drawing on a rich tradition of youth social action and citizenship, students develop youth voice and leadership skills, supporting their peers, and building a deep sense of agency and purpose to drive their learning and benefit the world around them.[27]

A recently published report from Edge (2021), compiled by Dr Lynne Rogers and Dr Susan McGrath from the University College, London, Institute of Education, summarises the international research evidence to date which overall suggests each of these approaches can be effective in promoting broader and deeper learning.[28]

One of the most sophisticated and well-researched curriculum frameworks, which synthesises many ideas from around the world, can be found in the work of the Centre for Curriculum Redesign in Boston USA. Over a period of years, they have researched, built and refined the model of a 4-Dimensional (4-D) curriculum, embracing knowledge, skills, character, and meta-learning, designed to educate the 'whole child for a whole world' (Figure 12).[29] It is now available in 23 languages.

---

27. Edge Foundation, 'Our Model'. Available at: https://edge.co.uk/edge-future-learning/.
28. Dr Lynne Rogers and Dr Susan McGrath (2021), *EFL Evidence Base*. Available at: https://www.edge.co.uk/edge-future-learning/efl-evidence-base/.
29. Fadel, C., et al. (2015), *Four-Dimensional Education*. Available at: https://curriculumredesign.org/our-work/four-dimensional-21st-century-education-learning-competencies-future-2030/.

Figure 12: Centre for Curriculum Redesign 4-D framework

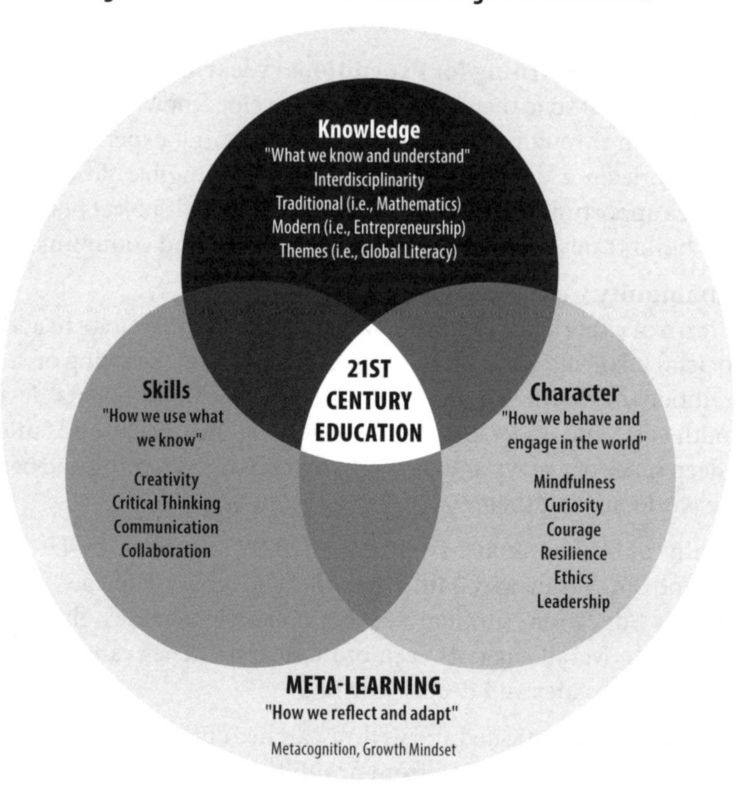

One key question in defining the nature of the curriculum is 'Are you a fox or a hedgehog?' This is the title of an essay by Isaiah Berlin that alludes to a proverb attributed to the Greek poet Archilochus: 'The fox knows many things, but the hedgehog knows one big thing'. In other words, should we aspire to breadth or depth?

The answer in terms of making the curriculum personally relevant to students is depth at the core combined with breadth in what might be best termed electives. That means a defined proportion of time working on the non-negotiables with the rest of the time following a personal learning pathway. The ratio between the required and chosen elements is determined by the needs of the learner and, hopefully, will change over time as the learner develops and matures as a self-managing learner.

The curriculum is only partly about amassing information and building knowledge. It must also focus on skills, behaviours, and personal qualities — it is about content and processes, as much about the how as the what.

A depressing number of sources define a curriculum as being the subjects taught at a school. Many schools compound the problem by referring to enrichment and extracurricular activities as beyond their core activities — to which surely the response should be that every aspect of what happens in school should be enriching and that it is wrong to imply that any learning is peripheral or marginal to the dominant hegemony of the subject.

The problem with subjects is that they can become bureaucratic — they take on a life of their own in terms of resources, the micro-political identity of subject specialists, and the Balkanization of subject silos. Thus, attempts to shift the emphasis of teaching to knowledge creation rather than replicating information by integrating subjects are often doomed, whether at school or university level. There are too many issues related to the subject-based culture to be optimistic about change. When career progression, professional status, and salary are all directly informed by the subject-focused structure, expecting change is naïve.

One of the key characteristics of deep learning is that it requires the ability to synthesise and integrate information to create knowledge. The various elements of subjects are the ingredients — not the cake. Without pushing the metaphor too strongly the ingredients need to be assembled in correct proportions and blended so that individual elements are subsumed and change their nature; if one element becomes dominant then it distorts and compromises the potential nature of the learning experience.

> We can't possibly understand everything, and the sane among us don't even try. We rely on abstract knowledge, vague and unanalysed. We've all seen the exceptions — people who cherish detail and love to talk about it at great length, sometimes in fascinating ways. And yet we all have domains in which we are experts, in which we know a lot in exquisite detail.
>
> (Fernbach & Sloman, 2017, p. 10)

So, the future-facing curriculum needs to be seen as the product of the interaction of the following component parts:

- Agreement, including all key stakeholders, on the overarching purpose of school, the values that should be espoused, and the young people we hope will emerge from our school.
- Definition of relevant educational outcomes related to cultural capital and well-being.
- Identification of the knowledge, strategies, and skills necessary to achieve the desired outcomes.
- Performance data used to inform improvement-focused strategies.
- Design of an assessment system that reinforces the focus on personal outcomes and is formative in nature, prioritising qualitative measures.

Assessment

Assessment is an area that can make or break any movement towards deeper learning. The need for some type of assessment is undeniable, but the use of an inappropriate model of assessment can have highly negative implications for the success of every antecedent stage of a learning strategy. The pivotal mantra here is that 'form follows function', in other words the purpose of something determines its design. This is why family saloon cars differ from racing cars. Deep learning requires different modes of assessment to shallow learning.

In the medieval world, academics had to participate in a viva or disputation in order to publicly demonstrate their fitness for an academic chair. In the same way journeymen in certain crafts had to produce a masterpiece in order to demonstrate their suitability to be recognised by the guild as a master. In 18th century France, such masterpieces produced by joiners were sometimes exquisite pieces of furniture in miniature. In these examples the final assessment was the ability to demonstrate work at the highest level, in other words, to apply in practical terms what had been learned. This is one of the distinguishing features of deep learning — the ability to demonstrate understanding and application. What is so worrying about the prevailing orthodoxy of assessment is that it is largely posited on shallow learning, although this is only rarely acknowledged. The assessment of shallow learning is essentially a binary process — it is largely focused on facts, nuggets of information, that can be tested by a learner's ability to replicate them accurately given that they are either right or wrong. As Joanne McCeachen (2017, p. 12) observes:

> The measurement of deep learning must be always informed by a wealth of underlying assessment evidence that captures the complete picture of who students are, what they know and whether they are prepared to use that knowledge to advance their lives and others.

The most basic analysis of the assessment of academic work is rooted in the distinction between formative and summative approaches. Summative approaches tend to have some or all of the following features:

- Tests are based on unseen papers.
- There is only limited guidance as to what an answer requires.
- Up to two years of work may be examined in two to four hours.
- Exams are individual and normally taken in silence without any interaction.
- Exam papers often assume a certain reading age, for instance in the UK one of 15 years 7 months, although the average actual reading age of students is 10 years.
- Summative assessment is essentially a memory test and as such compounds the possibility of cognitive overload.

Given the size and scope of the academic curriculum, as well as the means by which it is assessed, and the implications of poor performance, it is scarcely surprising that examinations take up a disproportionate amount of teaching and learning time in schools. This is not to mention the emotional burden on those taking an exam and those preparing them to take it.

Gardner (1999, pp. 130–40) offers an approach to assessment developed through long-term partnerships between higher education and schools and focused on learning for understanding. His approach has four elements:

1. The delineation of understanding goals — simple statements about the understandings to be achieved.
2. The 'essential questions' or provocations.
3. The identification and promulgation of 'performances of understanding'.
4. 'Ongoing assessment' rather than a final summative judgement.

Meanwhile, Bill Lucas (2021) suggests assessment focussed on creativity, critical thinking, collaboration, and aspects of communication. He comments:

> ... we may wish to evidence less of what is currently assessed. We need to have much more nuanced, strengths-based, multimodal descriptions of young people.
>
> We need to use some of the many new methods being pioneered across the world, always seeking to make the processes of evidencing progress, in all aspects of learning, visible and evidence-based. As we consider the inclusion of any new area, we will need to use evidence from the learning sciences to consider:
>
> - Its learnability.
> - Its usefulness in life.
> - The validity, reliability and practicality with which it can be assessed.
> - Its likely positive impact on the development of more expansive curricula.
>
> (Lucas, 2021, p. 36)

He concludes with the crucial point that we need to reunite assessment with curriculum and pedagogy, from which it has become harmfully separated.

Building a more personalised approach to learning

Personalisation has become the generally accepted term for an approach to education that is based on individual or personal needs and wants. It is a structured approach to reconciling generic provision with these personal needs and wants. It is not about individualisation but rather enabling access to all learning opportunities.

The *Gilbert Review* (2007) defined 'personalised learning' in the following terms:

> Personalising learning and teaching means taking a highly structured and responsive approach to each child's and young person's learning, in order that all are able to progress, achieve and participate. It means strengthening the link between learning and teaching by engaging pupils — and their parents — as partners in learning.[30]

The rationale for personalisation is partly moral — respect for the individual — and partly scientific, as demonstrated in the following quotation:

> Research is starting to investigate what gives rise to these large individual differences — the person's genes, their specific environment — and the consequences of the individual brain's developmental trajectory across adolescence.
>
> (Blakemore, 2018, p. 202)

Blakemore's analysis challenges a system that largely assumes the average is the most appropriate basis for designing education. This can be seen, for example, in the primacy of automatic cohort chronological progression — based on the myth that all children of a given age are at the same level of development. It means classrooms and schools work on a largely homogeneous basis when in fact they are highly heterogeneous. Gardner makes a similar point:

> Possessing different kinds of minds, individuals represent information and knowledge in idiosyncratic ways.
>
> (Gardner, 1999, p. 245)

A model of intelligence and its related assessment that focuses exclusively on mathematical, logical, and linguistic skills, which many believe are fixed for life and can only be measured by crude and narrow quantitative methods, is likely to be a barrier to both equity and excellence rather than fostering them.

---

30. Department for Education and Skills (2011), *2020 vision: report of the Teaching and Learning in 2020 Review Group*. Available at: http://dera.ioe.ac.uk/id/eprint/6347.

All learners are the product of a wide range of influences and experiences that lead to significant diversity in their life choices and learner identity. We are all very different, with unique profiles based on countless numbers of significant choices that have a cumulative impact on our learning profile. There is a strong case for developing what might be called a 'learning autobiography' that develops a cumulative record of all of the influences that inform our growth as learners.

One of the potential benefits of a personalised approach to teaching is the recognition and respect shown for 'idiosyncratic ways' that are expressed in almost every aspect of pupil's lives apart from their experience of school. It is the idiosyncratic that stops us being clones or automata and allows us to celebrate our humanity in respect for difference.

> The significance of our findings is that individual differences in educational achievement at the end of compulsory education are not primarily an index of the quality of teachers or schools: much more of the variance of GCSE scores can be attributed to genetics than to school or family environment.
>
> (Asbury & Plomin, 2014, p. 11)

The argument for a personalised approach does not come only from science — there is also a moral case to be made based on the value of and respect for the individual.

> ... we need a new framework to show how personal needs can be taken into account within universal equity and excellence in education. In recent years the policy agenda has grown to recognise the fact that in the context of greater diversity we can only understand these terms by putting the needs and wants of individual learners at the heart of the system.
>
> (Leadbeater, 2004, p. 6)

Leadbeater's optimism has not been borne out in recent years. In fact, education policy in England has taken quite the opposite course in a number of key respects, notably assessment and the nature of the curriculum experience. However, there are still significant opportunities to build approaches based on personalisation strategies, and both the moral and scientific case for doing so continues to grow in strength

In essence, personalisation is about negotiating agreement, working on the basis of an a la carte menu rather than a table d'hote or set menu. Even highly sophisticated diners might have an intolerance of fish or a deep aversion to celery. By respecting difference, we are more likely to secure engagement in deep learning. Thus, irrespective of age or ability, the learner is valued and respected on their own terms.

There are numerous variables that inform and influence our unique identity as learners. What makes the issue even more complex are the potential permutations emerging from the interaction of these variables. It is simply not practically possible or morally acceptable to subsume (in some sort of social blender) all the individual learner profiles in a class in a school to create an artificial sense of homogeneity.

> In times past, schools have been uniform, in the sense that they taught the same materials to all students, and even assessed all students in the same ways. This procedure may have offered the illusion of fairness, but in my view, it was not fair except for those few blessed students strong in the linguistic and logical domains.
>
> (Gardner, 1999, p. 72)

Gardner's conclusion that 'the educational process needs to be conceived quite differently' results in the imperative that schools should be 'individualised and personalised'. Hopefully Gardner is being ironic when he talks of schools 'in times past'; as Education policy in recent years has only reinforced a culture that fosters the notion of uniformity.

There are nevertheless two practical examples of personalisation currently working very successfully in the English school system — much of early years provision, and best practice in special education. In many ways it is a pity that the principles of early years and SEND learning and teaching are not sustained and spread across mainstream provision.

Those principles may be summarised as:

- Trust the learner's instincts about what they need.
- Respect the perceptions of learners and their parents.
- Focus on play and socialisation as the foundations for all learning.
- Work on the basis of personal readiness rather than cohort progression — stage not age.

- Agree the range of required and self-determined topics, for instance, literacy is not optional.
- Use formative assessment rather than summative testing.

If students are to assume greater responsibility for their own learning, then they also need to be able to articulate their significant characteristics as learners. This means developing models and a language that enables and supports personal reflection and shared dialogue. Personalising the curriculum can draw on a range of successful strategies, experience, and skills derived from the usage of Individual Learning Plans (ILP) or Individual Education Plans (IEP), such as those developed for pupils with particular special needs or disabilities.

In his model of 'powerful learning' (that shares many of the characteristics of deep learning) Brandt (1998, p. 12) argues for a range of necessary pre-conditions, which he classifies into the 'what, how, and where' of learning:

What They Learn

- What they learn is personally meaningful.
- What they learn is challenging and they accept the challenge.
- What they learn is appropriate for their developmental level.

How They Learn

- They can learn their own way, have choices, and feel in control.
- They use what they already know as they construct new knowledge.
- They have opportunities for social interaction.
- They get helpful feedback.
- They acquire and use strategies.

Where They Learn

- They experience a positive emotional climate.
- The environment supports the intended learning.

These form a good basis to build a more personalised, as well as joy-full, approach to learning.

Pedagogy

Perhaps one of the greatest challenges in the introduction of a learning culture based on deep learning is the fact that many teachers will not have experienced it as learners in their own experience of school. One of the key factors in how teachers develop their professional confidence and competence is how they were taught.

Obviously, teachers develop their own preferred style over time, but, if their personal modelling of successful teaching does not include experience of some of the components of deep learning, then it is more difficult for them to change basic assumptions and engage with alternative strategies:

> Teaching for deep understanding may conflict with deeply held beliefs about maths (e.g. that it is a fixed body of knowledge), about how students learn (e.g. you have to master the basics before you can tackle complex problems), and about the teacher's role (e.g. the sole knowledge expert in the classroom).
>
> (Leithwood et al., 2006, p. 37)

One of the most significant cliches in any discussion of teaching and learning is the exhortation to move from being 'sage on the stage to guide at the side'. The sage is typically defined in terms of the university lecture, while the guide is essentially tutoring and coaching. Although these images are stereotypes, their underpinning truth is very important in setting out a key issue in relating teaching to deep learning. They can be best understood as extremes on a continuum, whereas what is needed is flexibility across that continuum — deploying the strategy that is most appropriate to the topic being taught, the outcomes required, and the needs of the group being taught. There is a certain delight in an authoritatively delivered lecture that combines knowledge with appropriate delivery, wit, and humour. Equally, there are few educational experiences worse than the poorly delivered lecture that is solely on the lecturer's own terms, patronising, and either dogmatic or out of date. In just the same way prescriptive coaching can be counterproductive — when the views of the coach deny the needs of the learner.

The most effective teaching combines content and process, reconciling what is to be learned with how it is to be learned. The following summary and synthesis of the various sources of evidence on highly effective teaching is derived and paraphrased from Leithwood et al. (2006), Coe et al. (2014 and 2020), and Hattie and Zierer (2017):

- Teachers are committed to social justice in the classroom and believe that every human being has the potential to change, grow, and improve. They reject policies that imply arbitrary limits to human potential and design their interventions on the basis of a growth mindset.
- The most effective teachers are transparent in their practice and collaborate with students and colleagues in understanding and developing their practice. They create opportunities for sharing ideas and practice as part of working relationships and through the full range of virtual media.
- Students are helped to understand the criteria for success in any activity and use self and peer assessment as part of their learning strategies. They are helped to understand that intelligence, ability, and performance can be improved through hard work.
- Effective teachers work through challenge and feedback for their students and themselves. They share the vocabulary of challenge and feedback with their students and develop a portfolio of personal problem-solving strategies.
- The dominant mode of communication in the classroom is dialogue rather than monologue.
- Students' activities are carefully sequenced, respect prior learning, and use practice to consolidate long-term memory. Students are helped to develop a framework of subject information to develop understanding of the underlying conceptual structure and so create authentic knowledge.

Conclusion

Both the necessity and the possibility of re-imagining the 'what, how, and where' of learning in order to foster deep learning for future sustainability are suggested by a weight of evidence as well as through the lived experience of school leaders (as we shall see in part three). Where that might actually lead for any particular school will inevitably be shaped by a range of specific contextual factors. But it will also be the product of ambition and imagination. For example:

- Re-thinking the **what** of learning might include developing greater opportunities for personalised and relevant learning for children and young people.
- Re-imagining the **how** of learning might involve developing the agency of young people and their ability to understand and shape their futures in a changing world, as well as engaging more productively with parents as the first educators of their children.
- Re-focusing the **where** of learning might mean looking at flexing resourcing boundaries, particularly the use of time, use of space, location, and personnel, to better support a broad, flexible, and engaging education connected to employers and the community.

There are inevitably significant implications in making those evidence-informed changes for the way a school approaches changes to curriculum, assessment, personalisation, and pedagogy. There is, though, no reason not to make a start right now.

Opportunity for self-reflection and collaborative review

- *To what extent is the prevailing culture of your school open to innovation and challenge?*
- *Is the curriculum of your school seen primarily as the cocreation of knowledge or the transmission of information?*
- *What is the balance between summative and formative assessment in the learning experience of your students?*

- *To what extent do your students have a significant say in the Why, What, How, When, and Where of their learning?*
- *What changes would you like to see in:*
  - *Your school's curriculum?*
  - *Its approach to assessment?*
  - *The personalisation of learning?*
  - *The further development of pedagogy?*
- *Where do you think your particular starting points might be?*

CHAPTER 7

DEVELOPING TEACHING FIT FOR THE FUTURE

> *The more complex and uncertain the world in which we live, the more that alternative sources of knowledge and influence are available to students, the more open schools become to diverse clienteles, and the more varied the organisational and pedagogical strategies that teachers should deploy, the greater ... the levels of professional skill needed to meet them.*
>
> OECD, Back to the Future of Education (2001)

Before we turn in part three to look at how leaders can make such changes happen, we will review a range of evidence-informed techniques by which teachers themselves can make a significant contribution to the development of deep learning for future sustainability in their own classrooms. Our problem is often not that we do not know what we need to do to promote deep learning, but that we do not apply what we know systematically and rigorously enough.

This chapter is largely devoted to some of what a range of sources and evidence point to as some of the most effective and established teaching strategies which can enable and support deep learning. We hope this alphabetically organised review will help shape a more intensive, purposeful, and considered use of these techniques in those classrooms today that are getting ready to face the future.

In using this chapter please remember that pedagogy is not something done to learners, but instead requires their active engagement. Likewise, learning is not something to be imposed on learners, it requires involvement and agency on their part as well. One of the great myths in teaching is that it is possible for one human being to motivate another. The truth is rather that a person can discover what motivates others and support and reinforce their commitment to outcomes they themselves seek.

Some of the interventions we have included might be seen as contentious, and we try always to retain the deference to experience and rejection of absolute theoretical perspectives which offers the most reliable and authoritative source and justification of professional practice. It would be naïve to ignore the evidence that the classic lecture/presentation is still the default model for many providers of education as well as the various stakeholders — notably parents and employers. In fairness it must also be conceded that a well-designed lecture that is authoritative, relevant, and engagingly presented is, potentially, a powerful learning experience. The addition of humour, mild self-deprecation, and skilful use of PowerPoint almost guarantees high satisfaction. Sadly, however, by most criteria 'chalk and talk' teacher-centred approaches, based on monologue, do not work for all students and, when combined with summative models of assessment, the possibility of deep learning being inhibited, if not fundamentally compromised, is very real.

A key part of these approaches is that learners too need to understand the interventions that are available and to become active participants in the selection of appropriate strategies. In other words, they need to become consciously competent about the relationship between their needs as learners and the provision of appropriate intervention strategies. This can be a challenging aspect of such pedagogies, but also offers great rewards.

What follows is an overview of a range of interventions to increase access to effective learning, which, taken together, can be seen as a menu of possibilities to support deep learning. Between them they ensure that as much attention is devoted to the *how* of deep learning as to the *what*.

Challenge

Challenge, in all its forms, is fundamental to the development of deep and effective learning. In fact, it is one of the pivotal characteristics that distinguishes deep and shallow approaches to learning. The development of the confidence necessary to respond to the widely differing challenges that epitomise modern life is one of the most significant outcomes for learners of any age. Indeed, we suggest that human beings are at their most effective as learners when faced with a challenge, a problem to solve, or an inquiry to follow.

Learning for understanding requires the confidence and skills in order to be able to thrive in an increasingly complex world. Schools are complex and often challenging environments, but they are as nothing compared with a Saturday night in an A and E department in a hospital, finding accommodation for a homeless refugee family, or meeting courier delivery deadlines.

> Our daily lives routinely require sophisticated problem solving and our current point in social history places a premium on the possession of intellectual capital ... most of us are confronted daily with personal and social challenges made increasingly complex by the increasingly diverse communities in which we live.
>
> (Leithwood et al., 2006, p. 8)

Challenge-based approaches are how we move from shallow learning based on the replication of information to deep learning based on the creation of knowledge, personal understanding, and the ability to act and apply.

> Optimal experiences usually involve a fine balance between one's ability to act, and the available opportunities for action. If challenges are too high one gets frustrated, then worried and eventually anxious. If challenges are too low then relative to one's skills one gets relaxed, then bored. If both challenges and skills are perceived to be low, one gets to feel apathetic. But when high challenges are matched with high skills, then [there is] deep involvement.
>
> (Csikszentmihalyi, 1997, p. 30)

The critical relationship here is the balance between the level of challenge faced with the level of skill required. Only when the ratio is right does learning and engagement occur, and this balance is one of the key functions of effective teaching and facilitating.

Most human activity, whether at work, socially, or at recreation, is a form of problem-solving. From solitary puzzles like crosswords or sudoku, to team sports, or reading detective novels (perhaps a vicarious form of problem-solving), people love challenges. Some people play computer games; other people play bridge. Most work is, in essence, sequential problem-solving, usually shared with others. Indeed, one way of understanding human evolution is to see it in terms of an increasing capacity to solve problems collaboratively.

Let us return again for a moment of our metaphor of the double helix: one strand consists of the challenge (the knowledge to be acquired, understood and applied), the other strand is the skills and strategies necessary to create that knowledge (the cognitive curriculum), and these two strands are linked by challenges and inquiry (the learning process). If challenges and skills are in an appropriate ratio, then the outcome is 'flow'. That is variously described as being 'in the zone', 'ecstasy', 'rapture'.

The function of the teacher, coach, or facilitator is to match *what* must be learned with *how* it is to be learned. In particular, the most effective teachers are those who ensure that the relationship between challenge and skills is at the optimum level to achieve flow.

> Relaxed alertness is the optimal state of mind for meaningful learning. People in a state of relaxed alertness experience low threat and high challenge. Essentially the learner is both relaxed and to some extent excited or emotionally engaged at the same time. This is the foundation for taking risks in thinking, questioning and experimenting, all of which are essential. In this state the learner feels competent and confident and has a sense of meaning and purpose.
>
> (Caine et al., 2009, p. 21)

What Caine is describing here is the basis for moving from shallow to deep learning. A crucial function of challenge in learning is to facilitate this movement. In essence, this is moving from managing information to creating knowledge — from accurate replication to understanding and the ability to apply and use that knowledge in practice.

Students learn more deeply when they can apply classroom knowledge to real world problems. Inquiry and design-based approaches are an important way to nurture communication, collaboration, creative and deep thinking. Attention to the processes, as well as the content of learning is beneficial.

(Barron & Darling-Hammond, 2010, p. 215)

Activities and ideas to help create a culture of challenge:

- Start each day with 10–15 minutes of challenge based 'warm-up' activities e.g. anagrams, cryptic clues, memory tests, logic puzzles, sudoku, concentration exercises, speed quizzes — individual and shared, or personal and competitive.
- Build on learners' prior knowledge by getting them to identify issues and problematise the topic. Introduce topics in terms of challenges, questions, and problems rather than content. 'What do we need to learn about X?'.
- Provide graduated extension work to enable individuals to progress at their own rate (3 Chillies — hot, hotter, hottest).
- Engage in sustained research projects (that may form the basis of self-managed study) over a period of time, increasing in significance as students grow in confidence. See the International Baccalaureate for examples of research-based learning at primary, middle, and diploma levels.
- Use strategies and skills to support responding to learning challenges consistently across the school, giving all members of the school community regular support to embed these skills into consistent practice.
- Once a year, or even every term, run a 'Challenge Week' for the entire school. This could involve all students and adults being involved in activities outside the standard curriculum that involves a range of personal challenges and opportunities for new experiences and learning.
- In addition to sports day and house sports competitions, organise a 'Thinking Olympics'.

- Setting up a 'Challenge Committee' responsible for developing challenges across the school and curriculum.
- Instituting a 'Challenge of the Day' designed to get the entire school community focused on an issue or problem.
- Set up a chess club and/or other clubs to play games based on strategy and problem solving.
- Develop a repertoire of age-appropriate computer games that have a focus on challenge.
- Debating Competitions, see for example, the English-Speaking Union schools Mace competition and the Institute of Ideas Debating Matters competition.
- Set up reading circles to focus on key ideas and texts.
- Introduce philosophy for children.[31]
- Use assemblies, case studies, scenarios, and leadership tasks to develop community debates on moral issues and themes.

31. See for example Philosophy for Children (www.p4c.com).

Coaching, mentoring, and tutoring

Coaching and mentoring are essentially learning relationships and as such are primarily concerned with personal change through the creation of understanding. However, what is the difference between coaching and mentoring? Here we follow classical usage, the role of the character Mentor in Homer's *Odyssey* was guiding Telemachus in the absence of Odysseus. More historically, the philosopher Aristotle served as a mentor to Alexander the Great. Traditionally, mentoring is seen as a long-term developmental relationship and coaching as a specific short-term supportive intervention.

Increasingly it is the case that the theoretical boundaries between coaching and mentoring are seen as unhelpful or blurred because they are both part of a helping relationship. These relationships may also reflect changing priorities, for example, a new school principal may be offered broad support through mentoring, but may need coaching through specific challenges, for instance a performance management issue. Coaching and mentoring are, perhaps, the most 'natural' of learning relationships. When seen in combination with counselling they can be seen as a continuum of different types of helping relationship with different strategies to meet different outcomes.

This spectrum, shown in Table 4, covers a range of strategies from the specific intervention (coaching) to the non-directive support (counselling). What is important is to identify the most cost-effective strategy in terms of time and impact. Coaching in particular is a high impact and low leverage strategy — it can achieve more for less. However, it is important to recognise and respect the needs of the learner and deploy the most appropriate strategy.

Table 4: Definitions of coaching, mentoring, and counselling

Coaching	Mentoring	Counselling
A focused intervention or series of interventions to provide explicit support in developing specific skills, techniques and strategies.	A sustained, one-to-one relationship based in trust in which the mentor actively supports the learner to build capacity to enhance personal effectiveness.	A therapeutic relationship which is designed to support personal understanding and facilitate change and enhance well-being.

In their various guises, helping relationships appear throughout history and across cultures as the optimum means of enhancing individual learning and development. Most of us develop language as small children through an intensive one-to-one relationship; we learn to drive on the same basis. The greatest artists and musicians have usually had their innate ability developed in the same way. The concept of apprenticeship was central to most trades for centuries and reflects the balance of mentoring and coaching in effective learning and development. The transition from apprentice to master craftsperson reflects the movement from coaching to mentoring.

We can thus extend our discussion of coaching as a learning relationship into a more detailed model that explores the nature of learning for understanding in terms of its component elements. One of the great strengths of the coaching approach is its potential to enable the movement from replication into the demonstration and application of understanding. Two further theoretical models reinforce the potential of coaching: *scaffolding* and the *zone of proximal development.*

- Scaffolding in the learning relationship is concerned with how the coach or facilitator sets about:

- Securing interest and engagement.
- Clarifying the task.
- Maintaining motivation and focus.
- Providing feedback by modelling strategies and outcomes.
- Controlling frustration and risk.
- Confirming and reinforcing success.

Vygotsky's (1978) concept of the zone of proximal development (Figure 13) describes the gap between what the learner working alone can achieve and the greater performance possible with the support of a skilled helper, facilitator, mentor, or teacher.

Figure 13: Vygotsky's zone of proximal development

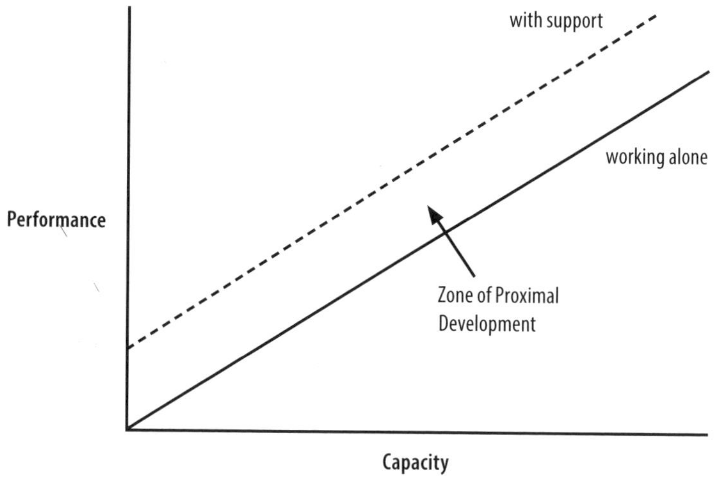

Joyce and Showers, Bloom, and Vygotsky all point to one central and fundamental theme — coaching and mentoring are about learning but also personal change. A key element therefore is that coaching is a fundamentally personalised activity based on the systematic analysis of the needs of the individual.

Strategies to develop a culture of one-to-one helping through coaching and mentoring:

- Developing a shared understanding of the theory and practice of coaching and mentoring, for example by using the Education Endowment Foundation's *Putting Evidence to Work.32*
- Leaders adopting the language of JPD (Joint Practice Development) rather than CPD (Continuing Professional Development).
- Introducing CMC (Coaching/Mentoring/Counselling) as a key leadership and learning strategy.
- Adding CMC to all school policies with appropriate definitions and exemplars.
- Introducing student CMC — peer coaching and academic support.
- Providing training and support for all adults and pupils, notably deep listening, negotiation, building consensus, review, and reflection.
- Monitoring and evaluating impact to secure and embed best practice.
- Creating time and space for meetings.

---

32. Education Endowment Foundation (2019), *Putting Evidence to Work – A School's Guide to Implementation.* Available at: https://educationendowmentfoundation.org.uk/education-evidence/guidance-reports/implementation.

Collaborative learning

There seems little doubt that it is easier to lead an autonomous institution (or classroom), with a traditional hierarchical structure, clear division of labour, and well-defined and logical bureaucratic procedures — than a complex collaborative network or a community. However, effective leadership and teaching has to be about engagement and connection:

> The best bosses understand and care about the social motivation of all members of the team. Bosses have to foster better connections between themselves and their team, among team members, and between the team and other outside groups and individuals critical to

> success … Creating this identification, this attachment to the group, is an essential component of successful leadership.
>
> (Lieberman, 2013, pp. 273–74)

Although there are numerous possible permutations of leadership styles and strategies, in the context of collaborative learning two behaviours are particularly appropriate. The first is dialogue: where the teacher or leader is both visible and available to engage in rich conversations in which they demonstrate effective communication, explain, enthuse, and help develop personal understanding and engagement. The second, closely related, strategy is modelling: where through their day-to-day behaviour teachers and leaders act as a tangible exemplar of the behaviours that are considered appropriate.

Although a great deal can be learned by an individual working on their own, there is abundant evidence that learning is an essentially social relationship — the long history of teachers, tutors, facilitators, mentors, and coaches bears abundant witness to the importance of relationships in learning. Equally the importance of parents, grandparents, and peer support is demonstrably a significant component of successful learning. This is in fact true beyond humans. There is clear evidence from comparative anatomical studies that in the higher apes brain size is directly correlated with the quality of social interaction. Learning requires interaction.

However, it is not enough just to have a teacher or equivalent. All learning relationships need to be positive in terms of their quality and integrity. It is important to stress that it is not only quality of relationships between teachers and learners that are important. Equally significant are the relationships between teachers and their colleagues and learners and their peers. Day and his colleagues capture the essence of the link between relationships and learning:

> Some recent studies show that trust remains a powerful and strong predictor of student achievement even after the effects of student background, prior achievement, race, and gender have been taken into account. Therefore, school leaders need to pay careful attention to the trust they engender in teachers, students, and parents if they wish to improve organisational performance still further.
>
> (Day et al., 2009, p. 244)

Trust is the essential prerequisite for any collaborative human activity from the most intimate relationships and deepest friendships, to professional relationships, working in teams, or living in a community. For learning to take place, then, alongside challenge, trust and empathy are critical elements, as are sensitivity, responsiveness, respect, and the core skills of listening and attending.

The emotional climate of the school might be best understood in terms of the emotional literacy of the school as a community. This embraces the behaviours, strategies, and norms that inform relationships, and the policies and resources that are devoted to optimising positive relationships. There are numerous formulations of the possible components of a model of emotional literacy — a generic framework might include the following elements:

- Recognising emotions in self and others and developing strategies to manage those emotions.
- Being aware of personal strengths and areas for development.
- Being empathic and sensitive to others articulating concern.
- Being sensitive to differences and respecting and valuing alternative perspectives.
- Listening and responding appropriately — 'Yes and ...' not 'Yes but ...'.
- Analysing problems and developing effective responses.
- Engaging with others and building positive relationships.
- Summarising and synthesising, building consensus.
- Cooperating, negotiating, and managing conflict using team-based approaches.
- Help-seeking and help-giving.
- Monitoring and reviewing task and processes.

These skills and behaviours are relevant and available for all members of the school community from five (and younger) to 50 (and older). They are essential to effective learning and to managing, leading, and being together in community. In essence, the skills for learning are the same as skills for living and working, and these need to be embedded in every dimension of a school's life. If one of the functions of a school is to prepare young people for a life in relationships, living in a community, and for employment, then it must be recognised that life involves collaborative working and learning. Success in relationships and as a member of any type of community requires emotional literacy. Most jobs involve collaborative problem-solving; most workers, right across the employment spectrum, cooperate to complete tasks, meet deadlines, and find effective solutions to a diverse range of issues.

Learning requires multiple alternative social relationships; in schools these necessarily include relationships with other learners. The school's structures and relationships need to optimise the opportunities for problem-based collaborative working if it is to be genuinely preparing people for lifc.

In practical terms this means that:

- The school recognises that personal relationships are primarily a moral issue at the heart of the school's values and purpose.
- The school works towards building a high trust culture as the essential precursor to improvement and learning.
- Leadership in the school is focused on developing an emotionally literate community, largely through modelling and dialogue.
- Training is provided to ensure consistent use of the interpersonal skills necessary to secure effective learning, notably listening and empathy.
- There is a deeply embedded culture of review and reflection that permeates learning activities, meetings and all social interactions.

Creativity and innovation

The first report of the Durham Commission on Creativity and Education (2019) defines creativity as:

> The capacity to imagine, conceive, express, or make something that was not there before.[33]

33. Durham Commission on Creativity in Education, 'First Report' (2019). Accessed at: https://www.dur.ac.uk/creativitycommission/report/firstreport/.

Meanwhile for Will Gompertz (2015, p. 194), the purpose of education is expressed this way:

> Students need to leave education as independently minded, intellectually curious, self-confident, and resourceful individuals who feel prepared for, and excited by the future.

Creativity and preparation to face the future successfully are inextricably linked. The development of skills and strategies to enhance creativity and innovation are fundamental to any model of a curriculum for the future and need to be reflected in appropriate teaching approaches. Creativity and innovation are also fundamental to any curriculum that is contributing to social, economic, artistic, and personal well-being.

'Create' is at the top of Bloom's taxonomy for a reason. As Alane Jordan Starko (2017) points out in her book *Creativity in the Classroom,* the strategies that support creativity — solving problems, exploring multiple options, and learning inquiry — also support depth of understanding.

The NACCCE report *All Our Futures: Creativity, Culture and Education* (1999), drew a useful distinction between 'teaching creatively' and 'teaching for creativity'. It defined the former as 'using imaginative approaches to make learning more interesting and effective', and the latter as 'forms of teaching that are intended to develop young people's own creative thinking or behaviour'.[34]

There is of course a close relationship between the two terms. The report states clearly that 'teaching for creativity involves teaching creatively' (p. 90) and notes that 'young people's creative abilities are most likely to be developed in an atmosphere in which the teacher's creative abilities are properly engaged'.

The Durham Report provides a detailed analysis of the research into the pedagogical issues that inform embedding creative thinking within the curriculum.

34. National Advisory Committee on Creative and Cultural Education (1999) *All Our Futures: Creativity, Culture and Education,* p. 102. Available at https://sirkenrobinson.com/pdf/allourfutures.pdf.

Strategies and interventions for teaching for creativity:

- Opportunities to 'fail without fear', to be reflective, and to try again, thereby developing resilience.
- A school culture which does not have a hierarchy of disciplines (such as over-privileging arts or mathematics) and offers a rich and varied curriculum, recognising the role played by creativity and the imagination in subjects such as physics or history, as well as subjects traditionally deemed to be creative.
- A classroom culture tolerant of ambiguity, paradox, and diverse points of view.
- Pedagogies which encourage experimentation, multiple perspectives, persistence, and collaboration.
- Opportunities for the unexpected.
- A system which rewards the creativity of students in all its aspects.

Durham Commission on Creativity and Education,
'Second Report' (2021, p. 66)

Growth Mindset

The concept of mindset is fundamental to a wide range of strategies relating to successful engagement with deep learning. The theory of mindsets as developed by Carol Dweck is primarily concerned with attitudes to success and failure and the implications for personal, team, and organisational culture.

Some believe that success is based on innate ability; they can be said to have a 'fixed' theory of intelligence (or fixed mindset). In contrast those with a 'growth' or 'incremental' theory of intelligence (a growth mindset) believe that success is based on hard work, learning, training, and doggedness.

Table 5: Characteristics of fixed and growth mindsets

Fixed Mindset	Growth Mindset
Intelligence is inherited and so is fixed	Intelligence is not fixed – nature via nurture
Avoids change	Welcomes innovation and opportunities
Avoids the possibility of making mistakes	Sees assessment as an opportunity to develop and grow.
Risk avoidance	Welcomes risks as an opportunity to extend learning experiences
I can't do this.	I can't do this yet.
Avoids engagement with other learners	Welcomes opportunities to learn with others

For feedback to make an impact on an individual's learning, potential achievement, and possible success, the teacher/facilitator/coach has to focus on their developing a growth mindset.

> We identified two different goals. The first is a 'performance goal'. This goal is about winning positive judgements of your competence and avoiding negative ones. (students) … want to look smart and avoid looking dumb. The other goal is a 'learning goal': the goal of increasing your competence. It reflects a desire to learn new skills, master new tasks, or understand new things. A desire to get smarter.
> (Dweck, 2000, p. 15)

Dweck's idea of the 'performance goal' fits exactly with the definition of shallow learning in chapter 4. Equally, their category of 'learning goal' coincides with the attributes of deep learning. The development of a growth mindset is a key characteristic of successful learning irrespective of age or perceived intellectual ability.

Contemporary research in neuroscience demonstrates that the brain is far more adaptable than was previously thought. Research on brain plasticity has shown how connectivity between neurons, the key to successful learning, can be changed by a range of environmental factors and specific interventions designed to modify brain functioning. With an appropriate programme, neural networks can be encouraged to grow new connections, strengthen existing ones, and build insulation that speeds the transmission of impulses. This enhances neural effectiveness and the potential for learning by asking questions, practicing, and following good nutrition and sleep habits.

However, the issue is as much psychological as neurological. Children often decide at a very early age whether they are bright or dim, and this view is reinforced (often unwittingly) by parents, peers, the language of some teachers, and the organisation of schools and classrooms. The essence of a growth mindset is moving from 'I can't' to 'I can't yet'.

Development of a growth mindset can be supported by focusing on the four areas indicated in Figure 14, remembering that the growth mindset school is a macrocosm of the growth mindset classroom.

Figure 14: Developing a growth mindset

Strategies to support the development of a growth mindset:

- Understanding the plasticity of intelligence.
- Setting demanding expectations and challenging quality criteria.
- Developing a language of growth and improvement focused on perseverance.

- Emphasising process over product.
- Recognising and celebrating work in progress and respecting that the struggle to improve requires effort.
- Building a portfolio of techniques and strategies focused on improvement.
- Providing structured displays of the process of producing high quality work.
- Creating a low-risk culture that accepts mistakes as opportunities to learn and improve.
- Developing a shared vocabulary that is used consistently across the school e.g. effort, persistence, challenge, stickability, feedback, challenge, risk, struggle.

Memory, practice, and learning

Fundamental to most learning situations is the relationship between learning and memory. The usefulness of the memorisation of facts (i.e. rote learning) as a teaching method is contested, but remains part of the portfolio of strategies of many teachers, not least in terms of summative assessment. We noted previously the danger of rote learning becoming an end in itself, and observed that the more complex a topic the less effective a strategy it is. But the role of memory in learning is nonetheless important.

Progress in any field of human activity is the result of the appropriate combination of a number of complex variables — intrinsic motivation, ability, appropriate teaching and coaching, and practice. Practice is sometimes demonised as being rote learning by another name, but in reality it is very difficult to conceptualise meaningful and sustainable progress without a commitment to practice.

Practice can help the learner master information, develop a repertoire of skills and techniques, and embed understanding so that it becomes intuitive. Perhaps above all it can help develop the confidence that comes from these newfound abilities. Any professional musician, athlete, dancer or craftsperson will stress the importance of a regular practice routine and, crucially, effort and application.

In his study of success and high performance, Malcolm Gladwell, put forward the concept of the '10,000-thousand-hour rule'. In essence, he describes how a variety of highly successful people, such as Bill Gates or the Beatles, have one overarching factor in common — over the years they practiced for a total of 10,000 hours or more. Gladwell cites a research project based on the development of young violinists at the Berlin Academy of Music. The students were divided into three groups — firstly those with the potential to become world class, secondly those who were good, and thirdly those who were destined for school teaching.

> In the first few years everybody practiced the same amount, about two or three hours per week … The students who would end up the best in their class began to practice more than everyone else; six hours a week by age nine; eight hours a week by age twelve; sixteen hours a week by age fourteen, and up and up until by the age of twenty they were practicing well over thirty hours per week.
>
> (Gladwell, 2008, p. 38)

Significantly Gladwell defines practice at the highest level as 'purposely and single-mindedly playing their instruments with the intent to get better'. The concert violinist Nicola Benedetti describes her work as creating:

> the feeling of enrichment that comes from making an effort. If I stick with one annoying finger movement, I know that the feeling the child will get at the end, when it works, is better than just being quickly satisfied by novelty.[35]

Benedetti says that children from different backgrounds are always amazed by the fact she has to practise for four to six hours a day. 'There are no shortcuts'.

The 10,000-hour model has its attractions — it also has significant detractors, not least those who contest the accuracy of counting the hours

35. Thorpe, V. (2013), 'Stick to one instrument, violinist Nichola Benedetti tells pushy parents', *Guardian*, 5 May. Available at: http://www.theguardian.com/education/2013/may/05/nicola-benedetti-violin-pushy-parents.

over such a protracted period. Equally, it ignores just how many variables are in play over that period — the quality of coaching, owning a decent violin, having parental support, and last but by no means least, intrinsic motivation. Simplistically, practice involves repetition in order to develop memory — whether kicking a ball or remembering the Periodic Table. Practice is equally important in language development, the more we use vocabulary, the more confident we become deploying it. The more we practice speaking, the more fluent we become — and this effect is essentially the same if we are five or 55.

However, practice in and of itself is not enough to ensure progress — how can we be certain that we are practicing the right things or executing the skills in question correctly — hence the importance of feedback. Feedback, drawing on Dweck's model of Growth Mindsets, ensures practice is developmental and secures and consolidates incremental improvement. Perhaps we need to allow for more time for learners to practice to enhance confidence and a sense of control leading to an enhanced sense of personal efficacy and well-being.

Alongside feedback, strengthening a sense of personal efficacy and well-being involves a range of everyday and sometimes quite mundane basic requirements, which, like any good sports coach, the effective teacher will encourage.

Personal wellbeing variables influencing effective learning include:

- A sense of personal well-being based on self-confidence, self-trust, and a belief in their potential to succeed.
- An emotional state of relaxed alertness — involved, interested, ready to work, and without negative pressures.
- Breakfast that provides a balance of carbohydrates and protein.
- A diet low in fat and sugar with access to fruit and water when required.
- Sufficient sleep — from 10 hours 30 minutes at age 6 to 8 hours at age 16.

- Most children will benefit from an hour of significant exercise every day — regular play, walking, cycling, or involvement in team sports.
- Confidence in being unconditionally loved and valued with very clear and shared values and expectations.

Metacognition

Metacognition is pivotal to deep learning because it focuses the learner on the process of understanding the *way* in which they learn as well as *what* they learn — in essence it is about how understanding learning enhances learner understanding. Another way of explaining this process is to see it in terms of reflexivity; that is critical review of one's own beliefs, norms, and practices, drawing conclusions about the appropriateness of their current state, and engagement with alternative perspectives if necessary.

Adey (2012) refers to programmes which have successfully demonstrated that better thinking can be positively affected by appropriate teaching strategies — convincing evidence of the plasticity of intelligence:

> A recent evaluation of the Philosophy for Children (P4C) programme in one local authority's schools showed an effect size on cognitive abilities of 0.48 … the gains made by the experimental group over the controls was maintained for at least two years …
>
> The cognitive acceleration (CA) approach has been demonstrating big effects for years … students who used CA in science … scored about 1 grade higher in their GCSE science, mathematics and English compared with matched controls.
>
> (Adey, 2012, p. 211)

His work demonstrates that carefully designed interventions can have a significant impact on a learner's cognitive capacity and thereby on their academic performance. Crucially he demonstrates that intelligence is not fixed and therefore appropriate interventions will raise achievement.

His work is reinforced by the Sutton Trust and Education Endowment Foundation investigation into teaching and learning strategies that make a significant difference to pupil attainment. That research identifies metacognition and self-regulation as one of the most potent and effective strategies.[36] In the classification of the full portfolio of strategies metacognition and self-regulation are identified as both high impact and low cost.

The report defines metacognition in the following terms:

> Metacognition is about the way learners monitor and purposefully direct their learning ... By metacognitive strategies we mean the strategies we use to monitor or control our cognition ...

It points to evidence-based strategies to enhance the potential contribution of metacognitive approaches:

- Acquiring the professional understanding and skills to develop pupils' metacognitive knowledge.
- Explicitly teaching pupils metacognitive strategies, including how to plan, monitor, and evaluate their learning.
- Support pupils to plan, monitor, and evaluate their learning.
- Setting an appropriate level of challenge to develop pupils' self-regulation and metacognition.
- Promoting and developing metacognitive discussion in the classroom.
- Explicitly teaching pupils how to organise and effectively manage their learning independently.

Finally, the report suggests that schools should support teachers to develop knowledge of these approaches and expect them to be applied appropriately. The potential impact of metacognitive strategies is also significantly enhanced if pupils are made to feel that they have a personal responsibility for their learning, moving away from a dependency culture, and working collaboratively with their peers.

In their meta-analysis of the key cognitive factors influencing successful learning, Schneider and Stern (2010, p. 85) identify ten key cognitive variables that, in various permutations, seem to determine the creation of understanding. Effective learning environments:

---

36. Education Endowment Foundation, 'Metacognition and self-regulation' in *Teaching and Learning Toolkit*. Available at: https://educationendowmentfoundation.org.uk/education-evidence/teaching-learning-toolkit/metacognition-and-self-regulation.

- Stimulate learners to be mentally active.
- Address prior knowledge.
- Integrate fragmented pieces of knowledge into meaningful structures.
- Balance concepts skills and meta-cognitive competence.
- Help people to organise knowledge hierarchically.
- Provide models and frameworks to help learners structure their knowledge, e.g. lesson structures, modelling, and displays.
- Recognise that successful learning may be inhibited by the limited capacity of working memory.
- Recognise that learning is the product of the complex interplay of cognition, motivation, and emotion.
- Create optimal learning environments that enable the learner to transfer knowledge between contexts.
- Recognise that time and effort invested in practising problem-solving and extending one's knowledge base are among the most important factors influencing the success of learning.

The practical implications of developing strategies to support thinking include:

- Providing training in metacognitive strategies for all pupils and all staff — become a thinking school so that lessons and meetings exemplify metacognitive principles in terms of review and application.
- School leaders modelling cognitive strategies in all aspects of the school's working — for example using restorative justice strategies rather than punishment-based approaches.[37]
- Embedding cognitive strategies across the curriculum, ensuring consistent application, and assuming their use in all activities.
- Pupil voice initiatives which focus on their involvement in developing and enhancing learning and teaching.

---

37. For example as applied by the approach and practice training group Restorative Justice 4 Schools, see www.restorativejustice4schools.co.uk.

Multilingual Thinking in Multicultural Classrooms

Schools are microcosms of society, and as such they draw upon the multilingual and multicultural richness of the societies in which they are based. How then do we best establish a culture in the school and classroom that reflects, celebrates, and embraces this richness to drive every aspect of the teaching and learning process (Staricoff, 2021)?

There are many studies asserting the benefits of establishing a multilingual approach to the teaching and learning process. For example, Marian and Shook (2012) state that 'today more of the world's population is bilingual than monolingual', and note this trend not only facilitates cross-cultural communication, but also that bilingualism has a positive impact on cognitive abilities, leading to better attention and task-switching capacities.[38]

They find this is true across the whole age spectrum and go on describe how managing multiple languages appears to have 'broad effects on neurological function' and how this leads to 'enriched cognitive control, improved metalinguistic awareness (ability to recognise and be playful with language), better memory, visual-spatial skills and creativity'. Moreover, these benefits are 'not exclusive to people who were raised bilingual; they are also seen in people who learn a second language later in life'. It is very powerful to note that research studies also demonstrate that establishing a multi-lingual classroom can go beyond having a direct benefit for multilingual students and in fact these environments actually benefit *all* children.

In an interview published on the Erasmus+ online platform Dr Dina Mehmedbegovic, from the University College, London, Institute of Education, discusses the importance of communicating to children and their families that every language a child speaks is important. She links this ability to greater success in terms of their future employability and their ability to convert their linguistic capital into economic capital for the good of society.[39]

---

38. Marian, V. and Shook, A. (2012) 'The cognitive benefits of being bilingual', *Cerebrum* 13. Accessed at: https://www.ncbi.nlm.nih.gov/pmc/articles/PMC3583091/.

39. Mehmedbegovic, D. (2016) 'Education Talks: Bilingualism in Education', *School Education Gateway*. Available at: https://www.schooleducationgateway.eu/en/pub/viewpoints/interviews/education-talks-bilingualism-.htm.

In a study conducted by Lauchlan (2012), researchers at the University of Strathclyde found that bilingualism also has a positive effect on children's ability to think creatively, which de Villa (2017) also sees as an essential tool for second language acquisition. This symbiotic relationship between critical thinking and a multilingual learning environment is at the heart of the multilingual thinking approach to the teaching and learning process and the presentation of the curriculum developed by JONK.[40]

In order to make a multilingual approach integral within the daily operation of the classroom, JONK defines three principal means of incorporation. The underlying principle is that at any time the children are able to access the learning and engage in thinking by calling upon their entire repertoire of language and culture, rather than feeling restricted to only engage, apply, and think in the language of instruction. These models are shared with the students so that they feel empowered to decide how to best learn at any one time. The models offer the students three ideas for engagement and problem-solving which are not mutually exclusive and may indeed be used in combination:

a. Completing a task in one language and then in another language(s).
b. Using more than one language to engage with a task in a structured approach with set parameters.
c. Using more than one language to engage with a task in a non-predetermined and non-structured approach where students feel free to use all their repertoire of language in any way they wish.

In the first of these situations, a child for whom the main language of instruction represents an additional language, may prefer to write a poem or plan a story, for example, in their first language and then translate the work into the language of instruction. This approach enables every individual to launch into a task by thinking and expressing themselves in the language that evokes the most emotion and provides the most meaning to them, reducing barriers to engagement and setting the scene for a personalised approach to the curriculum.

40. See Staricoff, M. (2021), *The Joy of Not Knowing*. Available at: https://www.jonklearning.co.uk/.

In the second scenario the child is offered the opportunity to use more than one language when thinking about a task and engaging in the learning process, but the way that the multiple languages are applied is pre-determined. For example, if writing a poem, the structure may involve writing alternate verses in alternate languages. If creating a Mind Map that contains six main branches, the student is tasked to creating three branches in one language and three in another. If playing scrabble with each other, each child can contribute words using two languages in an alternate sequence, etc.

In the third scenario, the child is completely free to 'trans-language' using a combination of their entire repertoire of language and cultural heritage to think through and engage with a task. There are no pre-set parameters or expectations. In solving a mathematical problem or checking the answer using an alternative method, for example, a child may use a cross-cultural approach, which may involve a different methodology to the ones being taught as part of the everyday curriculum.

Thinking, learning, and co-existing in a multilingual and multicultural school environment offers numerous emotional, cognitive, social and neurological benefits to both multilingual and monolingual students. Very importantly, it also helps to forge links with families. The inclusiveness of establishing a multilingual and multicultural environment for thinking and learning in schools has a tremendous impact on the emotional wellbeing of all, an aspect beautifully captured by Nelson Mandela when he said:

> If you talk to a man in a language that he understands, that goes to his head. If you talk to him in his language, that goes to his heart.

Project-based Learning and Expeditionary Learning

Project-based Learning (PBL) involves learners gaining knowledge and skills by working for an extended period to investigate and respond to an authentic, engaging, and complex question, problem, or challenge.

Students demonstrate their knowledge and skills by developing a public product or presentation for a real audience. As a result, students develop deep content knowledge as well as skills like critical thinking, creativity, collaboration, and communication in the context of doing an authentic, meaningful, project. Advocates argue that PBL unleashes a contagious, creative energy among students and teachers.

The closely connected concept of Expeditionary Learning (EL) is based on the educational ideas of German educator Kurt Hahn, the founder of Outward Bound. It is a model that emphasises high achievement through active learning, character growth, and teamwork. Rather than being tied to a traditional classroom setting, students engage in projects that challenge their thinking and teach them critical problem-solving skills. Work may be done inside or outside of the classroom, with a focus on journeys that help students discover their interests and passions, not just prepare them for tests.

According to ELeducation.org, there are ten core design principles of EL.

1. **The Primacy of Self Discovery:** Students discover their abilities, values, passions, and responsibilities in situations that are challenging and adventurous.
2. **The Having of Wonderful Ideas:** Curiosity about the world is fostered when learning situations provide something important to think about, time to experiment, and time to make sense of what is observed.
3. **The Responsibility for Learning:** Learning is both a personal process of discovery and a social activity. Everyone learns both individually and as part of a group.
4. **Empathy and Caring:** Learning is fostered best in communities where students feel physically and emotionally safe. Where students' and teachers' ideas are respected and where there is mutual trust.
5. **Success and Failure:** Students are encouraged to build the confidence to take risks, learn from their failures, persevere when things are hard, and turn limitations into opportunities.
6. **Collaboration and Competition:** Students are encouraged to compete against their own personal best, rather than each other, with rigorous standards of excellence.
7. **Diversity and Inclusion:** Both diversity and inclusion increase the richness of ideas, creative power, problem-solving ability, and respect for others.

8. **The Natural World:** A direct and respectful relationship with the natural world refreshes the human spirit and teaches the important ideas of recurring cycles and cause and effect.
9. **Solitude and Reflection:** Students and teachers need time alone to explore their own thoughts, make their own connections, and create their own ideas.
10. **Service and Compassion:** We are crew, not passengers. Students and teachers are strengthened by acts of consequential service to others.

One of the leading UK exponents of such a model is XP School in Doncaster, whose curriculum model is constructed around expeditions not subjects. When the school was inspected by Ofsted in 2017, it was rated as outstanding. Inspectors wrote:

> Pupils love their school. They attend well and enjoy learning. They appreciate the hard work and thought that goes into the work and the experiences staff plan for them. Pupils are impeccably behaved. They are kind, generous-spirited and aware of the needs of others, both at school and beyond. They are very well prepared for life in modern Britain. Parents are overwhelmingly positive about the work of the school and the positive impact it is having on their children's intellectual progress and moral well-being.

For XP, though, EL is not the same thing as PBL. For the school's founders, pure PBL:

> … focuses on creating beautiful, authentic work. Work that happens in the world outside schools. A pure PBL practitioner would argue that character growth and academic progress is the result of creating beautiful, authentic, work.
>
> (ap Harri & Sprakes, 2019, p. 161)

While they do not believe pure PBL is possible as such within the constraints of the English school inspection and accountability system, they nevertheless try to adopt both the principle of beautiful work and of supporting character growth to achieve academic progress. Their curriculum is therefore very carefully planned by cross-curricular group of teachers to incorporate national curriculum requirements into integrated units of work, each addressing a compelling guiding question.

This forms the basis of each 'expedition'. Importantly, teachers are expected to create the product of the expedition themselves before pupils attempt it.

A 2021 review of the international research evidence for project-based learning, carried out for the Edge Foundation, concludes:

> The research literature clearly indicates that project-based learning is beneficial, with positive outcomes, including increases in level of student engagement, heightened interest in content, more robust development of problem-solving strategies, and greater depth of learning and transfer of skills to new situations …
>
> (Rogers & McGrath, 2021, p. 13)

Successful project-based learning includes these elements:

- Use authentic project ideas.
- Plan with the end in mind.
- Promote student exploration of problems and questions.
- Plan for formative assessment.
- Ensure students create authentic products.
- Encourage students to make personal connections.
- Promote impact on authentic audiences.

Social pedagogy

Social pedagogy offers an integrated approach to well-being, education, and learning, that integrates principle and practice, and synthesises many of the key themes of this book.

Social pedagogy describes a holistic and relationship-centred way of working in care and educational settings with people across the course of their lives. In many countries across Europe, it has a long-standing tradition as a field of practice and academic discipline concerned with addressing issues focused on equity and securing social justice by enabling learning, well-being, and interdependence at individual, institutional, and community levels.

The term 'pedagogy' originates from the Greek *pais* (child) and *agein* (to bring up, or lead). The prefix 'social' emphasises that upbringing is not only the responsibility of parents but also the wider family, the village, and broader institutions and communities. In very broad terms, social pedagogy is an expression of the ethical foundations of liberal democracy, but avoiding the ghettoization that leads to professional silos competing for status, resources, and control of practice. Even more fundamentally, social pedagogy challenges the artificial divide between the academic and the pastoral, and between the curriculum and extracurricular activities.

Social pedagogy rejects traditional hierarchical relationships between children and adults as well as amongst adults. It is based on mutual respect for personal dignity, equity, and equality. Echoes of social pedagogy are found in the philosophy underpinning the work of Reggio Emilia, as well as in Montessori and Steiner based educational approaches that value the person irrespective of age, ability, or social status. It is a manifestation of a humanistic perspective applied to educational practice.

Social pedagogy offers a range of principles and practices that have been codified by Petrie et al. (2006). Adapting and applying those principles to deep learning gives us another perspective on the implications of social pedagogy for pupils, teachers, leaders, and the wider community.

The key features of this approach are:

- An holistic focus on the child as a person, based on support for the child's overall well-being.
- The principle that children and adults share a common humanity and habitus that informs all activities.
- Pedagogues constantly reflect on their practice and explore theory and experience to build understanding and so improve.
- Pedagogues are also practical; their training prepares them to share in many aspects of children's daily lives and activities, such as play, meal-times, and physical and mental well-being.

- Children's family and community is seen as an important resource: workers should foster and engage with this group.
- Pedagogy builds on an understanding of children's rights that is not restricted to bureaucratic or system formality.
- There is an emphasis on teamwork and effective relationships.

Conclusion

All of the pedagogic strategies explored in this chapter are evidence-informed. They can offer established, tried and tested ways of working. It is for each school and teacher to work out the appropriate blend together in their context, perhaps in the sort of systematic and considered way pursued by Thomas Tallis School in London in the development of their Pedagogy Wheel (Figure 15).[41]

All the strategies referenced in this chapter have the potential to make an important contribution to the development of deep learning for future sustainability in schools today, if we choose to draw on them and apply them in balanced and appropriate ways.

41. Thomas Tallis School, 'Tallis Habits'. Available at: https://www.thomastallisschool.com/tallis-habits.html.

Figure 15: The Thomas Tallis pedagogy wheel

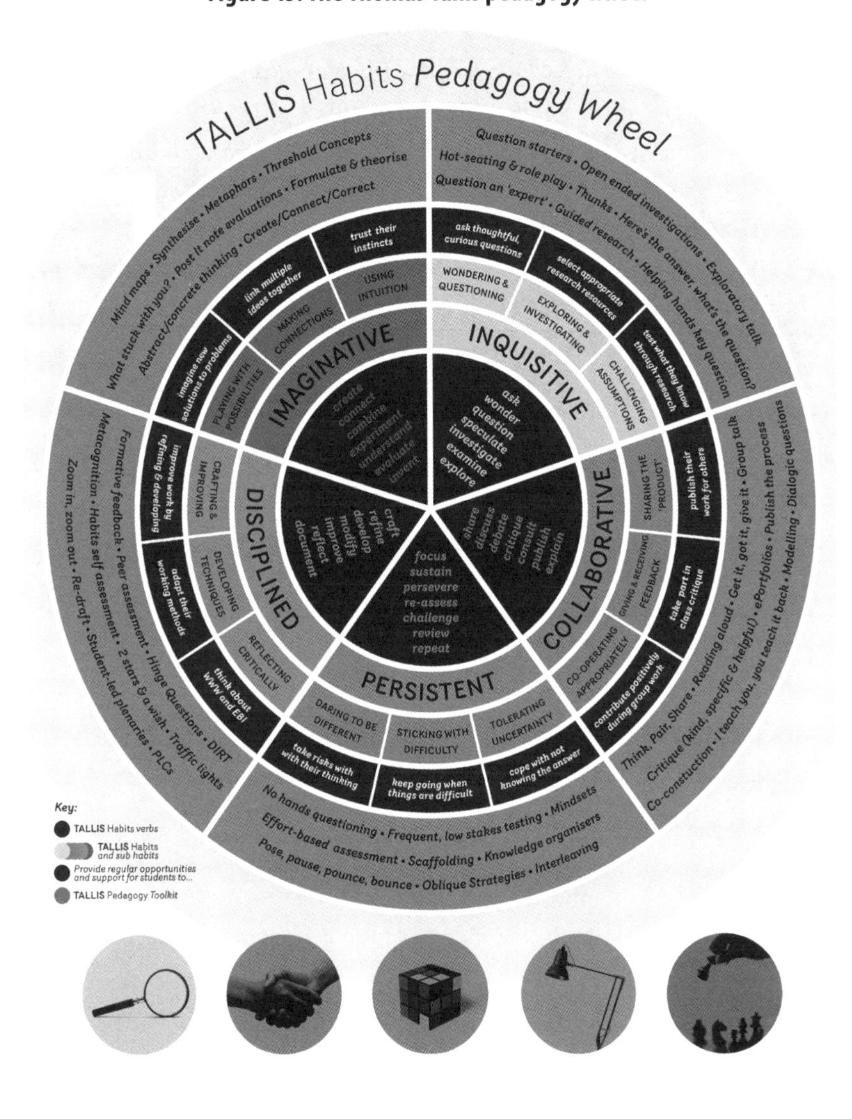

Opportunity for self-reflection and collaborative review

- *In your experience which of the strategies outlined in this chapter are most likely to support the embedding of deep learning?*
- *How confident would your school community be with an explicit advocacy of challenge, creativity, and a growth mindset, as the key elements of deep learning?*
- *What needs to happen to create a learning culture based on coaching and mentoring?*
- *Have you had experience of successful learning involving collaboration between pupils and teachers?*
- *Is it naïve to advocate social pedagogy as a way of enhancing well-being and academic success?*
- *Which of the strategies reviewed here has the greatest potential to help secure deep learning in your school? Which strategies would be most problematic?*

PART THREE

WHAT NOW?

THOUGHT PIECE: GWYN AP HARRI – CEO, XP TRUST

No Excuses

I saw High Tech High (HTH) in 2012 and I knew I had to create a similar school in the UK, then I visited Expeditionary Learning (EL) schools and knew I could.[42] Two years later, XP School opened in Doncaster, UK.

Like us, HTH & EL gets many visitors a year, and I wonder why there aren't more schools like HTH & EL in the world. How can you see those schools and then not replicate it?

I hear that the problem with XP is scale. It's ok to create one good school, but how does it go to scale? Hmm... yeah, it will ultimately fail because it can't go to 'scale'. You see, it's a small school and therefore can't be replicated at scale.

This, like a lot of other things I hear, is baloney. We have a natural propensity to look at the state of things now and believe things will never change. We also have a natural propensity to assume everything was always like this, and always was, straight after something has changed. Do you even remember when we all started recycling? I don't...

What I do know is that, before, only the hippies re-cycled and we all laughed at them. Now we all do it.

I think this phenomenon is something to do with 'owning the narrative'. Things have to fit our own successful narrative, or unsuccessful one, but it can't sound unsuccessful.

So, if something new comes along and it looks, smells, and sounds good, we have to have a reason why we are not part of it or doing it.

42. See https://www.hightechhigh.org/

We make excuses.

We used to say XP was a 'small' school. Now we say it is 'deliberately sized'. True, it is much smaller than most other secondary schools in the UK, but it's probably similar to a lot of privately funded schools. It's definitely similar to a primary school size.

And there's the rub. Most of the time, these excuses become 'memes', and get shared like a virus and accepted quickly. We can't all do XP because it can't scale. It's much too small for a secondary school. It's frustrating because these memes obviously are blatantly not true.

We have a network of primary schools all across the UK. They receive less money per pupil than secondary students. Yet they exist at scale and are a similar size to XP.

We have shown how you can scale locally by creating another small school right next to XP, called XP East. We could continue doing this on our patch of land in Doncaster if we wanted/were allowed.

We've now created a new school in Gateshead which is exactly the same model.

We get asked how we would turn a big secondary school into an XP school, and while our favoured route would be to bulldoze it, and build new smaller schools that actually work, there are many models of splitting big schools internally into smaller 'schools within schools'.

Yes, our school is financially viable. In fact, we pay for Outward Bound, Duke of Edinburgh and ALL the fieldwork our students experience, and ALL the experts that come into the school. All our staff have Apple devices paid for, including our learning coaches (teaching assistants). All our students have iPads. I can show you the spreadsheets.

Then it comes to demographics. To say we have a random lottery admissions process, and anyone who lives in Doncaster can apply, is not enough to convince people that we don't have an unfair advantage. The differences are apparently 'nuanced'. Well, I look at numbers to see the truth, and these are the numbers as of 9 October 2021:

We have 32.4% Pupil Premium students (The average is 34% locally and 16% nationally) with 17.6% Free School Meals — so we're pretty much bang on average for Doncaster and twice as high compared with the rest of the country for deprivation.

We have 22% Special Educational Needs students (The average is 11% locally and 12% nationally) with 3.2% students with Education Health Care Plans (1.8% locally and 1.7% nationally), so we have about twice as many high needs students. We have 6.4% Looked After Children, which is almost six times the local and national average of 1.2%. We have 8% of students who have English as an Additional Language. Finally, XP has taken three times more permanently excluded students from other schools than any other as a proportion through the local Fair Access Panel. XP hasn't permanently excluded a single student in the last seven years.

While we know there are other schools in more difficult contexts, including some primary schools in our Trust, and most definitely some Expeditionary Learning schools in the USA, I personally couldn't say that XP is only successful because of our context. But others will. I have heard that it's not necessarily our demographics, but that 'our parents are different'.

The truth is, to create and run a school like XP takes guts. It's very different from most other schools. This takes courage, which means taking risks. It has taken a lot of working out. A hell of a lot of design, and inevitably some failure and reiteration. It's hard work and you have to put the hours in.

And with differences, comes complexities, especially because our norms are different. We are solving different problems to most schools, and there are not many people who know how to do things the way we do, so we have to grow our own.

These are the real excuses; too scary, too hard, and too complicated. And these excuses are fine. It's not for everyone and there's no shame in that.

All the rest...bull.

Most school leaders cannot start with a completely new beginning as XP did. They have to build their new school piece by piece while it also runs day to day. This can feel rather like constructing an aeroplane while at the same time keeping it flying in the air. In part three we focus in particularly on the nature of change and on leadership in that context.

The urgency with which humankind must tackle the challenge of creating a different future is clear and has been firmly re-stated yet again in the most recent 2021 IPCC report.[43] We believe schools have a profoundly important and distinctive part to play in helping to meet this challenge.

The thrust of our case for a more future-facing school, one that can equip young people both to respond to the dramatic upheavals they will face in their lives and help them shape a better future for all, has been to focus on the process of learning. We have described a model of deep learning for future sustainability with the three key pillars: understanding, character, and agency.

This is most emphatically not an argument to create a new curriculum subject — climate science for example — although there is a strong case for specific curriculum or knowledge content pertinent to understanding our relationship with the natural world to have a higher profile. Rather we have proposed a deep-seated attitudinal change. The future and its challenge of change requires schools which are able to nurture young people capable of deep learning, with strength of character and resilience, and with the ability and confidence to act empathetically and effectively to secure change, while being mindful of their own impact on the generations that will hopefully come after them.

It is this insight which lies at the heart of the future-facing school. Many schools already make an important contribution on some or all of these levels, but the urgency and precariousness of the situation we outlined in chapter 1, now calls for a major step-change to power up the focus and priority this is given.

43. The Intergovernmental Panel on Climate Change (2021), *AR6 Climate Change 2021: The Physical Science Basis*. Available at: https://www.ipcc.ch/report/ar6/wg1/#FullReport.

So, in part 3 we look in some depth at three schools and their leaders, all grappling with change in the here and now, and at what we can learn from their leadership of change. We explore some of the wider implications we see flowing from this analysis. And outline how we can and must now all move, urgently yet in realistic and practical ways, towards a radical new understanding of schooling and its purpose.

CHAPTER 8

MAKING CHANGE HAPPEN — DEEP LEARNING IN PRACTICE

> *Educating for the unknown, far from an unapproachable paradox can be an alluring and inspiring agenda. Rather than counselling despair, education for the unknown favors a vision of learning aggressive in its effort to foster curiosity, enlightenment, empowerment, and responsibility in a complex and a dynamic world. It favors a broad and visionary reach for meaningful learning.*
>
> David Perkins (2014)

Any educational reform, whether at the micro or macro level, faces a number of specific problems that, while not unique to education, do hold particular significance for it. This is especially true of the sort of deep changes we are discussing here.

First, it is very rare for any school to be able to start with a clean sheet. School leaders usually have to build their new plane in the air while attempting to fly it. Second, the objects of reform, pupils, are themselves not static but constantly changing and developing. Nor are they mere objects, but people, and themselves are active participants in the change process. Thirdly, there are distinct ethical considerations related to the compulsory nature of schooling and the irreplaceability of time. Fourth, the aims of education are commonly contested and there is no unanimous agreement on them.

Together these create a drag effect making real change slow and difficult in many situations. On the other hand, the fact of a radically changed future for humankind, as set out in chapter 1, suggests we face a situation of considerable urgency, which requires rapid response just to alleviate its worst effects (never mind prevention or repair). We are past the point of preventing upheaval to established ways, even if all of these were worth preserving.

The argument we have presented thus far in this book faces an acute dilemma. That dilemma is sharpest for school leaders. On the one hand the need for significant change in the way that schools function is extremely pressing, on the other hand the range of immediate demands from the present is at times almost overwhelming for school leaders. It is in essence the dilemma we referred to in an earlier book as 'leading across the second horizon' (Groves et al., 2017).

A good analogy to help understand what we mean by this second horizon can be borrowed from the energy industry. According to Curry and Hodgson (2008), the challenge of achieving a sustainable energy supply for the future can be conceptualised using the lens of three different horizons. The first represents the way we generate and use energy at present. It is inefficient, damaging to the environment, short-term, and ultimately unsustainable. A third, far-off horizon represents the outlook of those who have seen these limitations and are trying to create alternative, viable, sustainable solutions to meet future energy needs. These might include, for example, solar and wind power, hydrogen cells, biofuels, and changing consumption patterns. Such solutions are currently still experimental, not yet proven, may be contradictory, and none are yet to scale or fully tested. However, at some point in the future, a new way forward will emerge from this experimental cauldron to supersede the unsustainable status quo.

Between these points lies another conceptual horizon, termed the second horizon, falling as it does between the here and now and the future. This is the space in which leaders try to make sense of how to navigate away from the failing, unsustainable present and towards the as yet uncertain, dimly glimpsed future in ways meaningful for their organisation, and, in the case of schools, for those in their care.

The parallel with the situation for schools addressing their currently failing models of effectiveness and accountability, is uncanny. For second-horizon school leaders, the role of leadership is therefore not confined simply to responding to the short-term demands of today, driven by government accountability alone. Leadership must combine this with a clear vision of what is needed for tomorrow and a determination to find practical and effective ways to start moving towards that future — despite the constraints of today. This involves living and leading in two worlds at one and the same time, and it means coping with the tension and ambiguity which this necessarily involves, recognising of course that the balance between the two worlds may shift according to context, circumstance, and capacity.

Over the last two years we have been working with the organisation Schools of Tomorrow to look at how schools can respond to the conditions created by a global pandemic to embrace necessary change.[44] We wanted to try to understand more about how individual school leaders, working both separately and collaboratively with each other, can stretch the boundaries of the second horizon.

We based this work on the premise that the step-change now needed is to give greater recognition to the contribution of a school to building social capital within and around itself, as we discussed in chapter 2. In chapter 6 suggested that this involves revisiting and reimagining the why, what, how, and where of learning. This argument builds upon our previous book *Flipping Schools!* (2020), which identified four building blocks for the changes now needed based on both the evidence of research and the observed practice of current school leaders. Summarising those findings, we believe the future-facing school needs:

- An unrelenting focus on the quality of relationships, on becoming a model of community itself. It is first and foremost a place of trust, mutual respect, and belonging.

44. See www.schoolsoftomorrow.org.

- A strong base of value and values, in which the curriculum is central but tailored to a much greater extent to the needs of each learner.
- A commitment to seeking anew the active and ongoing engagement of all stakeholders.
- A fresh understanding of the role of a school as a focal hub of support for learning and wellbeing more widely.

(Groves & West-Burnham, 2020)

It is the dynamic interaction of these elements that generates the social and cultural capital now vital to developing an education system grounded in deep learning and fit to help build a just and sustainable future.

It was the opportunity afforded by the pandemic to try to build back better along these principles that provided the impetus for our present work. We invited schools who shared our conviction to join a community of practice, meeting monthly online over a two-year period to develop and commit to take forward a relevant change initiative based on these ideas and which they identified as appropriate to their context. They would undertake some school-based action research, engage with stakeholders, and work steadily and purposefully to achieve their change goals. We asked them all to establish some clear success indicators, to justify these to the community of practice, and to record the progress of their journeys.

We also elected to follow three of these schools in greater depth in order to gather insights for this book and to help us understand more about how to address the dilemma of change. We conducted a series of in-depth research interviews with leaders, staff, and pupils in these schools, as well as, where possible, parents and community partners. These took place in November 2021, about two-thirds of the way through the programme. So, our analysis here does not attempt to gauge final impact, which would in any case take much longer to show through meaningfully. Rather we wanted to see whether they could afford us insights into the ongoing process of change along that second horizon which may help others to move forward more quickly.

These three schools were chosen for their variety. We wanted a primary school and a secondary school. We also felt an international perspective would be helpful, so we chose to include a Dutch secondary school with a bilingual track. We will consider each in turn in this chapter before taking an overview of what they might show us collectively.

Each of our three case studies follows a similar format. We begin with a brief description of the context of the school. We then look at leadership, and in particular, the role of the headteacher and their vision for change. We then home in on one or two specific changes that are under way and try to understand what they involve and how they contribute to wider development. Finally, we offer a reflection on what this initiative can help us understand about making change happen in the here and now, and some key specific learning points that may have wider application for anyone embarking on a process of change while also flying their plane.

As you read about these three schools, keep in mind the notion of deep learning for future sustainability and its three drivers for change. Consider how the schools, in ways that are both convergent and distinctive, are working to deepen understanding, character, and agency, and especially how these three interact in each setting.

CASE STUDY ONE

INTRODUCING STUDENTS AS AGENTS OF CHANGE

CALS COLLEGE, NIEUWEGEIN, NETHERLANDS

Background

CALS College is a large secondary school, of some 2200 pupils aged 12–18, serving a relatively prosperous area about 40 miles south east of Amsterdam. The college is founded on general Christian values, but open to all faiths. Its stated ethos has focused around cultivating an open atmosphere, with an emphasis on good relations between pupils and staff.

The school has a large and well-developed bilingual (Dutch and English) HAVO and VWO department, which forms the focus of our research. In the Netherlands HAVO provides pupils between the ages of 12 and 17 with a basic general education and prepares them for higher professional education. Pupils can also transfer to pre-university education (VWO), which last six years from ages 12 to 18. In the first three years of the optional bilingual programme, more than half of the subjects are taught in English. The aim is to help students to develop an excellent command of the English language and an international perspective.

The bilingual department organises a range of excursions and drama workshops with an international perspective. Second-year pupils go on a study tour to England, and in the third year there are exchanges between CALS students and schools across Europe. In the upper school, international work placements take pupils all over the world. Upper school pupils work toward an IB (International Baccalaureate) English certificate on top of their secondary school subjects.

Importantly, then, the three pillars of bilingual education — language proficiency, global citizenship, and personal growth — offer a balanced view of education and the curriculum, which is grounded in a clear set of values, summarised by the college as:

- We believe in each other, in each other's capabilities, and in each other's intentions. We have high expectations of each other, and we think and act in terms of opportunities and possibilities. In this way we offer our pupils the opportunity to develop cognitively, creatively, and in their understanding of this world.
- We feel a bond with each other. Acknowledging each other and being acknowledged are therefore important to us. We look out for each other. We feel responsible for ourselves and for each other.
- We are open to the ways in which other people can be different. This requires tolerance. We do so in dialogue with each other, on the basis of equality.
- We seek an atmosphere of openness. We respond to our environment with an open mind and are open to new ideas and insights.

We can see here a clear interlinking of our three drivers of change: understanding, character, and agency.

Leadership

Mirjam Heller is head of the bilingual track at CALS College. She has long felt a tension in the system around the 'boundaries we meet when we want to do things differently'. In particular this refers to the demands of the timetable, the fact that students are all expected to progress chronologically and learn in neat 65-minute packages at the same rate. She recognises it is not possible to escape these limitations completely but, equally, she wants to create 'more opportunities for students to choose and work in different ways'.

She had noticed that many bright students would switch off in lessons and become disengaged. 'It was almost as if the college was giving a message which turned students into passive consumers. "We decide what you do and at what pace. Do what we tell you and we will get you there"'. She continues, 'I cannot accept that 12–18-year-olds must do what we tell them every single day'. Consequently, she set herself the challenge to improve the climate for learning in classrooms.

The college aspires to be a 'learning organisation', and its climate of openness and professional trust allows staff to innovate and to take risks. As one explained to us, 'if you want to try something new, you can get the space to do it'.

But, as in any school, CALS contains a spectrum of staff opinion and Mirjam has been careful to seek a balance in which there is agreement on a common pathway and a degree of consistency, while continuing to explore avenues for change. She seeks to achieve a basic minimum on which everyone can agree, while allowing some colleagues to push ahead further and faster. Her strategy has been to take small steps, combined with lots of professional development to constantly remind people what is behind the direction of travel, especially in terms of research evidence, why this route is being followed, and how the journey can be undertaken.

Change

The focus on improving the classroom experience of students began by addressing the quality of lessons and expanding choice and opportunity for students. These were exemplified in change initiatives that the college was then in the process of undertaking, clearly rooted in the values of the college and aimed at better preparing students to understand and shape their futures.

The first strand of change began with the launch of *learning ambassadors* in 2017, and well illustrates the push-pull dynamic for effecting meaningful change that Mirjam described.

Learning Ambassadors

This is an idea which Mirjam took from the English school network Schools of Tomorrow, following a conference presentation they gave. After observing the idea in operation at Pershore High School in Worcestershire, where it had been introduced by then headteacher Clive

Corbett, Mirjam saw it as central to the developments she was looking for at CALS. It all started with a small group of students who grew into a core team of about twenty.

The learning ambassadors (LAs) today act as a feedback group and discussion partner for all levels within the school. But in the early days they simply observed lessons (other than their own) using an observation tool adapted by Mirjam. LAs receive training and are now increasingly being included in the training for the college's programme of didactic coaching. LAs apply for the position, often at the prompting of friends, and are interviewed for the role by existing ambassadors.

It was, and remains, entirely voluntary to be included in the programme on the part of the teacher being observed. The focus of the exercise is on the learning experience and there is no sense of assessment or judgement. Mirjam describes the work of the learning ambassadors as follows:

> As an observer they analyze the lesson and describe the interaction between teacher and students. They will discuss the observations with the teacher and with leaders in general terms. We have got back that students appreciate interactive lessons, in which the teacher asks a lot of questions. In the language classes they prefer to talk about current affairs in the relevant language than to read texts from a book. They also want to know clearly which learning objectives they are working towards. These are points of attention that teachers can do something with. It also fits in with the formative learning process that we want to apply school-wide. We want to take the students' voice seriously.

As both staff and students grew more accustomed to this dialogue, the number of ambassadors and the range of their influence has increased. There are now learning ambassadors linked to most college departments through a network of committees. These are gradually becoming a structural part of planning and decisions. Mirjam notes:

> It is slowly beginning to work in both directions and we are now seeing that departments are also starting to ask their committee to contribute ideas and discuss developments with them.

Most recently the pre-existing school council — which was previously viewed by students and some staff as lacking focus and influence — has been combined with the learning ambassador structures to provide a more effective student voice. The current chairs of this merged group are Marah and Sven. They talked to us positively about the successes and challenges of the role from their office in the college. For Marah:

> As a learning ambassador you learn that you have to substantiate something in order to change it. Pushing through your point of view doesn't work, but a good presentation with the how and why does. I've developed a more realistic view of what can be changed, but also that it's important to be ambitious and assertive …

Sven adds that ambassadorship teaches him to look more realistically at learning.

> Education is there for us, so it's good that we're involved. I also like to learn how the school works and how we can improve education.

The learning ambassadors are perhaps currently operating at around Stage 6 of the sun model of co-agency (See Figure 4). They are being taken increasingly seriously, but Mirjam also recognises that the idea needs to grow further at school.

> The advantage lies in the fact that teachers and students are not opposed to each other but talk constructively about education and we all reap the benefits … Pupils are important stakeholders, but they are often at the back of the queue of people we talk to about education. It's not bad intentions, but it's weird. What do they think is important to learn and what do they think will benefit them in their future? We want to take the student's voice seriously. Student agency, the feeling that you as a student are in control and are allowed to participate, goes hand in hand with motivation.

In the times of pandemic and lockdown, the input of the learning ambassadors has been particularly important. Marah and Sven, the current president and vice-president of the team, noticed:

> Last year before lockdown we were already concerned about the lack of social interaction and conducted a survey among the students. This showed that there is a need for clubs such as a cooking club, film club and chemistry and physics club. We have drawn up a plan and submitted it to the school management. They are now looking at how

> they can use post-Covid catch-up funds to facilitate six clubs and have them supervised by teachers. In doing so, we want to encourage social interaction between students.

The voice of students has also been powerful in relation to assessment, another strand of change on which the college had recently embarked. The Dutch education system builds towards a common set of exams in the final year of schooling. Students graduate from secondary school by passing both school and national exams. School exams are usually taken between mid-autumn and mid-spring of the last year, and amount to 50% of their final mark. National written examinations are taken from mid to late spring of the final year and are standardised for each subject and programme stream. The government specifies which subjects must be taught during the exam year. All Dutch secondary school students get the results of their combined school and national exams on the same day in early June and find out whether they have high enough marks to get passes for all the various subjects.

Some teachers we spoke to feel these requirements acted as a brake on change. They reduced flexibility in the curriculum, and they narrowed motivation as students would only focus on work directly associated with marks in assignments and tests. As a result, and after considerable thought and debate, the college has begun moving towards making greater use of formative assessment through direct and specific feedback and less reliance on regular in-course grades and marks.

This is a highly complex endeavour requiring significant buy-in from both staff and students.

Those we spoke to were highly sympathetic to the change and its potential benefits. They were also aware that, at this early stage, progress had been uneven and sometimes difficult.

Marah and Sven felt the rationale of the change was 'not yet fully understood by all teachers or students. It's about much more than no grades. Everyone has a different idea at the moment'. They felt inconsistencies in the implementation of the changes meant the quality of personal feedback some students received was on occasions limited. There were also students who felt they did not know how successfully they were on track for their national exams. In any case the college makes a switch back to using only summative assessment techniques in the final year, which in turn can create a confusing or jarring experience for some students. Such constructive and early feedback is enabling more rapid and effective action to address the inevitable issues which arise when implementing change on this scale.

In addition to trying to re-think approaches to assessment in ways that would give students greater ownership of the process, the college has tried over a number of years to introduce curriculum elements that showed greater reliance on skills-based rather than knowledge-based content. Some students were taking the International Baccalaureate in addition to national requirements. A Global Perspectives course, using the Cambridge syllabus, also provides opportunities for other students to develop the skill set to look at major issues facing the world through different perspectives.[45]

As a result of the pandemic, there is also a growing awareness of the importance of student mental health. One student told us how she, like many others, was struggling with the return to college after lockdown. She was having difficulty meeting new people and making friends. She felt her social and communication skills had been set back considerably by the experience of lockdown.

To give one example of the impact on schooling, shortly after students returned from the period of lockdown in September 2021, the college arranged its usual week of baseline attainment tests. Many students were unhappy about the speed and nature of this return to tests. They felt strongly that the college did not appear to have recognised how many of them had struggled during lockdown and that they were not at the same point they would have been without the pandemic. They also felt this situation was not recognised by the government, who appeared to think catching up would be quick and easy. As one put it to us: 'Students have changed, education hasn't'.

Learning ambassadors took up the issue with senior leaders. Senior leaders told us they were shocked to hear this, as they had not been aware

45. For Cambridge Global Perspectives see, https://www.cambridgeinternational.org/programmes-and-qualifications/cambridge-global-perspectives/.

of the issue. However, they listened and realised that there was a serious problem that they had not thought through. At the time of our research, discussions were underway to seek a better approach to balancing the needs of students and the demands of the system. But for one of the earliest learning ambassadors, Elise, the key point she has taken from her engagement in observing and reflecting on the learning experience of other students was clear: 'Let each school look at each pupil more individually — we need a more personalised approach'.

Reflection

Change lesson 1: Acknowledge messiness and the need for a constant conversation

Schools are complex places. From the smallest early years provision to large multi-site secondary schools, the leadership of change is subject to a wide range of complex and constantly shifting variables. It will almost inevitably appear chaotic to some degree and move at different paces in different places. It requires leadership not just management. There are two images that we find helpful in understanding how change happens through good leadership and why this is necessarily messy.

The first is that managers occupy the high ground, while leaders are found actively at work in the swamp. The high ground offers control and clarity. Leadership by contrast, especially across the second horizon, is engaged with the messiness of values, strategy, and human relationships. It operates in this swamp because that is where change springs from.

The second image reinforces this point by extending the metaphor to swimming in a carefully regulated pool compared with wild swimming in rivers and ponds. These analogies represent fundamentally different ways of working and being. The pool is essentially (and necessarily) a product of managerial perspectives, i.e. the effective maintenance of an essentially sterile environment. It is about the continuation of the status quo. In contrast, the pond or river, is not managed, it changes with the seasons, and as some life forms grow, others die. It is essentially a complex and adaptive system — the result of a wide range of variables interacting in a way that is understandable but not replicable. We can seek to understand, but we may not be able to predict, patterns of change. A leader here can foster the conditions for growth, but not necessarily control them. While the essential integrity of the pond is preserved, alternative futures are constantly being developed and encouraged.

Only this second approach can bring meaningful lasting change. That is what we see emerging in this case study under Mirjam's leadership. Only in this way will it be possible to secure deep learning for future sustainability, utilising its three drivers for change.

Some key learning points for consideration from this case study:

- The importance of long-term vision, while moving in carefully paced, sure steps, relentlessly taken.
- The necessity for tangible high-level leadership commitment.
- The primacy of working to establish and sustain high-quality relationships, including professional trust.
- The need for regular reinforcement and conversation about change and the direction of travel, with both staff and students, allied to building rapidly on small successes.
- The potency of co-agency, even when it involves challenge to school leaders.
- A continuing investment in professional development, combined with a constant willingness to innovate and challenge assumptions.

CASE STUDY TWO

BUILDING A CULTURE OF CARING AND LEARNING TOGETHER

ST AUGUSTINE'S ACADEMY, DUNSTABLE, UNITED KINGDOM

Background

St. Augustine's Academy is a one form entry primary school with 177 pupils on roll, serving the highly disadvantaged community of Downside on the southern side of Dunstable. The school has a diverse population, including children and families who have special educational needs and disabilities, those who are disadvantaged, those who speak English as an additional language, and those who have protected characteristics.

St Augustine's became a voluntary controlled church school and stand-alone academy in 2012 and a primary school in 2014. The present head and deputy took up post in September 2017. Prior to that, outcomes had been very low and declining for the previous three years during a period of leadership turbulence after reorganisation and the death in post of the serving headteacher.

Leadership

When Amanda Howes took up the post of headteacher in 2017, undaunted by the challenges it appeared to present, she found a school that had become too heavily focused on the nurture of its pupils rather than their achievement — to the extent that in the previous year no pupil had achieved the national expectation in their standard assessment tests at the age of 11. She also knew this was not an either/or proposition. It was possible to be both caring and have high expectations.

She began by re-shaping the school's values and behaviour policy, using these to drive improvement, and then moving quickly on to learning strategies, including paced reflection, knowledge organisers, and ensuring learning for long-term memory.

A focus was equally placed on extending the range of children's experiences. One key initiative has involved developing an outdoor forest school in an area of the grounds to give them an understanding of nature and to be active outdoors, but also to give them a sense of worth and belonging. Every pupil has planted a tree to encourage ownership and a sense of pride. The area is now home to dozens of trees and woodland, as well as a wild grass meadow. The forest school is also beginning a focus upon sustainability, which is now being integrated into school life.

On entering the school every child receives a 'vision box' to remind them of the school's values. It contains a seed (for growth), a safety pin (well-being), a Lego child (you are the heart of all we do), a jigsaw piece (relationships), a crayon (creativity), a balloon (high expectations), and an elastic band (stretching to reach our potential). The school's ethos is centred around Christian and British values and 'The St Augustine's Way' has as its 'Golden Rules': 'Show Respect, Be Kind, Try Our Best'.

Four years on pupils' progress is now good, notwithstanding the disruption of Covid, though attainment remains below average. In June 2018, after a year under its new leadership, the school was rated by Ofsted as good.

Change

The changes at St Augustine's have been driven by a strong set of values which places the child at the centre. Whereas previously many purchases for the school were of second-hand items to save money and library books could not be taken home, changes to these policies now mean that children now know they matter, they are trusted, and their learning is fully supported, no matter what. To give but one small example, when the annual Bike-ability training came round, it became clear some children would miss out because their families could not afford bikes. So, the school Business Manager was dispatched to purchase some bikes to ensure no one would lose out. During the pandemic lockdown, every family received photocopied worksheets and stationery items delivered to their door, and families in receipt of the pupil premium also received food parcels.

An ethos of everyone working together to improve their learning encourages every child to follow suit. This ethos of learning together, applied to both pupils and staff, is especially evident in the programme on which we focus here.

Vocabulary Velociraptors

Amanda set out to undertake a transformative piece of school-based action research designed to improve children's language. She posed the question: 'If we improve children's visual cognisance and expressive vocabulary, will the quality and depth of their vocabulary improve'. The outcomes of this were, importantly, used to develop the teaching strategies and modelling of vocabulary use of teachers and teaching assistants, as well as supporting parents to extend vocabulary use, beyond the initial outcomes sought for the children. The initiative involved the whole school. For all, the goal was a 'renewed hunger for words', hence the name by which children came to know the work, 'Vocabulary Velociraptors'.

After initial staff training led by Amanda, the idea was introduced to children at a special school assembly. Every week a shared focus is given to a letter of the alphabet, beginning in week one with the letter A. Every class receives an A3-sized poster taken from the book *The Ultimate Alphabet* (1986) by Mike Wilks. Each page of the book contains a vivid whole-page illustration in which are hidden often hundreds of objects whose names begin with a given letter. One of the children's tasks is to recognise as many as they can by the end of the week.

In addition, one object is selected for an intense focus, including a special WOW day. For instance, furniture was chosen for the letter F and the school hall filled with different pieces of furniture, for children to view. In addition, the site manager spent all day in the hall making a bookcase, showing children the skills and tools that he used. Dwellings was chosen for the letter D and the programme included a walk round the local area to spot as many different types of dwelling as possible.

The feedback from parents has been hugely positive. As one said, 'it's helped my vocabulary too'. Another spoke about taking their child into town and spotting types of dwelling together. Prior to the pandemic, the reluctance of parents to come into school for meetings had begun to be overcome in the early years class by inviting them to come in and play with their children while staff joined in alongside them, modelling for parents how to play and how to speak to their children, rather than talking at them. This approach was so successful that multiple sessions across the year were introduced. Once pandemic restrictions ease, the school sees that approach of inviting parents to work alongside their child as the next stage of parental engagement with the Vocabulary Velociraptors initiative.

Children's use of words in writing is being enriched through the programme and the school measures their increase in word knowledge through quizzes and other tools at the beginning and end of each week. These records show a typical increase in children's knowledge of and use of words of at least 200 % and in some year groups considerably more. All children also have their individual score to improve on and they take real pride in their achievement.

The initiative requires teachers and assistants to use appropriate language all the time (while also informally trying to outdo each in terms of the words derived from the week's letter). This sense of engagement for everyone, of excitement and of variety within a consistent structure, form key ingredients in the program securing the quality and depth of learning evident. Staff are also learning at the same time, and this is clear to the children. As one teaching assistant explained to us: 'We are modelling learning behaviour and showing children that we're not giving up either!'

Reflection

Change lesson 2 — Grow a community of learners

A key ingredient in the implementation of deep learning for pupils is that teachers and leaders practice deep learning for themselves.

One of the pivotal criteria for professional status is a commitment to professional learning and development. In most education systems, various forms of CPD are seen as both an entitlement and an obligation. However, there is considerable caution as to the extent to which various models of professional learning make a difference in terms of student outcomes and school performance. A significant cause for concern with the traditional approach to professional learning is the lack of consensus as to what the available evidence actually says. A great deal of provision pre-Covid operated on the basis attending courses, and listening to experts, but then with little or very limited application or follow-up.

This is not what we have seen in this case study. Here, learning is embedded into 'the way they do things'. Learning is valued, supported by leaders, and people help each other learn constantly.

A 'learning culture' can be defined as a mindset within an organisation where learning and improvement are at the heart of how people prioritise their time, do their jobs, and interact with one another. Where people are actively seeking opportunities to develop themselves and others, and to explore new ways for the organisation to improve. This is a self-sustaining culture that produces more energy than it consumes. It is grown through a combination of leadership by example, trust, structure, and support. This is what we clearly see evident in in the changes continuing to take place at St Augustine's and becoming embedded at every level for staff as well as for pupils.

Key learning points suggested by this case study:

- The crucial role of values as the driver of change.
- The importance of care for individuals, and of fostering a sense of belonging and shared purpose.
- Consistent modelling and positive reinforcement of good behaviour and learning.
- High-quality relationships do not preclude, but actually require, high expectations and challenge.
- The value attached to the involvement of parents as co-educators.
- The centrality of first-hand experience in deep learning.

CASE STUDY THREE

UNLEASHING COMPELLING LEARNING AND THE POWER OF COMMUNITY PARTNERSHIP

FALINGE PARK HIGH, SCHOOL, ROCHDALE, UNITED KINGDOM

Background

Falinge Park High School is an 11–16 mixed local authority comprehensive school in the centre of Rochdale in the north west of England. It is a large school with over 1350 pupils. A very high proportion of those students come from families who do not have English as a first language and the proportion of pupils needing additional support is also above the national average. At its last Ofsted inspection in 2018, the school was rated as good.

Leadership

Janice Allen joined Falinge Park as its headteacher in 2015. She had previously had some distressing experiences in the way she had been treated by line managers in other leadership positions and was determined that, under her leadership, no one would be made to feel bad about themselves at Falinge Park. She saw no necessary conflict between having high expectations of people and showing kindness in the way they are treated.

She came to the school with one objective, which has not changed — to create a compelling learning experience. She told us:

> We focused on improving learning in those initial years and ensuring the highest quality professional learning for our staff and we are very proud that we have been awarded the highest status of professional learning by the Teacher Development Trust. We've built a compelling school together through being open, honest and transparent — we get things wrong sometimes, but when we do, we admit it and make changes.

This deliberate culture of openness and trust was evident throughout our engagement with the school and is a crucial underpinning of its change strategy. It allows everyone to work collaboratively in a positive environment.

The school website describes compelling learning as:

> ... engrossing, irresistible and creative. It is like a book you can't put down. It is gripping, riveting, enthralling, absorbing and thrilling. It is characterised by curiosity, relevance and rigour.

This vision is supported by the promotion of explicit learning behaviours, which form expectations of all pupils as well as staff. They involve showing kindness and empathy, being curious, being responsible, and taking action. Together they neatly connect our three drivers of understanding, character, and agency.

The commitment to compelling learning is underpinned by four key values: ensuring equity; building community; strengthening communication; and celebrating diversity. It is worth briefly exploring each.

The first value of *equity* means recognising explicitly that there is inequity when pupils first arrive in school. This can come from socioeconomic issues such as poverty; trauma in childhood, with at least a tenth of a cohort experiencing prior trauma, neglect, or abuse; religious and cultural inequities, which are being played out nationally and globally; and academic inequity, which plays out in terms of exposure to vocabulary, cultural capital, cognitive and learning difficulties; and EAL. With regards to EAL a key piece of thinking is that pupils may be bilingual — but they are often not academically fluent in any of the languages they speak. As a result:

> Whatever we do, we have to remember that we are driven to make improvements through a strong sense of social justice. When we talk about equity therefore it encompasses all aspects of school life.

The second value of *community* recognises that school plays an important part in any community in terms of regeneration, equity building, and social cohesion. It acknowledges there are many communities in school (year groups, friendship groups, ethnic groups, gender groups, disability groups, LGBT groups, staff team groups, and staff friendship groups) and that the school is part of a local, national, and global community. Community is understood in both its narrow and wider senses. As a result, the school is:

> ... talking about identifying how we want our community to be and what it can be, fostering a sense of connectedness which builds social capital and ensures equity.

The school believes its third value of improving communication is the cornerstone of addressing equity and supporting community cohesion, because improved oral, written, academic, and social communication helps build the positive relationships to bring about change. This building of positive relationships, both with the community and between professionals, makes it possible to create a sense of connectedness and work on a strength-finding approach rather than a deficit model.

During the Covid pandemic, Falinge Park significantly strengthened its partnerships with parents, families, and the community using technology as well as social media to communicate and supporting the distribution of food parcels. They also developed a Community Wing to the school, working together with charitable and voluntary organisations to provide a wide variety of opportunities and support for pupils and the wider Falinge Family. We will return to this in a moment.

The multi-faith, multi-ethnic, and multicultural nature of the school makes the fourth value of *celebrating diversity* central to achieving a harmonious culture in the school and its wider communities. In order to celebrate diversity fully, the environment must be safe and calm, with clear boundaries for adults and children to thrive in. A focus on wellbeing for all is key to this thinking:

We cannot ensure equity if we are not secure in ourselves and our communities, and if we lack the communication skills to express ourselves in an increasingly complex world. As one of our Year 7 eloquently expressed it, 'it's not possible to change the world if you're not feeling emotionally healthy and secure'.

Change

We have chosen to explore the change programme implicit in developing the compelling learning approach through two themes, *community partnerships* and *student agency* in the curriculum.

Community partnerships

Lucy Tasker was appointed in 2018 to the new post of assistant headteacher — creative partnerships and community cohesion. This role was described to her at interview as 'the last missing piece of the jigsaw' in Janice's vision for the school.

This role was initially to involve:

- Building links with voluntary organisations within and around Rochdale.
- Working closely with youth organisations.
- Developing supportive groups for parents, and advocates for these groups, to strengthen the home-school partnership.
- Identifying contextual issues and working with the rest of the team in building these into the taught curriculum.

There were several important features of this role which were integral to its design and success. It was located strategically within the senior leadership. It was allocated time, in particular two non-teaching days, in which to be available for meeting and working with groups in the community. Rather than being see as a quick fix the role was part of long-term relationship-building, coherent with a fully thought-through whole-school vision. Importantly it incorporated a direct involvement in both the taught and hidden curriculum of the school.

Lucy approached the role first by seeking to understand the local area, its demography and its challenges, of which there were many, including deprivation, a history of grooming gangs, and racial unrest. Crucially, she saw her task as listening, not imposing. Although this required a genuine humility on her part, it led into an organic process of co-creation to identify key issues where the school might have a contribution to offer: language, ICT, and personal attitudes.

Over the next three years, seven strong community partnerships have been built. One of the most significant is Action Together, an overarching umbrella body for voluntary community groups, bringing them together to share issues and opportunities, including shared bids for funding. What characterises all Falinge Park's partnerships is their grounding in careful listening, building and maintaining respectful reciprocal relationships, their quality and frequency of communication, and their clarity of focus. A couple of examples may help to make this clear.

The school engages constructively with both the statutory and voluntary youth service sectors. Rochdale Youth Service staff work closely with key school staff in respect of targeted young people who need support with emotional regulation, communication skills, respecting diversity, developing confidence and self-esteem, or who are having difficulties forming effective relationships with staff or other pupils. They work with some of these young people in specific sessions during the school day as well as more informally at lunchtime. There is a half-termly meeting between all parties, including the young person, to review progress and agree next steps. The clear recognition, by both organisations, of the professionalism and complementary roles of the other, which when combined with their trust in each other, serves to enhance the effectiveness of both to the benefit of the young people they work with.

Early Break is a voluntary sector partner, a charity working with young people with emotional and behavioural difficulties. Their Fresh Start project supports pupils coming into year 7 who have been identified in their primary schools as either perpetrators or victims of bullying, while they are still in year 6, along with their families. The project aims to help those pupils make a successful transition to secondary school through a combination of individual and group sessions, adopting a 'relational' approach to counselling.[46] Early Break is also working with a small number of Y8 pupils who have a parent currently or recently in prison.

Through work such as this the school is endeavouring to take a preventative approach to well-being and discipline, seeking to 'catch' behaviour issues before they develop into a problem. The project enhances both its capacity and skill base though partnership working, and adopts an educational rather than a punitive approach in order to increase its long-term effectiveness. Achieving this requires regular, ongoing, and open communication about each case, as well as joint staff training to build shared understanding.

The role of curriculum and student agency

A significant part of the whole community engagement strategy rests on the school's commitment to and use of tutoring time, to which 2 hours a week is allocated. Half of that time is built around recognising the importance of human rights. This program was developed by the staff collectively, overseen by Lucy, and is delivered by form tutors with their group. Through encouraging skills of critical thinking and providing a safe space for dialogue the programme aims to give pupils a voice to engage in difficult conversations, challenge misconceptions, and become advocates for those who can't speak for themselves. In the words of the school's curriculum statement:

> So what do we see in compelling tutor time? We will walk past a room and be drawn in because the form is engaged in a discussion related to a topic or theme shared via the Robert F Kennedy Human Rights Programme. They are leading the discussion, offering opinions and listening to others. We will see a tutor helping pupils develop their vocabulary and delivering support in instructional vocabulary; we will see them reading together and learning collaboratively; we will see them reflecting on their learning behaviours and their successes; we might simply see the tutor group talking together about contemporary issues.

46. On Relational Psychotherapy see, https://www.goodtherapy.org/learn-about-therapy/types/relational-psychotherapy.

Assemblies are planned to complement and support this programme, and within each unit there is a special focus on extending the vocabulary of the pupils, particularly in relation to their understanding of human rights and social justice. It is also expected that at key moments pupils will engage in some form of social action, for instance writing letters to the council about an issue of concern, organising a festival of hope, or planting trees to improve the environment.

The notion of student agency is deeply embedded in the curriculum, and this finds practical expression in a rich variety of opportunities for pupil leadership, and through structured and professionally managed avenues for pupil voice. Currently some 200 pupils are involved in a range of roles and in issue-based groups.

Pupils we spoke to were working as mental health ambassadors, eco-champions, and as democratic ambassadors acting as the voice of their form group. Perhaps one of the most interesting examples was the White Ribbon Ambassadors: a group of male students in years 9 and 10, who had just received two days training from Rochdale Women's Welfare to explore and understand attitudes to girls and women and the roots of domestic abuse and violence. They group were now working out how best to share the understanding and insights they had gained more widely within the school and outside in the community, aiming to help change potentially harmful male mindsets. Notable here is the school's commitment to the co-creation of the programme, to training for young leaders, to making time available, and to supporting and expecting pupils to take on a wider community role in effecting meaningful change.

The school is now in the process of building a comprehensive Pupil Parliament, drawing all of these activities into an over-arching democratic framework, reflecting local and national government structures, as outlined in Figure 16. One of the significant things about this is that the structure is not simply an artificial replica. It has a clear purpose connected both to the learning in which pupils are engaged as well as to the wellbeing and development of both the school and wider community. In doing that, it is offering pupils real and meaningful roles and an education in democracy.

Figure 16: Pupil Parliament Design at Falinge Park High School

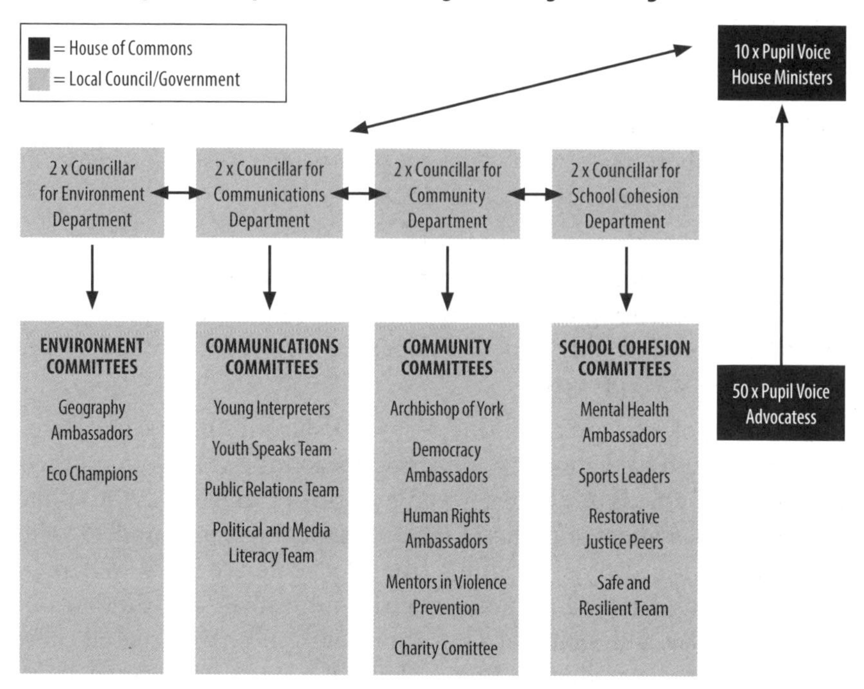

Reflection

Change lesson 3: Draw on a combination of individual and collective agency

In chapter 3 we identified agency and co-agency as pivotal components of deep learning.

Agency is about the capacity to set goals, reflect, and act responsibly to effect change. It involves students and adults, as well as schools and communities. A combination of collective and individual agency lies at the heart of the OECD sun model (Figure 4), described in chapter 3. Getting this combination and balance right is crucial to the chances of young people being able to secure a sustainable and just future for all.

A directly example of how personal and collective agency might work is found in Gladwell's study *The Tipping Point* (2006). Gladwell identifies three essential components of what he calls 'stickiness'. For Gladwell success, in terms of completion, requires the involvement of connectors, mavens, and salesmen (sic). Across several examples, he demonstrates the factors that increase the likelihood of a project or event being translated from principle into practice, and from aspiration into concrete outcomes.

> **Connectors** build networks and relationships — they know lots of other people and delight in building and maintaining bridges. Connectors are people with a special gift for bringing the world together — they are gregarious and intensely social (p. 38).
>
> **Mavens** are information brokers — sharing and trading what they know. They are assiduous in collecting information and disseminating it. They are open and generous (p. 69).
>
> **Salesmen** work through persuasion — they are intuitively skilled and sensitive to non-verbal communication. They are sensitive to emotional contagion to enhance their reception and to successfully achieve their desired outcome (p. 259).

There seems little doubt that Janice's leadership has fostered and harnessed a significant number of connectors, mavens, and salespeople. A shared vision and clear, explicit common values, routinely reinforced and integrated consistently into everyday thinking and being, have been critical components of her success.

Key learning points suggested by this case study:

- High quality relationships and partnerships are rooted in reciprocity.
- Ongoing regular communication is essential in partnership working.
- Clarity of purpose is essential to the choice of partners.
- Strong networking underpins the building of effective partnerships.
- Effective partnership working has resourcing implications in terms of people and time, which need to be recognised from the outset.

- Students are key agents of change, given the right support and training.
- The curriculum, and its goal of compelling learning, lies at the heart of change. These are not bolt-on activities.

Conclusion

Our three case studies clearly demonstrate that purposeful, deep change, even in this most challenging of times, is possible. None of them started with a blank canvas, unlike XP, yet all are managing to make meaningful deep changes while also still keeping their plane aloft. Each of these schools began the process of change prior to the pandemic, but each has continued with their strategy during and beyond the period of lockdown. They have looked to turn that setback to advantage and have made clear their intentions not to retreat back into old ways.

These schools have moved forward by drawing on the building blocks of change identified at the start of the chapter. They are strongly focused on the quality of relationships, on values, and the way that these are embedded within the curriculum. They are working to develop meaningful engagement with all their stakeholders. They all understand the role of the school as acting beyond its immediate walls to influence their communities and to grow social capital.

All three began from a learner-centred, community-focused mindset. Each has placed the learner front and centre in their thinking. However, they also all saw that this was not enough if detached from a sense of wider community. Each, in their different ways, is seeking to help children and young people understand and shape a better future both for themselves and, crucially, for others. In each we can see evidence of a coming together of understanding, character, and agency, within and beyond the formal curriculum. Each school is also working positively with their stakeholders, in order to give the children and young people in their charge experience of and insight into aspects of deep learning for future sustainability.

We have also used each case study to draw attention to particular features necessary in any process of change — the acknowledgement of messiness and the need for a constant conversation, the establishment of a culture of shared learning, and the combination of individual and collective agency. Although we have highlighted each of these in relation a particular school, they are present to a degree in all three. There is a fourth important characteristic all share — a commitment by leaders to deep listening and embedding this approach throughout their organisations.

Change lesson 4 — Practice deep listening

Listening is part of all types of human interaction, ranging from basic formal courtesy to the deepest levels of human engagement. 'Deep listening' is a fundamental component of deep change; indeed deep learning rests on deep listening.

Deep listening, openness to admit ignorance, and the acceptance of guidance, advice, and challenges, all contribute to both personal and social engagement and the development of understanding. This involves:

> ... individuals with remarkable empathy, who are continuously focused on other people's feelings to check on these and be supportive. It is as if their empathy circuit is in a constant state of hyper-arousal; such that other people are never off their radar
>
> (Baron-Cohen, 2011, p. 18)

Mirjam, Amanda, and Janice are such individuals, and that is part of the secret of their success. What also distinguishes them is the way that they manage disagreement through ongoing dialogue.

David Bohm and colleagues (1991) argue for the importance of ongoing dialogue as:

> ... a way of observing, collectively, how hidden values and intentions can control our behavior, and how unnoticed cultural differences can clash without our realising what is occurring.[47]
>
> In their view, ongoing dialogue provides a space in which individuals and organisations can identify and understand the processes that fragment and interfere with real communication.

47. Bohm, D., et al. (1991), *Dialogue — A proposal*. Available at: http://www.david-bohm.net/dialogue/dialogue_proposal.html.

Dialogue then is an arena in which collective learning takes place, and out of which a sense of increased harmony, fellowship, and creativity can arise. For Bohm, dialogue is a key tool in liberating creativity in groups and organisations, and fundamental to investigating the crises facing society. While he has developed a specific structured approach for this work, these core points also apply equally to less formal exchanges rooted in deep listening.

The processes of change evident in our case studies — reflecting as they do, messiness, learning, agency, and a constant dialogue — derive from the leadership provided by Mirjam, Amanda, and Janice. We believe the contribution of these leaders is distinctive and different, and such contributions are hugely necessary for the change now needed in our schools. The nature of such leadership forms the theme of our next chapter.

Opportunity for self-reflection and collaborative review

- *In what ways do change strategies in your school resemble the three case study schools? What lessons can they offer you?*
- *What excuses might be offered to avoid necessary change? How can you best overcome these?*
- *Consider the three-horizon model. Which horizon do you and colleagues spend the most time in? Why?*
- *Is there a culture of deep and respectful listening across your whole school?*
- *Is there agency and resources available to initiate and support conversations across the whole school community?*
- *How much time do you spend on the high ground and how much in the swamp?*

CHAPTER 9

LEADING INTO THE FUTURE

Historically, pandemics have forced humans to break with the past and imagine their world anew. This one is no different. It is a portal, a gateway between one world and the next. We can choose to walk through it, dragging the carcasses of our prejudice and hatred, our data banks and dead ideas, dead rivers and smoky skies behind us. Or we can walk through lightly, with little luggage ready to imagine another world. And ready to fight for it.[48]

Arundhati Roy (2020)

The future-facing school will not be created without leadership at school level. Change at a system level can both support and stimulate this and would be most welcome. But the most significant impact will come from school leaders at a local level who take the initiative without waiting to be asked by the system. The system will catch up one day, but it may be too late by then.

We are at an almost unprecedented juncture, a moment of *chairos*, a time for change. The combination of the pandemic and the climate crisis, together with pre-existing issues such as poverty, has led to one

48. Roy, A. (2020), 'The pandemic is a portal', *Financial Times*, 3 April. Available at: https://www.ft.com/content/10d8f5e8-74eb-11ea-95fe-fcd274e920ca/.

of the most challenging environments known in modern times. This combination of negative and challenging forces has created a critical nexus, without parallel in modern history outside the world wars, in which each component has a multiplier effect.

This combination of the pandemic and climate change also has global implications. It means there is no hiding place in terms of geography or social status. Both negative forces are inclusive and democratic in that they affect societies at all levels and involve education as much as any other sphere of human activity. Just as medicine must develop new responses from respirators to mass vaccination and new drugs, so education is having to develop strategies to face a unique situation in order to minimise the negative impact on children.

The process of re-assessing many aspects of how we live now, and what we will have to change in our lives in the near future is already in hand. However, the full impact of the combination of Covid-19 and the climate crisis has yet to be fully understood, accepted, or acted on. As Lupton and Hayes observe:

> No generation in the past has been handed the legacy of a world with severely damaged ecosystems and unstable climatic conditions, at the same time as being faced with a pandemic-induced global economic crisis of huge proportions and rapidly accelerating economic transformation due to the advance of artificial intelligence, which will likely have lasting effects on labour conditions and the way we live our lives. **Education will be changed by these conditions and can shape their evolution** [our emphasis].
>
> (Lupton & Hayes, 2021, p. 10)

In many significant respects those born after the second world war, in many countries, have led lives characterised by historically unparalleled levels of personal, social, and economic wellbeing. There have been periods of peace without precedent, and a powerful combination of medical innovation, improved agriculture, and relative political stability, underpinned by full employment and cultural richness. As Pinker puts it:

> For all the tribulations in our lives, for all the troubles that remain in the world, the decline of violence is an accomplishment we can savour

> and an impetus to cherish the forces of civilization and enlightenment that make it possible.
>
> (Pinker, 2011, p. 841)

On the other hand, George Monbiot argues:

> We have been induced by certain politicians, economists, and commentators to accept a vicious ideology of extreme competition and individualism that pits us against each other, encourages us to fear and mistrust each other and weakens the social bonds that make our lives worth living.
>
> (Monbiot, 2017, p. 25)

The net result of this situation is, according to Monbiot, 'an epidemic of unhappiness and of psychological and physical illness'. Indeed, according to 'Nip in the Bud', about 10% of children in the UK experience at least one mental health problem during childhood and about 75% of mental illnesses are thought to start before the age of 25.[49] In practical terms this means that there could be at least three children with diagnosable mental illness in any school class.

According to Marks and Hickman (2021), surveying 10,000 young people in 10 countries, 59% of respondents were very or extremely worried about climate change. Over 50% felt sad, anxious, angry, powerless, helpless, and guilty. Over 45% said their feelings about climate change negatively affected their daily life and functioning, and many reported a high number of negative thoughts about climate change. Respondents overall rated governmental response to climate change negatively and reported greater feelings of betrayal than reassurance. Correlations indicated that climate anxiety and distress were significantly related to the perception of inadequate government response and associated with feelings of betrayal.

The truth of the matter is of course that the impacts of the climate emergency and pandemic are not evenly distributed — social class, wealth and poverty, north and south combine to literally polarise society. According to the World Bank the repercussions of climate change and

49. Cited from www.nipinthebud.org.

the pandemic are closely intertwined with patterns of inequality.[50] The pandemic has demonstrated that the most vulnerable groups have limited access to resources to respond to crisis. There is also a lack of knowledge and understanding about the causes and implications of these combined threats, hence, perhaps, the number of people who have rejected the opportunities for vaccination. Many countries lack the necessary infrastructure in terms of planning, distribution, logistics, and information management. Strategic policy-making often ignores the voice of communities and vulnerable groups, such as children, persons with disabilities, indigenous peoples, and ethnic minorities.

Crises at this level cannot be sufficiently addressed through short term emergency responses. To take one example, the floods across Germany, Luxembourg and Belgium in July 2021 also reinforced a sense of victimhood, being out of control, and facing great uncertainty. While these floods were devastating, they were also a clear warning of what is to come as the climate crisis worsens. Ad hoc reactive measures such as distribution of sandbags, preventing building on flood plains, and improving the forecasting of possible floods are of only marginal value here in the grand scheme of things. As Lupton and Hayes (2021, p. 11) acidly observe:

> In this context, small additive reforms that keep a broken system creaking along are a waste of money, a denial of the facts, and a failed response to young people who will bear the responsibility of finding solutions to the world's many problems.

All of this has fundamental implications for the theory and practice of educational leadership. As with other public and private sector services, education systems have, perhaps understandably, tended to be largely reactive, with no clear consensus about the components of educational responses to either the climate crisis or Covid-19. This reflects the general tendency for education policy to focus on short-term fixes rather than long-term prevention.

---

50. Hallegatte, S. and Walsh, B. (2020), 'Covid, climate change and poverty: Avoiding the worst impacts', *World Bank Blogs*. Accessed at: https://blogs.worldbank.org/climatechange/covid-climate-change-and-poverty-avoiding-worst-impacts.

The overwhelming imperative for school leaders and educational administrators though the pandemic has been to secure quality educational provision in situations without precedent. The demands made on school leaders have ranged from literally life-saving interventions to low-level administrative chores; all involving decisions necessarily made with only limited confidence in the efficacy and effectiveness of any given choice and no authoritative consensus as to their long-term effects. Claims that government policies were evidence-based in this context only served to question the trustworthiness, validity, and reliability of that evidence.

Equally, the emotional impact of lockdown has often been hidden. The limited communication with pupils and families that was available to schools often exacerbated deep-rooted fears and tensions. School leaders, quite apart from their personal concerns about their own families, were on the one hand responding to high levels of stress and ambiguity, and on the other maintaining necessary but basic school procedures. The challenges ahead — of which the pandemic has been in many respects just a foretaste — mean we cannot continue with the same patched-up, creaking, and broken models. That applies equally to leadership as it does to schooling.

In considering appropriate leadership responses to the combined crises of the pandemic and climate emergency, we have identified from the available evidence these four significant elements:

- Rethinking leadership and management roles for complex times.
- Releasing the power of positive leadership.
- Focusing on the importance of social and emotional relationships.
- Emphasising collaboration.

We will now examine each of these in turn.

1. Rethinking leadership and management roles for complex times

Most thinking about schools as organisations is posited on the assumption of order, structure, predictability, and consistency. Deviations from those norms, for whatever reason, can lead to significant personal and organisational stress. Complexity and chaos have the potential to traumatise.

VUCA (short for volatility, uncertainty, complexity, and ambiguity) emerged from the work of Warren Bennis and Burt Nanus (1986) on the role of the military in a post-cold war world. Originally it was used to help understand the implications of moving from the 'simple' binary world of the cold war to the shifting alliances, terrorism, economic warfare, and territorial disputes, which characterised the post-cold war period. The cold war had led to a culture of control and prescription, with no room for negotiation or modification. There was no room for ambiguity because of the disastrous consequences of mistakes in understanding or interpretation between nuclear powers. VUCA is an analytical tool that supports the development of organisational responses to external change that requires initiative, flexibility, and crucially, the acceptance of personal choice and responsibility.

Most importantly VUCA explores the interaction between the ability to control a given situation and the ability to understand its complexity. That interaction is described in various ways:

Volatility: the situation is inherently unstable, unpredictable, and difficult to manage.

Uncertainty: there is lack of clarity and limited potential to understand or control the situation.

Complexity: there are multiple interdependent variables at work. Some information is available, but its volume inhibits and compromises understanding.

Ambiguity: there are contradictory and uncertain relationships between actors in the situation. There are no precedents or guidelines to support understanding.

Responses to the four components of VUCA might include, for example, addressing root causes by increasing transparency and sharing information; developing intelligence-gathering systems; and exploring cause and effect.

The systematic use of the VUCA model has the potential to support:

- Developing a sense of awareness and readiness.
- Anticipation of emerging issues.

- Gaining understanding of consequences and implications.
- Recognition of significant variables and their potential interactions.
- Developing awareness of alternative future scenarios and changing realities to identify and interpret potential opportunities.

In responses to complex situations, such as the climate emergency and the pandemic, our concept of leadership itself may have to change to reflect evolving social norms. For Harris and Jones (2020, p. 246):

> Distributed leadership has now become the default leadership response in this current crisis, requiring more school leaders, *at all levels* [our emphasis], to connect share, learn and network their way through issues.

Gemma Moss argues in a 2020 blog for the British Education Research Association:

> Key fragilities in the way that the English education system currently operates stem from over-centralisation, a lack of awareness of problems on the ground and a preference for pressure-driven management.[51]

A powerful antidote to personal and organisational stress and dysfunctionality is leadership that builds confidence and a sense of shared purpose, combined with management that gets things done and solves problems. In times of crisis, it important that leadership and management are seen as complementing and reinforcing each other, in other words managerial leadership, where strategy is clear and practical, solves problems, and restores confidence. As Ron Glatter (1997, p. 189) argues:

> Erecting [a] kind of dichotomy between something pure called 'leadership' and something 'dirty' called 'management' ... would be disastrous

51. Moss, G. (2020), 'The fragilities in the English education system revealed by Covid-19, and how to put them right', *British Educational Research Association*. Available at: https://www.bera.ac.uk/blog/the-fragilities-in-the-english-education-system-revealed-by-covid-19-and-how-to-put-them-right.

Peter Senge goes even further:

> I have come to see our obsession with the hero-CEO as a type of cultural addiction. Faced with the practical needs for significant change, we opt for the hero-leader rather than eliciting and developing leadership capacity throughout the organization.[52]

What might such change look like in a school? Wendy Hemmingsley, headteacher at Henry Box School, describes just one example:

Henry Box School in Witney, Oxfordshire school is a popular, highly subscribed 11–18 mixed comprehensive school that has academy status and is part of a small MAT. It is an historic foundation with the prevailing orthodoxy for curriculum and leadership and management models. Although a 'Good' school in Ofsted terms the headteacher, (also CEO of the MAT) the leadership team, and trustees shared a view that the prevailing management structure was not fit for purpose in terms of its effectiveness and impact.

A major review of the school's systems and structures was followed by a radical restructuring that challenged a range of prevailing orthodoxies for leadership in large schools. The historic leadership model comprised:

1 headteacher, 2/3 deputy heads, 3/4 assistant heads and a business manager, senior curriculum leaders (English and Maths), 1 senior pastoral leader (head of 6 Form), 30 middle managers (renamed middle leaders, e.g. heads of subject and heads of year), and just 25 classroom teachers.

The headteacher, deputies, and senior staff came together in a senior leadership team. The cost of senior leadership (with on-costs) was £574,000 per annum. A cost-benefit review revealed a significant imbalance in terms of roles, and a lack of consistency and impact.

52. Senge, P. (2000), 'The Leadership of Profound Change', *SPC Ink*. Available at https://docs.google.com/viewer?url=http%3A%2F%2Fwww.spcpress.com%2Fpdf%2Fother%2FSenge.pdf.

Following a period of negotiation and consultation, the leadership structure was reduced to a headteacher and deputy. Traditional SLT roles were removed entirely and replaced with school leaders all on Leadership Pay Spine. This resulted in savings of £350,000. The new structure reduced the size of the SLT to the head and deputy with all other posts with a leadership function being subsumed into the new role of school leader covering key leadership and management functions — Maths, English, Science, International and Innovation, Creativity and Performance, Social Sciences, Post 16 Education, Inclusion, and Teaching.

At the same time the traditional year group pastoral system (5 heads of year) was replaced with vertical tutoring in four 'houses'. Four school leaders are heads of house. All teachers have a tutor group (including the deputy head). This means vertical tutor groups of a maximum of 22, as opposed to 28–30 previously.

All operational work, the day-to-day management of the school, is divided between this team: for example, the School Leader English leads on PR; the School Leader Maths on whole school data; the School Leader Science prepares the timetable; and the School Leader Social Sciences organises parents' evenings.

The process of allocating these responsibilities used Andy Buck's 'Whose Name's on the Tin' system. School Leaders chose the 'tins' that they would manage — this process was essential in securing their engagement and commitment. The aggregation of these personal 'tins' provides a clear and exhaustive definition of management and leadership functions.

This large team now 'runs the school' operationally. Smaller teams (often mixed) meet to problem solve and/or develop systems, often in time-limited projects.

Benefits of the changes:

- Improving the focus and application of professional development.
- Retaining high performing staff through increased opportunities for them to gain leadership experience.

- Freeing up financial resources from expensive traditional SLT model to employ and deploy a large 'Learner Engagement Team', making more resources available for working with families and the most vulnerable.
- Significantly improving operational effectiveness — including a sense of enhanced agency and the ability to deliver on the school's promises among staff.

The message is very clear — a layer of bureaucracy has been removed. Specialists apply their knowledge, skills, experience at whole school level. Talent density in the school leadership team has increased and everyone is closer to the work that needs doing and the problems that need solving.

Impact of change

The rapid response challenge of the Covid19 years was managed very successfully under this distributed model. Decisions were taken quickly and definitively by the very people who were going to implement and manage significant change within a very short timescale. The bureaucracy of another layer of leadership was removed. Parent and staff feedback (through surveys) have been positive and show improvements on previous surveys.

Implications for school leaders

Change has supported the strategy of recruiting and retaining the best people and freeing up scarce resource to allocate to front line needs. It has removed the 'balkanisation' that can often be seen in secondary school 'subject departments'. The School Leader Team is 'the first team' — all have an overview of the whole school operation. Trust is high and this means that work can be undertaken at a rapid pace where necessary.

Key conclusions

Traditional structures and ways of operating in schools need to be reviewed. Schools are traditionally very hierarchical. Changing the way they are organised can achieve great benefits in terms of leadership understanding, buy-in, recruitment and retention, reduction in 'groupthink', and increases in the will and skill to lead change. Decision-makers can see and understand what needs to be done because they are in the 'engine room' of the school.

Such distributed managerial leadership integrates traditional roles — values and relationships — with the management functions of planning and implementation in a symbiotic approach that optimises their potential combined impact. This approach is about creating fresh connections between the high ground and the swamp, the swimming pool and the pond. This innovative approach addresses both strategies for leadership capacity and effectiveness and the impact of leadership in terms of managing systemic change.

However, it is important to recognise that there are examples of schools that have worked with a de facto 'managerial leadership' approach for almost as long as there have been schools in a modern sense — notably in early years provision, primary schools, and special schools. The vulnerability and immaturity of children in these schools precludes what might be caricatured as the dignity and status of the 'headmaster' tradition. Small children are profoundly democratic and iconoclastic. They work on their own terms and will secure help from the nearest adult — irrespective of their status. Watching play in an early years setting, or observing a special needs classroom at work, provides a clear demonstration of some of the key characteristics of such managerial leadership:

- It is learner-centred, responding to practical needs, in particular the translation of theory into practice — in essence keeping promises.
- It is an essentially democratic and humanist approach to organisational structures and relationships.
- It assumes equity and fairness in the deployment of staff and allocation of tasks.
- It prioritises expertise and commitment over historic norms and relationships.

We see clearly here how it is perfectly possible to combine high performance with positive human relationships. Educational success does not require performativity, rather it develops through shared values and vision underpinned with positive relationships. Effective managerial leadership is thus also positive leadership.

2. Releasing the power of positive leadership

The prevailing and historic model of leadership language is based on the key themes of competition and winning; strategy and tactics; hierarchy and control. This language is redolent of military and corporate environments and may not helpfully contribute to the creation of an authentic learning culture. Learning for understanding requires a level of emotional engagement that may not be possible in a culture of performativity and narrowly defined answerability. In essence we need kinder and gentler schools rather than more efficient delivery of a narrow and outmoded curriculum.

An organisation should implicitly model the vocabulary and behaviours that are necessary for its core purpose. Is the vocabulary of military, hedge fund, or research organisations compatible with, or appropriate to, a school? Equally is the language of early years provision appropriate to post-16 education or vice versa? The language of leadership is about more than the transmission of information — in this context it needs to model creation of knowledge, based in deep learning. What are the appropriate leadership behaviours and vocabulary to consolidate a culture of deep learning and respond to a combination of a health and environmental crises?

Table 6: Comparing historic and positive models of leadership

Historic Model	Positive Model
Pachyderm	Self-aware, vulnerable, open
Outcomes-focused	Relationships-focused, caring
Competitive	Collaborative
Logical, rational, quantitative	Intuitive, qualitative
Strategic	Visionary, utopian
Independence, autonomy	Interdependent
Formal	Friendship, warmth
Functional, practical	Care, kindness, compassion

Table 6 is not a series of alternatives, nor are the columns in any way mutually exclusive. Rather, it should be read as a set of possible relationships that may be right for a given context. If 'deep learning for future sustainability' is to become a significant option for school leadership and governance, then there has to be a parallel emphasis on 'learning and leadership' — these have to be reciprocal and interdependent and, crucially, mutually reinforcing.

Csikszentmihalyi and Csikszentmihalyi describe a 'new direction':

> If we imagine human experience as following along a bell curve with illness and despair at the left tail of the slope, joy and creativity at the other end and the great majority of experiences around a middle neutral point, one could say that for the past half century or so psychology in the United States has been focusing almost exclusively on the left-hand tail of the curve.
>
> (Csikszentmihalyi & Csikszentmihalyi, 2006, p. 3)

They go on to argue for greater emphasis to be placed on the right-hand side of the curve working with people who want a better life and to become better persons.

And educational leadership does indeed often seem to focus more towards the left-hand side of this curve — sometimes, perhaps too often, taking a negative approach that can even take the form of toxicity rather than emphasising the potential gains of a positive approach.

An increased focus on the positive in turn requires the development of an alternative vocabulary. It involves moving:

- From viewing the school as an organisation towards understanding the school as a community.
- From behaviour and discipline towards a culture of love, kindness, and caring.
- From emphasis on rules towards positive relationships based on empathy.
- From controlling outcomes towards processes based on trust.
- From punishment towards restorative justice.
- From control towards courtesy, dignity, and respect.

The transition from left to right on the Csikszentmihalyi distribution curve is significantly facilitated by the extent to which such a new vocabulary comes into use confidently and rooted in shared definitions. In effect, this is learning a new language by matching key concepts to shared observations and experiences.

There are two concepts taken from the Total Quality movement in business that might have application to education in this context. They are 'fitness for purpose' and 'form following function'. Both of these ideas are derived from a definition of quality as 'what the customer says it is'. The criterion for effectiveness in any product or process is judged by the extent 'it does what it says on the tin'. Thus, a racing car and a family saloon can both be quality vehicles if their design and operation promote their core function and if their performance is appropriate to the context in which they are used.

Central tenets of this book are that much of contemporary policy and practice in education is not fit for purpose, and the conceptual framework informing them is an example of function following form rather than vice versa. The currently dominant model of schooling patently only works for a limited cohort of the population.

An alternative to the historic model of school improvement might be best approached by engaging with some pivotal ideas from a positive perspective, notably kindness, vulnerability, care, empathy, and friendship. Significantly, these virtues or qualities are often referred to as 'soft' or 'person-centred' behaviours. There is an implicit assumption that these soft behaviours are in some way less significant or appropriate, whereas 'hard' behaviours are in some way more natural or appropriate.

The child as a product is implicit to the thinking underpinning the Global Education Reform Movement (GERM) model, as characterised by Sahlberg and prevalent in much school system thinking around the world.[53] This model in turn is derived from the military via business and deeply embedded theories of society and hence leadership. Examples include Plato's philosopher kings and Machiavelli's Prince, as well as the

53. Sahlberg, P. (2012), 'How GERM is infecting schools around the world?'. Available at: https://pasisahlberg.com/text-test/.

prevailing neoliberal, managerialist culture in government. The primary reason for moving away from this towards a more positive view of society and of the importance of social and emotional relationships is because these are fundamental to both personal well-being and to engaging with deep learning.

3. Focussing on social and emotional relationships

> Our energies are overwhelmingly directed towards material, scientific and technical subjects — and away from psychological and emotional ones. Much anxiety surrounds the question of how good the next generation will be at maths; very little around their abilities at marriage or kindness. We devote inordinate hours to learning about tectonic plates and cloud formations, and relatively few fathoming shame or rage.
>
> (de Botton, 2019, p. 1)

In a memorable insight, de Botton goes on there to argue that:

> We have the appetites and destructive furies of primitive primates who have come into the possession of thermonuclear warheads.

Our emotional development has not kept pace with our social and technical complexity. In emotional terms we are naïve and often simplistic and in educational terms we are avoiding, or even denying, that idea education should be equally concerned with emotional literacy as oracy and reading. The need for this shift to happen as a pre-requisite for a just and sustainable future is echoed by the eminent political philosopher, Michael Sandel:

> There but for the grace of God, or accident of birth, or the mystery of fate, go I. Such humility is the beginning of the way back from the harsh ethic of success that drives us apart. It points beyond the tyranny of merit toward a less rancorous, more generous public life.
>
> (Sandel, 2020, p. 227)

The movement towards a positive culture, ethos, language, and associated behaviours has to start with an emphasis on love, and a shared focus on friendship and kindness between partners, across communities, villages, and organisations of all types. The conceptual map for a school culture based on positive principles might look like Figure 17 below.

Let us look at each of these elements in a bit more detail.

Figure 17: Conceptual map of positive school culture

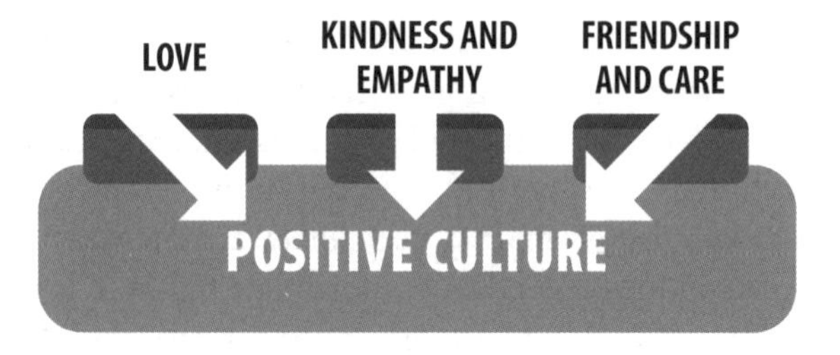

Love

Imagine a classroom or workplace where the tension is palpable, students or workers are clearly in fear of making a mistake, relationships are very formal, permission is being sought for the most basic activities, and there is clearly no trust, no care, or kindness. In essence there is no love. Such an environment would be seen as negative by any group of people, young or old.

This is an extreme example, there are obviously degrees of control and negativity, and of lack of care, trust, and respect. However, it could be argued that any conceptualisation of children's rights should include an entitlement to unconditional love — no matter how complex the definitions and practical implications of this are. After all we manage this in other aspects of life. Emotionally competent communities develop a sophisticated language, so that it is possible to love a Mozart symphony, your preferred football team, one's colleagues and students, without fear of ambiguity or misinterpretation.

We hear sentiments such as 'I love my class', 'I love teaching my subject', 'I love my teacher' on a regular basis in most schools. But imagine the horror of a teacher saying I am in love with one of my students. For obvious reasons we find it very difficult to use love as a key concept in the language we use in talking about leadership in schools. But hopefully common sense prevails, and the context provides reassurance as to the appropriateness of the usage. The Ancient Greeks were very clear about the variety of different usages of love — love of God or humanity, erotic love, love between friends, and love between child and parent.

This perspective challenges many of the orthodoxies surrounding the moral dimension of leadership; love and imaginative engagement are at the heart of the creation of a just society. Layard reinforces this perspective:

> We need other people, and we need to be needed. Increasingly research confirms the dominating importance of love.
>
> (Layard, 2005, p. 66)

The introduction of love as a key element in a discourse about leadership raises many problems and challenges. Love is a complex and subjective topic with so many levels of understanding and connotations that introducing it into the vocabulary of leadership might well be counterproductive in the same way that critical analysis can compromise the intrinsic beauty of a poem or painting. One way of understanding love is to compare and contrast it with one of its traditional diametric opposites — power.

Power without love is abuse, love without power is impotence. The basis of reconciling and integrating love and power is, in Kahane's terms, to:

> ... consciously and carefully observe both our power and our love and, and neither confuse, nor choose between, nor forcibly use them.
>
> (Kahane, 2010, p. 129)

The optimum situation is obviously where love and power are mutually positive and symbiotically linked with a high degree of reinforcement. Aspiring to the combination of love and power might seem to be a counsel of perfection, but history tells us of people who aimed at exactly that and in doing so, begin to adopt and adapt new ways of talking and behaving. The melding of love and power is essentially a learning process that manifests itself most recognisably in how we understand wisdom. Indeed, one way of understanding wisdom is to see the various skills and qualities outlined in Figure 17 as its constituent elements. Notwithstanding that, it is inevitably very difficult to conceive of all of the positive aspects of love and power being present in one person all the time!

Kindness and empathy

> There are places in the world where rules are less important than kindness.
>
> (Rovelli, 2018 p. 212).

Carlo Rovelli, the Italian physicist, uses this phrase to describe an incident in North Africa when rules were broken in order to respond positively to the request of a guest.

The concept of kindness covers a wide range of applications from offering a simple courtesy (holding a door) to life changing altruism (donating a kidney). Motivation to be kind can range from pragmatic self-interest to higher order empathy and altruism. Some acts of kindness might be examples of 'doing the right deed for the wrong reason', to quote T. S. Eliot. However, these seeming moral complexities might be a biological rather than a philosophical issue:

> Perhaps because of evolution, it turns out that humans are hardwired to give. Giving releases hormones such as oxytocin which produces a natural high. In one study people were given the choice to keep $128 or donate it to charity; the researchers found that those who donated it activated the regions of the brain associated with positive reward, pleasure, trust and social connection ...
>
> (Cole, 2020, p. 302)

Kindness is behaviour that is marked by acts of generosity, consideration, or concern for others, initiated without having an expectation of recognition, praise, or reward. Kindness is found in various guises in all of the great faiths and philosophies. In the philosophy of the classical world, Aristotle defines kindness as 'helpfulness towards someone in need, not in return for anything, nor for the advantage of the helper himself, but for that of the person helped'. The Christian New Testament contains the parable of Good Samaritan. Nietzsche considered kindness and love to be the 'most curative herbs and agents in human intercourse'. Kindness is often seen as closely allied to altruism and as a practical manifestation of empathy:

Empathy is our ability to identify what someone else is thinking or feeling and respond to their thoughts and feelings with an appropriate emotion

> Empathy is like a universal solvent. Any problem immersed on empathy becomes soluble. It is effective as a way of anticipating and resolving interpersonal problems whether this is a marital conflict, an international conflict, a problem at work, difficulties in a friendship, political deadlocks, a family dispute or a problem with a neighbour.
> (Baron-Cohen, 2011, p. 127)

Empathy, in turn, requires a range of behaviours and attitudes: active listening; optimum engagement; non-judgmental; metacognition; and understanding of how others see us. This is true of both leaders and followers.

Friendship and care

Research after the Second World War found that soldiers were not motivated by idealism or ideology:

> An American soldier wasn't fuelled by patriotic spirit any more than a British one was by the democratic rule of law. It wasn't so much for their countries that these men fought as for their comrades.
> (Bregman, 2020, p. 206)

Friendship is fundamental to human relationships, and it manifests itself in a wide range of permutations. In the context of this discussion, it seems pertinent to argue that friendship is expressed in terms of degrees of attachment or engagement. Friendship can be positive but limited in terms of time and engagement, i.e. as in a professional relationship with clear boundaries and explicit limits in terms of emotional openness and commitment. At the other extreme the concept of friendship can help us to articulate the profound nature of authentic relationships that transcend the formal or symbolic components of human interaction.

Dunbar (2021, p. 91) describes our social world in terms of degrees of intimacy or engagement:

> The innermost group consists of three to five people These seem to constitute a small nucleus of really good friends to whom you go in times of trouble — for advice, comfort or perhaps even a loan of money or help.

Moving from the innermost circle to the outer sees a significant change in terms of intimacy, confidentiality, trust, disclosure and amount of interaction. Dunbar identifies 150 people as the optimum group size for human effectiveness, and this appears to apply to a wide range of human activities. As such it has implications for the way we choose to organise our schools.

Caring is instinctual human behaviour that is expressed in two, closely related, ways. Firstly, it is a morally inspired behaviour that is concerned with either safety, well-being, and protection from harm, or an expression of tenderness and kindness. Secondly, it is a legal relationship that sets out the accountability of organisations and individuals for the safety and welfare of dependents, employees, and clients — as expressed by health and safety, safeguarding, and other policies outlining expectations and entitlements. Schools will usually have statements of their shared and espoused values, but these will be reinforced and expressed through a range of policies, strategies, norms, and expectations both implicit and explicit.

We are increasingly aware of the fundamental importance of authenticity in leadership — a key element of this authenticity is the consistent use of appropriate language and behaviours without compromise or contradiction. Leaders are highly effective when they work through modelling and dialogue, developing a mutual vocabulary that is based in shared understanding and usage.

However, to focus on the emotional dimension of living and working in an authentic community inevitably also leads to a high level of personal vulnerability, as Brene Brown identifies:

> The real barrier to daring leadership is our armour — the thoughts, emotions, and behaviours that we use to protect ourselves when we aren't able to rumble with vulnerability. A rumble is a discussion, conversation or meeting defined by a commitment to lean into vulnerability, to stay curious and generous, to stick with the messy middle of problem identification and solving.
>
> (Brown, 2018, p. 12)

4. Emphasising collaboration

The history of education in England over the past 25 years could be interpreted as the growth in significance of two apparently contradictory imperatives — autonomy and collaboration. One of the defining characteristics of professional status is a degree of personal autonomy — the ability to make appropriate decisions and judgements on the basis of personal authority and expertise. This has always been a cornerstone of professional practice in education. From the late 1980s this principle has been increasingly applied to schools as institutions with the gradual emergence of Local Management of Schools (LMS), Grant Maintained Schools (GMS), specialist schools and colleges, and then academies and free schools.

In many respects the English education system is now moving towards a structure of government-funded independent schools far removed from the relationship with local education authorities that dominated the system a generation ago. One of the defining characteristics of academies is their legal status as autonomous bodies. The accountability model that prevails in England reinforces this autonomy through the way in which in which Ofsted, irrespective of any relationship a school or academy might enter into, only inspects the individual school. In other words, accountability cannot be shared.

Parallel to this growth in autonomy though has been an increasing emphasis on collaboration, which is seen as the foundation for the emergence of the self-improving school system (SISS) — the epitome of school autonomy.

> Once established, a SISS potentially reduces the need for extensive bureaucratic, top-down systems of monitoring to check on school quality, the imposition of improvement strategies that are relatively insensitive to local context, with out-of-school in-service courses not tailored to individual professional needs, and external, last-ditch interventions to remedy schools in difficulties, all of which are very costly and often only partially successful.
>
> (Hargreaves, 2010, p. 23)

The clear implication of the emergence of a SISS is a significant increase in the range and complexity of professional relationships. This perspective is reinforced by Ken Leithwood and his colleagues when they write:

> There is evidence that the process of change is more resilient and improvement more sustainable when schools collaborate and learn from other schools. Schools that sustain improvement are usually well networked and have a good structure of internal support.
>
> While such schools may be considered to be leading the way for others to follow, the reciprocal nature of the relationship and the opportunities for schools to innovate together means there is added value in both directions from these forms of collaboration.
>
> (Leithwood et al., 2010, p. 238)

This raises interesting challenges. How do we ensure high levels of collaboration between schools when, by definition, levels of engagement are limited by how easily meetings can take place and how much significance they are afforded? It is worth reflecting on the quality of relationships within schools before considering relationships between schools.

Schools themselves can be run with high degrees of personal and structural autonomy, for instance, a subject department in a secondary school. A prerequisite to effective partnership working in chains, federations, or trusts might be the development of an internal culture of openness and transparency. Even a basic analysis of the various types of partnership working that collaboration implies for schools indicates the potential challenges in terms of the breadth of effective relationships needed. Indeed, the nature of a school's relationships and partnerships will be determined by a complex series of interactions that are the product of a range of dynamic variables. Each of these will influence the nature of social interactions:

- The moral relationship — the centrality of the learner.
- The contractual relationship — e.g. the parent as client.
- The professional relationship — working with colleagues.
- The accountability relationship — being held and holding others to account.

- The learning relationship — learning communities.
- The geographical relationship — the school in context.

Matthew Taylor, then Chief Executive of the Royal Society for the Encouragement of the Arts, offered an analysis of successful collaboration derived from social anthropology theory:

- From an individualistic perspective, collaboration must be seen to be in the interests of those engaged.
- From a solidaristic perspective, collaboration needs to be underpinned by trust based on sufficiently shared norms and values.
- From a hierarchical perspective, system and organisation leaders — recognising how hard it is to establish and maintain — have to enable, incentivise and support collaboration.

(Taylor, 2013)

Taylor argues that, in almost any human context, collaboration will only work to the extent to which individuals are engaged and motivated, there is trust rooted in shared norms and values, and leadership prioritises collaboration as a priority. Taylor then goes on to explore the implications and potential benefits of this broad social analysis for education. Effective collaboration could enable a step change in the functioning of the school's system at six distinct levels:

- Relationships between the centre, localities, and schools, which are too often characterised by suspicion, misunderstanding, and resentment.
- Relationships between schools, which are rarely as robust and committed as they should be.
- Relationships between teachers, which are too often absent or shallow but could be the foundation for continuously improving professional practice.
- Relationships between schools and other local bodies, which tend to be weak or merely transactional.
- Relationships between teachers and pupils; learning is still too often seen as something that is done to pupils rather than with them.
- Relationships between pupils; even though team working is vital in

> the modern workplace, and children can powerfully support each other, we still see schooling primarily as a process of individual endeavour and ranking.
>
> (Taylor, 2012)

For most aspects of educational leadership, the future has to be collaborative; from the integrated approaches being developed by federations and trusts in the UK, to the introduction of joint practice development both within and across schools, the focus is increasingly on collaboration and cooperation.

However, the importance of collaboration is not unique to education. The history of human success is essentially the story of genuine and inclusive collaboration and cooperation and the recognition and adoption of appropriate behaviours and skills necessary for social success. Likewise, the history of human failure can usually be attributed to the failure to collaborate through a lack of appropriate effective social strategies. From the earliest hunter-gatherers to the triumphs of civilizations, progress has most been rapid through collaboration, albeit often in response to external hostile threat or challenge. We are essentially social animals and are at our best (and sometimes our worst) when we are working for mutual benefit.

> This behaviour is instantly recognizable in chimpanzees grooming one another, children building a sandcastle, or men and women laying sandbags against an impending flood. Instantly recognizable, because mutual support is built into the genes of all social animals; they cooperate to accomplish what they can't do alone.
>
> (Sennett, 2012, p. 5)

This is not to advocate mutual grooming as a strategy for leadership teams and governing bodies — although that might be an interesting alternative on the agenda. In fact, of course, mutual grooming is found in every successful human social interaction. Eye contact, shaking hands, position at the board meeting, positive reinforcement through body language, positive feedback and endorsement.

It is a myth that collaboration and cooperation involve some sort of denial of individuality or can only function in a competition free environment. Miller draws lessons for collaboration and communication from observing group behaviours in nature:

> In this respect swarms in nature have taught us two lessons. The first is that, by working together in smart groups, we too can lessen the impact of uncertainty, complexity, and change …
>
> The second lesson of smart swarms is that we don't have to surrender our individuality. In nature, good decision-making comes as much from competition as from compromise, from disagreement as much as from consensus.
>
> (Miller, 2010, pp. 267–68)

Perversely education and schooling has historically tended to reject the idea of collaboration. Teachers have long worked as essentially autonomous professionals; schools have always aspired to be highly autonomous institutions; and pupils, their parents, and other stakeholders have been subject to partial or conditional involvement. Increasing collaboration in schools and efforts to move from mere parental involvement in attending school-organised events to a deeper parental engagement focused on learning are therefore challenging. Indeed, often the school system seems to do the opposite. Many parents are initially highly engaged with their children, until school structures, procedures, and norms become involved, and seem to compromise aspects of this engagement.

The problem with a history and culture focused on autonomy is that it means that we may lose access to one of the most powerful qualities and strategies available to human beings — collaborative working, through which:

> … we have to learn not to be too inward looking, petty minded, and competitive. When it comes to the structure of society, for example we have to step out of the narrow confinement of looking after our relatives or our own kind.
>
> (Nowak, 2012, p. 283)

Collaboration and cooperation are deeply rooted in what it means to be human, but that does not mean that they are automatic or easy. One way of understanding the importance of collaboration is to see it in terms of problem-solving — people come together to collaborate and cooperate in order to solve problems. Whether it is the nomadic hunter-gatherer clan working in unison in order to hunt, the different disciplines of engineering coming together to solve problems encountered in building a bridge, or a group of schools working collaboratively to close the gap in achievement across the community, the issue is one of joint, consensual, problem solving. It could be argued that, irrespective of context, culture, or era, people spend most of their lives working with others to solve problems of varying degrees of significance and complexity.

Hargreaves and Harris in their study 'Performance beyond Expectations' identify collaboration and cooperation as fundamental to high performance:

> ... organisations that perform beyond expectations relate to their peers and even their opponents through creative and counter-intuitive combinations of competition and collaboration where success partly rests on the success of others and a sense of social justice inspires service to neighbours who are less fortunate.
>
> (Hargreaves & Harris, 2011, p. 58)

Across the spectrum of human social activity, the ability to collaborate and build effective relationships is an essential precondition to successful innovation. What is consistent are the strategies, behaviours, and skills that are necessary to make collaboration work. Success in nature, in business, in community, in health promotion, and in scientific innovation all seem to be directly related to collaboration and the ability to cooperate. It also appears to be the case that the greater the focus on innovation and creativity in an organisation, the more it works through collaboration and cooperation and the less it uses hierarchy and control systems. In such organisations a very clear sense of purpose and high levels of trust enable rich and complex networks with an openness and willingness to share.

Conclusion

Perhaps the single most important manifestation of the essential relationship between deep learning and leadership is that leaders are themselves deep learners and, crucially, model this in their practice.

Although it is important to have an explicit set of criteria for effective leadership in the context of deep learning, those criteria need to be seen in terms of capacity across the community rather than personal status. In other words, leadership that is positive and collaborative demonstrates most of the following characteristics:

- Builds a culture focused on love, friendship, care, kindness, empathy, trust, and based on restorative justice.
- Engages in futures thinking that is an iterative process rather than an event.
- Works towards collaborative and emergent understandings of the nature and implications of deep learning.
- Provides opportunities to work collaboratively in the design and delivery of deep learning in the community.
- Adopts policy that is evidence-informed and based on regular engagement with the literature, research-informed CPD, and evaluation based on formative models of assessment, so that both leadership and professional development reinforce deep learning.
- Uses a skills-based approach to problem-solving, and so models higher order skills to inform the daily working practices of adults and students.
- Is willing to 'speak truth to power' and challenge orthodoxy when necessary — including being radical and prepared to take necessary risks.
- Builds networks to optimise positive relationships, develop access to alternative perspectives, and support and enhance innovation.
- Works to enhance social and cultural capital — developing the school as a community, and reaching personal potential.

Opportunity for self-reflection and collaborative review

- *Consider the VUCA model — what do you feel are its implications for leadership and management?*
- *For each implication that you identify, what practical strategies derived from your reflections on positive leadership might help you address them?*
    - *The level of knowledge about it.*
    - *The evidence base that is available.*
    - *The degree to which it is predictable.*
    - *Precedents for responding from other systems and historic examples.*
    - *The resources that can be committed.*

Use the chart below to capture your thoughts.

Table 7: Applying the VUCA model

Category Causes and symptoms	Implications for managerial leadership	Practical strategies for positive leadership
Volatility: the speed and intensity of change.		
Uncertainty: the confidence with which we can predict the future.		
Complexity: the nature of significant variables and how they interact.		
Ambiguity: the fuzziness of variables.		

CHAPTER 10

THE FUTURE-FACING SCHOOL

> *I used to think that environmental problems were biodiversity loss, ecosystem collapse and climate change. I thought that thirty years of good science could address these problems. I was wrong. The top environmental problems are selfishness, greed and apathy, and to deal with these we need a cultural and spiritual transformation.*
>
> Gus Speth (2014, quoted in Coles & Gent, 2020, p. 140)

It is of course possible that Gus Speth, former US climate adviser and Yale Professor, takes an unduly pessimistic view of human nature. Rutger Bregman, in his book *Humankind* (2020), argues that while humans are clearly capable of great evil in certain circumstances, this is not their intrinsic nature. They are in fact hard-wired to be kind. Our own experience of parenting leaves us only partly convinced by this. It seems more reasonable to assume that the greater truth lies somewhere between these two views of human nature. If so, the role of upbringing and of education in helping to determine which side of a person's character is more likely and able to prevail takes on a special importance.

The responsibility for fostering the inner transformation Speth suggests rests heavily, though by no means absolutely, with schools. Notwithstanding the serious systemic problems we identified in chapter 2, there is no other social institution as well placed, or with such relevant experience, to contribute to this task. The pandemic and its associated lockdowns has been a vivid reminder of the vital role many schools play in their communities. We have tried in the preceding chapters to discuss what a school response to the challenges of the future might look like through an exploration of the notion of deep learning. It is time to draw these insights together into a more systematic account of the future-facing school and what this implies for school leaders.

We attempt this with a degree of ambivalence. On the one hand, the urgency of the human predicament is clear and there is no time to be wasted in trying to respond. On the other hand, for schools and their leaders there are already huge competing pressures in the form of the status quo of accountability. It is also not possible to start afresh with a completely blank sheet. Schools are firmly in the territory of the 'second horizon'.

Somehow our response to the challenge of change needs to balance being both radical and realistic. Moreover, effective solutions will also necessarily depend heavily on local contexts. It is helpful to start from first principles. It is rare to find a totally unique idea in any sphere of human activity — indeed most ideas in education can usually be traced back to the Greeks! It is therefore no surprise that our core model of deep learning — understanding, action, and character — has a significant precedent in the more recent past, in this case in the words and deeds of Johann Heinrich Pestalozzi (1746–1827).

Pestalozzi is best known today for the Pestalozzi villages and the scholarship programme for able students from developing countries that bear his name. Fundamental to both activities is Pestalozzi's principle of education of the 'Heart, Hand, and Head'.

The Pestalozzi Society website defines this principle in the following terms:

> Firstly, the child should feel moral life (heart), then it should do good (hand) and finally it should reflect on morality (head).

Importantly, Pestalozzi stressed the interconnectedness and interdependence of these domains. It is the work of educators to develop strategies that treat the three aspects equally so that the learner can develop as their own unique person:

Heart (i.e. character): the moral and relational dimension of education based on recognition of everyone's deep seated individuality and social awareness.

Hand (i.e. agency): working in collaboration with others to understand and so control nature with an emphasis on action.

Head (i.e. understanding): the application of reason to reflect on learning experiences and demonstrate understanding through the development of concepts and ideas.

Figure 18: The Pestalozzi model of education

Pestalozzi was a radical in social and educational thought, following in the steps of Rousseau and the interaction of romantic idealism with an empirical, experimental approach. His ideas on the nature of childhood, the rights of children, and the development of teaching and learning strategies, derived from his own practice, making him a remarkably modern figure. In particular, he was concerned with how school-based education can translate into moral virtue and in turn social change and improvement.

When Pestalozzi writes of the development of the heart, he writes of 'upbringing', whereas he usually refers to the development and strengthening of mental and physical powers as 'formative education'. A more modern perspective would be that upbringing and formative education should not be separated but connected with each other in such a way that the former supports the latter. School and family are thus inextricably linked.

It is a key responsibility of the educator — irrespective of the context of the learner in terms of time, place, or organisation — to keep the three elements of heart/character, head/understanding, and hand/agency in equilibrium. It is not enough to simply teach a subject. Rather, teachers have a responsibility to harmonise intellectual, artistic, and technical activities in such a way that children can take increasing responsibility for their own learning.

The most important idea here is balance across these three aspects. A similar point is made more recently by Gert Biesta (2021) when he talks about three functions of education: qualification (by which he means knowledge and skills); socialisation (ways of being and doing); and subjectification (the formation of the person). Finding and maintaining a proper balance between these functions requires three-dimensional thinking and practice rather than the more simplistic views which inform much educational policy-making at a national level. As he observes:

> Right now, qualification seems to occupy the centre of the educational universe. Socialisation tends to enter the scene when there are concerns about the behaviour of children and young people, which often is the rationale for the inclusion of such things as values education, character education, citizenship education, or environmental education. In such a set-up, the concern for the student-as-subject and for the subject-ness of the student often appears at the very end, as a kind of luxury, when the alleged basics have been taken care of and there is still some time left — which means that it may happen for some and not for others, or may only happen haphazardly.[54]

The Pestalozzi Society website (https://www.jhpestalozzi.org/) identifies a wide range of aspects of current educational significance, which we have organised in Table 8 to focus on the key themes of Pestalozzi's influence.

---

54. Biesta, G. (2021), *World-Centred Education: A View for the Present*. Available from: https://www.researchgate.net/publication/352809159_World-Centred_Education_A_View_for_the_Present.

While drawing on the past, they provide a highly relevant summary of the most important characteristics of the future-facing school. We see strong echoes of them in our case study schools and they relate closely to the three drivers of change we have identified as the prime characteristics of deep learning for future sustainability.

Table 8: Pestalozzi principles adapted for the future-facing school

Core values

- Authority based on love, not fear - a culture of kindness and gentleness.
- The interests and needs of the child define the learning experience.
- A child-centred rather than teacher-centred approach to teaching.

Principles of curriculum design

- The importance of an all-round education – an education of the head, the heart, and the hands, but which is led by the heart.
- The use of systemised subjects of instruction, which are also carefully graduated and illustrated.
- Learning which is cross-curricular and includes a varied school life.

Principles of pedagogy and learning

- Education which puts emphasis on how things are taught as well as what is taught.
- The freedom of the child based on his or her natural development balanced with the self-discipline to function well as an individual and in society.
- Active rather than passive participation in the learning experience.
- The use of all the senses in training pupils in observation and judgement.

Education in context

- The child having direct experience of the world and the use of natural objects in teaching.
- Cooperation between the school and the home and between parents and teachers.
- Teachers as deep learners about education.

It would be easy, but wrong, to misrepresent and dismiss these statements as simply offering a child-centred view of education. Even though the term appears in the list, it refers here to learning rather than teaching! Terms such as 'child-centred' have often been used to create a falsely polarised view; Dewey himself noted that a purely child-centred education would be 'really stupid' (Dewey, 1984, p. 59). That is because to educate is fundamentally to intervene, having made a value judgement about the direction of learning that is desirable. Education involves teaching, and teaching specifics, as Pestalozzi also makes absolutely clear.

At the same time, however, as Biesta acutely observes:

> Pure curriculum-centred education ... is equally 'stupid', because just trying to get curriculum content into children and monitor retention and reproduction, without any concern for who they are and for what they might do with all the content they are acquiring, misses the existential point of education as well, and would, in my view, therefore miss the point of education altogether.

Biesta prefers the term 'world-centred education':

> .... that is, focused on equipping and encouraging the next generation to exist 'in' and 'with' the world, and do so in their own right. This is not to suggest, of course, that existing in one's own right is the same as 'just doing what one wants to do'. On the contrary, to exist as subject 'in' and 'with' the world is about acknowledging that the world, natural and social, puts limits and limitations on what we can desire from it and can do with it — which is both the question of democracy and the question of ecology.

The future-facing school is, in this sense, world-centred, and as part of its core business is concerned with questions of both democracy and ecology.

Connecting what we know and what we do

We know from multiple sources that balance between the different functions of education matters. Yet, as George Monbiot observed in a recent article, 'There is no connection between what we know and what we do ... [indeed, we have to] close the gap between knowing and doing'.[55] Although he was talking about change for a sustainable future in a much broader context than education, those words are particularly powerful when applied to 'what we know' about learning compared the reality of 'what we do' (or do not do) in schools.

Closing the gap between knowing and doing for the school that is setting out to turn its face towards the future, to become world-centred in its education, and child-centred in its teaching, means paying attention to

55. Monbiot, G. (2021), 'Why is life on Earth still taking second place to fossil fuel companies?', *Guardian*, 19 August. Available at: https://www.theguardian.com/commentisfree/2021/aug/19/life-earth-second-place-fossil-fuel-climate-breakdown.

three key lessons. These are about looking beyond itself; modelling wider change within itself; and integrating and balancing the three drivers of understanding, character and agency across its curriculum. Inevitably, and necessarily, they overlap, and these connections are important. For each, we attempt to identify some possible responses for schools who wish to turn their face towards the future. These responses are not intended to be prescriptive or definitive, but rather as triggers or points of departure. While we would encourage every school to turn its focus in this direction, there is no single right path to take. Context always matters. It is better to do something than nothing, and it is better to light a candle than rage at the darkness.

Lesson 1: The future-facing school cannot succeed in isolation

Engaging with stakeholders

Because it cannot act alone and because meaningful change cannot be imposed on others, the school which is turning its face towards the future must begin with, and remain fundamentally rooted in, deep listening. It chooses to orchestrate an ongoing conversation with all its stakeholders, students, parents, staff, and community, to build a shared understanding of purpose, and continually renew this. The future-facing school is thus engaged in a process of co-creation. The task of leadership is to facilitate and nurture this process, influencing and shaping it of course, but not seeking to control it.

The thrust of that ongoing conversation with stakeholders is about the world our children will live in and how we equip them to understand and shape it for their own wellbeing as well as for the good of all. It is important that those conversations are:

- Genuine, not contrived.
- Open, not closed.
- Creative, not sterile.
- Inclusive, not exclusive.
- Purposeful, not pointless.

The role of parents as co-educators is central to this task. However, adopting a strategy of engaging with families as co-educators begins with the recognition by the school that its relationship with families is qualitatively changed as a result of parents' role and influence in educating their children. It goes well beyond the simplistic notions of parental choice which have governed national education policy for several decades. It means:

- Developing systematic and continuous engagement right from the very beginning.
- Looking to include all families, not just the advantaged.
- Recognising that children's learning extends beyond school.
- Shifting our mindset from doing 'for' and 'to', towards actively co-creating opportunities to engage with parents.

None of this is easy. Parents are also affected, indeed bombarded, by the deficit model of education and schools that is promoted by some policy-makers and media. Many carry with them their own negative associations of school and of 'authority' more generally. But by building supportive and sympathetic relationships carefully from the earliest moment of contact — based on mutual trust and respect — and by making changes in day-to-day practice to match, a clear and shared focus on supporting children's learning and recognising each other's contribution can be built.

Nurturing wider partnerships for learning and sustainability

The future-facing school will also need to foster a wider partnership network of all those with an interest in young people. That of course should be everyone. As the traditional Masai greeting reminds us; *Kasserian Ingera* — How goes it with *our* children?

But there are also a wide range of more focused partners with special interest in the upbringing and education of the young with whom the school needs to nurture relationships as it seeks to equip young people for the future.

This is of course not as straightforward as it sounds and far from being just an easy soundbite. The language of partnership can mask both conceptual and practical difficulties. As Guest and Peccei pointed out a while back, partnership 'is an idea with which anyone can agree, without having any clear idea what they are agreeing about' (Guest & Peccei, 2001, p. 207).

Gray (1989, p. 5) defined collaboration as:

> ... a process through which parties who see different aspects of a problem can explore constructively their differences and search for solutions that go beyond their own limited vision of what is possible.

We choose to use two terms to describe different but complementary approaches to collaboration: *partnership*, by which we mean formal arrangements to collaborate with those who are not already key stakeholders; and *networks*, by which we mean looser and less formal collaboration across a wider span. Both have a part to play. Dhillon (2009) teases out the relationship of partnerships and networks further by suggesting that the effectiveness and sustainability of a partnership depends not just on the quantity of contacts in a network but also their quality in terms of the power, influence, and trustworthiness.

Lasker, Weiss, and Miller (2001, p. 182) helpfully use the term 'synergy' to describe the magic ingredient for effective partnerships. They feel there is a need to define 'the mechanism that enables partnerships to accomplish more than individuals and organisations'. Consequently, they look for 'a pathway through which partnership functioning influences partnership effectiveness'. Synergy is the concept with which they seek to fill the void. The combined perspectives, resources, and skills of each organisation in the partnership create synergy, which in turn creates a new entity that is greater than its individual components. That is precisely what we saw demonstrated in practice in our case study of Falinge Park High School in chapter 8.

Creating such synergy is not easy, but it is clearly possible. Huxham and Vangen (2005) describe the potentially frustrating nature of collaborative working through their concept of 'collaborative inertia'. They conclude that collaboration is a seriously resource-consuming activity, only to be considered when the stakes are worth pursuing. We think the stakes here are indeed that high. Nevertheless, the development of effective partnerships represents a considerable leadership challenge that requires specific skills.

At the heart of these skills is an awareness of relationships, but this involves more than simply looking upwards (towards the goal) and looking downwards (towards followers). It involves looking sideways and around as well. It is not just focused on the self-interest of the individual school. Such leadership also displays insight into how the school for which the leader has responsibility is, itself, part of a wider fabric, to which it actively contributes, and from which it consciously draws.

Becoming a good ancestor

Finally, in the same way that our individual decisions can make a contribution to a more sustainable future but need to be accompanied by equally vigorous social action, so the future-facing school mirrors these individual characteristics in its organisational life by seeking to gauge and take account of long-term wider impact in all its decisions and structures. This might range from the simplest purchasing decisions to planning the most advanced building changes, from the way its members are fed to the way it organises transport, from how it avoids waste and manages rubbish to its use of energy. By engaging all its stakeholders in this process, a school can again help to create a multiplier effect. Its example encourages others to do the same for themselves.

In his book *The Good Ancestor*, Roman Krznaric argues that the survival of our species and planet requires us to shift from the short-termism of current political and business thinking to incorporate a much longer-term view of our impact on future generations. Among a range of strategies to work towards this, he cites the example of the Future Design movement in Japan:

> The idea is simple: if there is no one to protect the interests of future generations, then designate people to 'take on the role of future generations' and have them stand in for future generations. This is the same reasoning as role playing scenarios used frequently in things such as war games (table-top exercises in war). Tatsuyoshi Saijo, a professor at Kochi University of Technology and his colleagues called these people whom are to take on the role of future generations the 'imaginary future generation' or 'imaginary future persons.'
>
> (Krznaric, 2020, p. 181)

We also wonder if it is possible to take this idea further — beyond role play — and equip the actual future generation, the children and young people who are in our classrooms right now, with the skills and understanding to represent successor generations in key decisions about the development of their school and community. Why not? In this way they may develop the habits of long-term thinking and individual and collective agency needed to navigate successfully to a just and sustainable future. It could offer a powerful new way to develop student leadership in schools.

Lesson 2: The future-facing school models within itself the changes it seeks in others

As Mahatma Gandhi said: 'Be the change that you wish to see in the world'. The second requirement of the future-facing school is that it models within itself the transformation it seeks in its pupils. For transformation is not a purely academic exercise, it requires the integration of heart, hand, and head (or character, agency, and understanding). It is caught more than it is taught, and this can be expressed in three ways in particular: relationships matter; a culture of deep learning; and empowering leadership.

Relationships matter

It is no coincidence that the motto of XP school is 'Above all compassion'. High quality relationships, at every level, and the values which necessarily underpin these, hold primacy in the future-facing school. In the words of one headteacher we spoke to: 'You have to build the relationships first. Nobody cares what you know until they know that you care.' The building blocks of these relationships are care, expectation, habit, and structure.

Founders of the CoEd Foundation, which seeks to promote the development of a more compassionate education, define compassion as 'a way of seeing the world that places love-in-action at the heart of everything' (Coles & Gent, 2020, p. 7).[56] The concept embraces care for self, others, place, and planet, and has a remarkable resonance with the thinking of our case study schools. For instance, Falinge Park has its five big learning behaviours: show kindness; show empathy; be curious; be responsible; and take positive action. There are strong echoes too in St Augustine's Academy's golden rules: 'show respect, be kind, try our best'. In other words, in both schools rules are both few in number and they are focused on positive behaviour and character. These qualities are not developed through rigid conformity or punishment. Neither do they happen by accident. Falinge Park is clear:

56. See also, https://www.coedfoundation.org.uk.

> We will plan so these are 'caught, taught and sought.' These are our learning behaviours and we will make sure that we can achieve this by planning carefully and not assuming they will appear through chance or at random.

There is constant reinforcement, catching people out being good rather than looking out for the bad. Of course, young people will make mistakes in the way they behave. In those cases the emphasis is not on punishment but rather on working to put right what went wrong and helping them to get back up again (i.e. restorative justice).

That means designing school structures which make it possible for every student to be well-known to staff and supported by peers and adults, as well as ensuring that they and their families have a significant and valued relationship with at least one key member of staff. It means giving this the highest priority and making space for those relationships to grow and flourish over time.

In the model of Expeditionary Learning (see chapter 7), the core structure for achieving such relationships is termed 'Crew'. This is derived from the thinking of Outward Bound founder Kurt Hahn, who stated: 'We are crew, not passengers, strengthened by acts of consequential service to others' (Berger et al., 2021). The culture of crew impels all members of a school community to work together as a team, to pitch in, to help others. Staff and students help their colleagues and peers to get 'up the mountain together' — individual success, whether academically or in other ways, is not enough. Yet too many pastoral arrangements in our schools treat children and young people as mere passengers rather than as active participants in a shared adventure.

The structure of Crew is centred on daily meetings specifically intended to support everyone's learning and growth. This regular commitment allows time for students to build meaningful relationships with their peers and their Crew leader, to reflect on and monitor academic progress, and to focus on character development. The future-facing school similarly needs to find ways to give real priority and time to this focused building of positive relationships.

A culture of deep learning

A second aspect of modelling change is that all who are part of the school understand and practice deep learning in their personal as well as their 'professional' lives.

Success in academic terms is often measured in terms of comfort and ease with abstract concepts. Indeed, the process of developing mastery in any given subject can be directly related to fluency in that subject's specialist language. Such a language is usually expressed in terms of concepts, for instance moving from being able to recite the causes of the First World War to understanding the concept of causality and being able to explain it, apply it in differing contexts, and offer alternative explanations.

A.C. Grayling sets out the key issue here:

> It is a common view, and one much acted on, that education consists in the transfer of knowledge and skills from teachers to pupils ... [However,] it is important that students should understand, how partial, incomplete and open-ended almost all enquiry is and that in many areas of enquiry there are no right and wrong answers, only better and worse reasons ...
>
> (quoted in Birch, 2014, p. ii)

Effective teaching and facilitation enable deep learning that moves us from compliance to informed and questioning engagement. All children, including the very youngest, the most challenging, and the least engaged, need skills to:

- Reveal and question underlying assumptions.
- Figure out the perhaps unforeseen consequences of a moral decision or point of view.
- Spot and diagnose faulty reasoning.
- Weigh up evidence fairly and impartially.
- Make a point clearly and concisely.
- Take turns in a debate and listen attentively without interrupting.
- Argue without personalizing a dispute.
- Look at issues from the point of view of others.

The same characteristics must feature in the life of their teachers as well.

Empowering leadership

We have argued that for students to develop as learners of and for the future, they need to be not just involved and engaged but also able to exercise agency. This in turn requires teachers who understand and experience agency themselves. It is for leaders to create the climate and conditions in which this is possible.

The exercise of agency, in any context, is challenging to existing authority. It offers different opinions, asks questions, and suggests different solutions. The exercise of agency inevitably means that people are no longer willing to be compliant, not because they wish to disagree and oppose, but in order to work together to learn, to be creative, to share in the excitement of exploration, and to find better ways.

An agency mindset will be characterised by the courage to make mistakes and learn from them; to be creative; to be resilient; and to persevere. It implies a collective commitment to engage in dialogue with the learners for whom we share a responsibility, and to take time to find different ways through seemingly intransient problems.

Lesson 3: The future-facing school integrates and balances the three domains of understanding, character, and agency (head, heart, and hand) across its curriculum

Too often, at least in policy discourses, the curriculum is considered to be little more than a list of subjects. To be clear, our argument is not about adding another subject, say climate science, to an already over-crowded school timetable. Although equally, that is not to say there is no place for some specific focus within the curriculum on issues of sustainability. Recent research has suggested that if only 16 % of high school students in high and middle-income countries were to receive climate change education, we might see a nearly 19 gigaton reduction of carbon dioxide by 2050.[57] When education helps students develop a strong personal connection to climate solutions, as well as a sense of personal agency and empowerment, it can have a consequential impact on their daily

57. Cordero, E. C., et al. (2020) 'The role of climate change education on individual lifetime carbon emissions', *PLoS ONE* 15(2). Available at: https://doi.org/10.1371/journal.pone.0206266.

behaviours and decision-making that also reduces their overall lifetime carbon footprint.

However, at root this is not about a syllabus to be covered, but about a future-thinking mindset and awareness which permeates across everything. Rather than seeing the curriculum as a set of subjects, however defined, Tony Breslin offers a much better definition when he argues 'curriculum is the total learned experience of the child: formal, informal, within the classroom and beyond'.[58] Such a curriculum, one which looks to properly face the future, has three notable characteristics in its approach: it is holistic; personal; and looks beyond the here and now.

A holistic approach

By this we mean an approach which secures a real balance across the curriculum by addressing all three domains of understanding, character, and agency (head, heart, and hand).

We have argued that our collective failure so far to find an adequate balance between these three domains within upbringing and education lies at the root of wider societal dysfunction. In his 2021 study *Head, Hand, Heart*, David Goodhart analyses the nature and implications of the deep malaise in British and American society caused by the need for a better balance between these aptitudes:

> The three aptitudes overlap to differing degrees, but the modern knowledge economy has produced ever rising returns for 'Head' workers ... reduced the pay and status of much manual ('Hand') work ... at the same time, many aspects of caring (Heart) work continue to be undervalued.
>
> (Goodhart, 2021, p. 4)

Along the way, he argues, we have undervalued both technical and practical abilities (hand), and social and empathetic skills (heart), while alienating and demoralising the people who do the jobs that require them. We have seen in the experience of the pandemic how out of kilter our valuations of different types of work truly are.

58. Breslin, T. (2018), 'The new Ofsted framework', *British Educational Research Association*. Available at: https://www.bera.ac.uk/blog/the-new-ofsted-framework.

Finding a more just and honest balance between the three domains lies at the very core of the future-facing school's challenge and is the key to them playing their part in the 'cultural and spiritual' transformation Speth called for if we are to establish and secure a just and sustainable future for all.

A personal approach

Lockdown has forcibly reminded us that school is not the only place where learning can happen, and that individuals have different needs, even within the same age range. Beyond personal relationships and interactions, there is scope to adjust the balance of in and out of school learning in order to make learning both real and personal.

The issues around a more blended model of learning are only partly a matter of technology. They are fundamentally about the recognition that learning happens both within and without school, and at the direction and instigation of both the teacher and learner. We need a much more personalised approach to identifying the balance appropriate for each learner at each stage of their individual journey.

One part of this involves what we might term flipping motivation, where the young person takes charge of determining their own ambitions and what success will look like for them. We saw this approach in action in the XP story. Indeed, in all three case studies we glimpsed in different ways how children and young people can be helped and encouraged to set their own goals and challenges, rather than having these imposed externally through the pursuit of test scores or qualifications in the abstract. None of these three schools implement this approach in a hands-off way, but rather work through fostering a long-term embedded mindset of respect for individuals, combined with challenge and support.

In their paper on the implications of Covid for education, Yong Zhao and Jim Watterston (2021) suggest that schools might use discretion in relaxing the intense requirements of curriculum.

> Schools could start by allowing students to negotiate part of their curriculum instead of requiring all students learn the same content ... Students should be enabled to have certain levels of autonomy over what they want to learn, how they learn, where they learn and how they want to be assessed.

Significantly for us, they go on to comment:

> When students have such autonomy, they are more likely to be less constrained by the local contexts they are born into. The impact of their home background and local schools may be less powerful.
> (Zhao & Watterston, 2021, p. 7)

This shift would not of course have to happen all at once. It is possible to envisage a developmental progression as a child matures, as well as a systemic progression as a school gains confidence in its own ability to work in this way.

An approach which looks beyond the here and now

We are just at the beginning of what Klaus Schwab, the Chair of the World Economic Forum, has termed the fourth industrial revolution.[59] This, he argues, will be driven largely by the convergence of digital, biological, and physical innovations. Technologies, such as artificial intelligence, genome editing, augmented reality, robotics, and 3-D printing, are already rapidly changing the way humans create, exchange, and distribute value. As in the previous industrial revolutions, this process will profoundly transform institutions, industries, and individuals. He concludes:

> More importantly, this revolution will be guided by the choices that people make today: the world in 50 to 100 years from now will owe a lot of its character to how we think about, invest in, and deploy these powerful new technologies.

In *21 Lessons for the 21 Century* Yuval Harrari (2018) summarises his most important advice to young people to prepare them for the associated deluge of change as 'to know yourself better first.' This is of course ancient wisdom and was inscribed over the entrance of the Greek temple of the oracle at Delphi to greet those who travelled there to learn of the future. Today, Harari warns, this is more important than ever because of the rapidly increasing power of biotechnology and machine learning to manipulate peoples' deepest emotions and desires, and because of the ways in which this can be (mis)appropriated by advertisers as well as by politicians.

---

59. Schwab, K. 'The Fourth Industrial Revolution', *Encyclopedia Britannica*. Available at: https://www.britannica.com/topic/The-Fourth-Industrial-Revolution-2119734.

Such technology is inevitably beginning to impact schools. Rachel Sylvester, Chair of The Times Education Commission, summarised some of this in an article for her newspaper in November 2021.[60] Estonia holds most exams online and pupils study robotics from age seven. In Silicon Valley pupils are using virtual reality glasses to visit the Arctic Circle or the Pyramids for history, to experience erupting volcanoes or marauding dinosaurs. That sounds like fun, but other developments may be more insidious. Sylvester cites researchers who are looking at how brain sensors contained in a baseball cap could let a teacher see which part of their pupils' brain are most active during lesson. The ethical implications are profound. One Chinese primary school has already made children wear head-scanning headbands to measure their attention span with the results being sent back to a central computer. The experiment was stopped once someone realised where it might lead in a surveillance state.

If these dangers are to be avoided, and a better future created, then it is vital that young people are helped 'to know yourself before they do', as Harari puts it. In other words, if schools are to equip young people for this set of future challenges, it means a strong focus on developing their humanity and their individuality. As Zhao and Watterston put it:

> For humans to thrive in the age of smart machines, it is essential they do not compete with machines. Instead they need to be more human.
> (Zhao & Watterston, 2021, p. 5)

That, for them, means recognising each child's uniqueness as well as fostering their social-emotional intelligence. This in turn means schools can no longer 'pre-impose all that is needed for the future before students graduate'. Students should have more control over their learning and be helped to develop their own unique pathways. While this would lead to much greater flexibility in both the pace and routes of learning, as well as the curriculum, it does require an acceptance of a greater level of learner control and co-agency than is currently thought permissible.

60. Sylvester, R. (2021), 'The AI revolution can supercharge learning in schools', *The Times*, 26 November. https://www.thetimes.co.uk/article/the-ai-revolution-can-supercharge-learning-in-school-xnv0vql8r.

Conclusion

The doughnut model of education sketched in chapter 3 is an attempt to capture the task ahead for the future-facing school which shares in the mission to create a just and sustainable future for all. Education forms just one part of the dramatic social and economic realignment implicit in Raworth's model of doughnut economics. The case for such change is in our view overwhelming. Schools that take seriously their responsibility to prepare students effectively to understand and shape their futures need to move ahead now with intent and purpose.

The three systemic weaknesses of the school system that we identified in part 1 (a neglect of family; a failure of equity; and a flawed approach to accountability) are not fixable solely by the work of individual schools. There are nevertheless important ways in which an individual school that understands the nature of these weaknesses can work to mitigate their effects and help to counteract them for their students. Doing so is part of the key to unlocking a just and sustainable future for all.

We have tried to set out some of the directions of those changes, which we think are both possible with commitment in the here and now, as well as having a positive effect in moving us towards that goal. We have attempted to put some flesh on these ideas without being over-prescriptive, and to describe the ways in which a school which turns its face to the future is different, most especially by emphasising the experience of a learning community offered to its pupils and to their parents.

We have, as we admitted earlier, done this with a degree of ambivalence. We are very mindful of the extent to which the directions in which we are pointing run counter to both the prevailing policy and what passes for wisdom in the English school system of today. But if we believe in a caring, participative, and sustainable world we must educate towards that end, using first-hand experience as the most important ingredient in the educative process. A future-facing school has the potential to be the most powerful catalyst in accelerating that process — if it so chooses.

Opportunity for self-reflection and collaborative review

- *How can your school embed a care agenda — care for oneself, care for others, care for place, and care for the planet — as a distinctive commitment?*
- *How can your school involve all its stakeholders in decision-making about sustainable development — balancing short-term interests with longer-term goals — while considering the needs of the environment, future generations, and other communities?*
- *How can your school develop individuals with the knowledge, values, skills, and self-confidence to make positive contributions to their family, their community, their job, the environment, and a dramatically changing world?*
- *How can your school's curriculum best comply with statutory requirements while re-balancing its emphasis between the domains of head, heart, and hand so as to promote each pupil's deep learning?*

CHAPTER 11

YES WE CAN!

Education is the point at which we decide whether we love the world enough to assume responsibility for it and by the same token save it.
Hannah Arendt (1954)

Can a school save the world? No, of course it can't, at least not on its own. Can a school make a difference if it focuses intensely on the future? Yes, we believe it can, but not if it just carries on with business as usual.

It is not the role of schools to solve the climate crisis, or any of the other multiple crises now facing humankind. But they can, if they so choose, equip young people as well as possible to deal with the consequences of the serious problems they will be inheriting from their elders, not betters.

The school which will make a difference, the future-facing school, is one which firstly recognises the need to change without waiting to be told by government. It recognises of course it has an accountability to government and works to fulfil that minimum requirement as effectively as possible. But it sees this as a secondary purpose, subordinate to and subsumed within, its main accountability to its learners and their future.

The second feature of the school which can make a difference is that it has the courage to change and to continually re-assess itself rigorously and on the basis of evidence. It is in other words a learning community.

We have suggested in the previous chapter that schools which are confident and courageous in these ways have a number of common features in how they engage with and support their students, families, and communities to face the future positively.

Because they know they cannot do this in isolation, they work pro-actively with all their stakeholders to build a sense of shared purpose. They carefully nurture wider partnerships for education and for sustainability. They are aware of their responsibility to become a good ancestor and to help others do likewise.

Because they model within themselves the changes they seek in others, they place the highest emphasis on forging high-quality relationships at every level and they commit the time and resources to making sure this happens. They actively build a positive culture of deep learning among staff, pupils, and families. Both of these strategies are enabled through their culture of empowering leadership.

Finally, because they understand the need to create a balance of learning across the domains of head, heart, and hand (understanding, character, and agency), they build a holistic approach within their whole curriculum. They understand that such a curriculum must also be personalised and relevant to each learner to a much greater extent than is currently practised. And they look beyond the here and now to grow their awareness of the challenges on the horizon for the learners they are educating.

Taking these principles seriously will also mean that a school recognises the part it can and must play in addressing the three systemic weaknesses with which we began our analysis in chapter 2. It recognises the importance of family. It takes seriously the need for equity and for social justice. It is robust but balanced and measured in its understanding of accountability.

None of this is radical in the sense of being extreme, although it is indeed 'radical' in its original Latinate sense of going back to the root of things. This argument is also not imagined or made-up, but rather robustly evidence-informed. But are any of these changes possible? Well, they are certainly not possible if we do nothing differently. The great question is whether enough schools and school leaders can make enough of a difference quickly enough, seizing the moment for change. There are, of course, seeds of hope, as we have identified in all the schools we have described.

It is, though, not easy to be optimistic. And it is certainly possible to argue we are only in our current predicament because of the business cynicism and shallow optimism of older generations who hoped that something would turn up or that someone else would fix these problems. Winston Churchill once said: 'A pessimist sees the difficulty in opportunity; an optimist sees the opportunity in every difficulty'. We have tried to be clear both about the extent of difficulty which we face and also the opportunity we believe is contained therein. But we can now no longer, if we ever could, leave it to others to fix.

For Jane Goodall, the primateologist and anthropologist, hope is the key. She understands well enough the bleak projections from climate scientists, as well as the economic and political structures that hinder change. But she argues that hope is essential for the survival of humanity. 'If you don't hope that your actions can make a difference, then you sink into apathy', she says. And, importantly for educators, she continues: 'If young people succumb to the doom and gloom—if *they* lose hope—that's the end'.

Young people themselves, indeed, are one of her main sources of hope, along with 'the amazing human intellect, the resilience of nature .... and the indomitable human spirit'.[61] That is why the role of schools and their commitment to deep learning for future sustainability is of such crucial importance at this time of *chairos*.

It is not possible, even if it were desirable, to wait for governments to catch up. Too often their leadership for change has been wanting in this regard, following the crowd with simplistic slogans and quick fixes rather than undertaking the in-depth strategic thinking and policy development that has been needed for years. And as Marks and Hickman have demonstrated, young people see this clearly and feel badly let down.

So, we believe, the onus and the responsibility to act now rests on the leaders and teachers in our schools today to play their part unasked. This requires bravery and it means taking risks. That is demanding in itself, but it is also possible, as we have seen in the examples of school leaders we

---

61. Nugent, C. (2021), 'The enduring hope of Jane Goodall', *Time Magazine*, 30 September. Available at: https://time.com/6102640/jane-goodall-environment-hope/.

have spoken to and whose work we have tried to capture in this book. The call to action we are making is not, however, an extra burden to be taken on; it is in reality the very work of education itself. And the response that each of us makes to that call will make a difference. It remains up to each of us, however, to decide what sort of difference that will be.

Hope, though, is not blind. As we write this final chapter, the ground has been shifting under our feet again in ways we would not have imagined when we started on the book two years ago. The Russian invasion of Ukraine has released unpredictable consequences, including reawakening the threat of nuclear catastrophe, while diverting minds and energy away from all those urgent planetary crises that demand out attention. Indeed, on the fifth day of that invasion, at the end of February 2022, the IPCC published an update to its 2021 report which concludes: 'Any further delay in concerted global action will miss a brief and rapidly closing window to secure a liveable future'.[62] The synchronicity of these two events makes it very hard to be confident there can be any positive future.

The American writer Anne Lamott (1995) says: 'Hope begins in the dark, the stubborn hope that if you just show up and try to do the right thing, the dawn will come. You wait and watch and work: you don't give up'. West-Burnham (2002) and Flintham (2010) developed the concept of a reservoir of hope that we each need in responding to the potentially negative implications of leading such change in the context of a VUCA world. That leadership requires both personal resilience and sustainability:

> The foundations of the 'reservoir of hope', the spiritual, moral and ethical bases on which individual leadership stands and which provide the well-spring which motivates, replenishes and renews the capacity for spiritual and moral leadership, are provided by a clearly articulated value system which explicitly or implicitly underpins leadership actions by providing the reason why.
>
> (Flintham, 2010, p. 55)

62. Harvey, F., 'IPCC issues 'bleakest warning yet' on impacts of climate breakdown', *Guardian*, 28 February. Available at: https://www.theguardian.com/environment/2022/feb/28/ipcc-issues-bleakest-warning-yet-impacts-climate-breakdown?CMP=Share_iOSApp_Other.

Becoming personally effective and developing authenticity depends on the creation and nurturing of such a reservoir of hope. Hope empowers us to take on new challenges, to make commitments, to trust, and to approach the future with confidence. From hope comes both courage and the desire to learn and grow. The reservoir is kept filled by creating time and space to focus on a sense of hope, optimism, peace, and personal well-being.

A full reservoir enables capacity and sustainability, but it needs to be nurtured and refilled. An empty reservoir leads to the loss of personal and professional effectiveness and authenticity. The leadership of change starts with personal change, it is neither possible nor morally acceptable to lead change without modelling that change in terms of language, beliefs, and behaviours.

The challenge ahead requires changemaker leaders with both tenacity and audacity. Robert Reich, Professor of Public Policy at Berkeley and former US Secretary of Labour, argues in a recent blog that the secret of tenacity for changemakers is threefold.[63] He cites an example, drawn from Adam Hochschild's book *Bury the Chains*, of the true story of twelve people (a printer, a lawyer, a clergyman, and nine others united by their hatred of slavery) who in early 1787 came together in a London printing shop and began a grass-roots movement to convince the British public to end the slave trade.

It seemed impossible at the time. The slave trade was hugely profitable. It enriched the British establishment. But the leaders of that movement stuck with it. In 1807 legislation was passed in both the Commons and the Lords prohibiting the trading of enslaved people in the British Empire. However, it took until August 1, 1838 for the final Abolition of Slavery Act to grant full emancipation across British territories.

How did these campaigners bring this about this shift in public support? Not only did they innovate, pioneering a variety of techniques that have been adopted by social movements ever since (from consumer boycotts to wall posters and lapel buttons to celebrity endorsements), but they

63. Reich, R. (2021), 'The Secret to tenacity'. Available at: https://robertreich.substack.com/p/tenacity.

also persevered against the odds. Reich suggests they had three secrets to success that are vital to all tenacious changemakers.

First, they pace themselves. They understand they are in a marathon which they cannot possibly win if they go all out, continuously. They are patient with themselves and recognise the importance of work-life balance. They keep re-filling their reservoir of hope.

Second, they are part of a team or group that helps one another. They trade off the hardest work among themselves, so that no single member of the group has to do it continuously. They buoy each other's spirits. They share jokes and humorous anecdotes. They watch out for each other's mental and physical health.

Third, they find opportunities to celebrate victories, no matter how small. Big victories are rare, but small ones do occur. And when they do, those who are in it for the long haul celebrate them, boosting everyone's morale and illustrating the possibilities for larger victories.

We do not have as long as those twelve needed to make a difference. We have to be just as tenacious, but we need to move faster, and perhaps therefore we need to be even more audacious in order to do that. The audacity of hope was the phrase, borrowed from a preacher, chosen by Barack Obama for the book he wrote prior to running for the US Presidency. He defined its meaning as:

> The audacity to believe ... that despite all the evidence to the contrary, we have some control — and therefore responsibility — over our own fate.
>
> (Obama, 2006, p. 256)

Whatever your take on Obama's achievements as US President, that message remains an important one. It is at the heart of our message as we approach our final page. We as educators have to take responsibility for our fate and for the world.

If not now, when?

If not us, who?

Yes we can!

Opportunity for self-reflection and collaborative review

How full is your personal reservoir of hope right now? What steps are you taking to re-fill?

Robert Reich described some of the essential qualities of tenacious changemakers. Applying these lessons to deep learning for future sustainability:

- *Do you have a clear picture of your preferred outcomes and a realistic time-scale?*
- *Have you developed a team with high quality relationships?*
- *Have you worked with your colleagues and stakeholders to develop preferred future scenarios?*
- *Do you celebrate success at every opportunity?*
- *Are you systematically building social and cultural capital as part of your commitment to equity and well-being?*

ACKNOWLEDGEMENTS

This book had its origins in the experience of lockdown in response to the Covid-19 pandemic, and the consequent need to change many established ways of being and doing, at both a personal and at a school level. It coincided with the build-up to and subsequent relative failure of COP 26, the global climate summit, in 2021.

We began writing in the middle of 2020 and we finished in February 2022. Across that period our message has been sharpened both by our own reflections and the range of global events and changes that have occurred over that period. For example, we cite the IPCC 2018 climate report early on, yet we refer to their 2021 report in part 3. However, fundamentally nothing of substance has yet changed in between, indeed much about the crisis they describe has deepened.

Nothing in the space between starting and finishing writing has changed our conviction in the underlying message of the book for schools or the crucial importance of their response. Living through that whole experience served to bring into sharp relief for us both the urgency and the necessity for deeper change, as well as further stimulating our thinking about the implications that this has for schools and the contribution they can make.

A great many people have given us support and encouragement in that challenging task. Among them we have to single out in particular the three headteachers who have opened up their schools and their hearts to us. We were awed by the time we spent talking with Janice Allen, Mirjam Heller, and Amanda Howes, their colleagues and students, and at what they had been able to achieve in such difficult times.

A host of others have shared thoughts and commented on earlier manuscripts to help shape our thinking, in particular Matthew Audley, Katalin Cserna, Charles Fadel, Maggie Farrar, Laura Hay, Mel Hewitt, Brian Lightman, Olly Newton, Hilarie Owen, Isra'a Qaddourah, Julie Taylor, Megan Thoms, and Mick Waters. We are especially grateful to the heads who gave us permission to use pieces from their blogs as thought pieces, Clare Flintoff, Gwyn Ap Harri, Marcelo Staricoff, and to Wendy Hemmingsley and Carolyn Roberts.

While we could not have completed this book without all their help, what we have done with that help in the end, of course, remains our responsibility. We hope we have found the right balance between pessimism and optimism, between theory and practice, between urgency and pace. Above all we hope we have left you, the reader, with greater understanding, motivation, and determination to act now to make learning in your school fit to face a highly challenging future, and to ensure the learners you send out to meet that future go forward better able to confront it in ways that are both sustainable and just.

Malcolm and John

February 2022

REFERENCES

Abel, S. (2019) *How Britain Really Works.* London: John Murray.

Ackoff, R. L. (1989) 'From data to wisdom,' *Journal of Applied Systems Analysis* 16/1, pp. 3–9.

Adey, P. (2012) 'From fixed IQ to multiple intelligences' in P. Adey and J. Dillon (eds), *Bad Education: Debunking myths in education.* Maidenhead: Open University Press, pp. 199–214.

Ap Harri, G. and Sprakes, A. (2019) *How we XP.* Doncaster: XP Trust.

Arendt, H. (1968) *Between Past and Future: Eight exercises in political thought.* New York: Penguin.

Asbury, K. and Plomin, R. (2014) *G is for Genes.* London: Wiley.

Attenborough, D. (2021) *A Life on Our Planet.* London: Witness Books.

Atwood, G. and Croll, P. (2014) 'Truancy and well-being among secondary school pupils in England', *Educational Studies* 41/1, pp. 14–28.

Baron-Cohen, S. (2011) *Zero Degrees of Empathy.* London: Allen Lane

Barron, B. and Darling-Hammond, L. (2010) 'Prospects and challenges for inquiry-based approaches to learning' in Dumont, H. et al (eds), *The Nature of Learning: Using research to inspire practice.* Paris: OECD Publishing, pp. 199–225.

Benjamin, H. R. W. (1939) *Saber-tooth curriculum, including other lectures in the History of Palaeolithic Education.* New York: McGraw Hill.

Bennis, W. G. and Nanus, B. (1986) *Leaders: The strategies for taking charge.* New York: Harper & Row.

Berger, R., Vilen, A., & Woodfin, L. (2021) *We Are Crew: A Teamwork Approach to School Culture.* EL Education.

Berry, W. (1992) *Sex, Economy, Freedom and Community.* New York: Pantheon.

Biesta, G. (2021) *World-Centred Education: A view for the present*, 1st edn. New York: Routledge.

Birch, D. (2014) *The Philosophy Foundation Provocations: Philosophy for secondary school.* Carmarthen: Crown House Publishing.

Blakemore, S-J. and Frith, U. (2005) *The Learning Brain.* Oxford: Blackwell.

Blakemore, S-J. (2018) *Inventing Ourselves.* London: Doubleday.

Bowring-Carr, C. and West-Burnham, J. (1997) *Effective Learning in Schools: How to integrate learning and leadership for a successful school.* London: Pearson Education.

Brandt, R. S. (1998) *Powerful Learning.* Alexandria, VA: ASCD.

Bregman, R. (2020) *Humankind: A hopeful history.* London: Bloomsbury.

Brown, B. (2018) *Dare to lead.* London: Vermillion Publishing.

Brinkman, S. A. et al. (2016) 'Efficacy of infant simulator programmes to prevent teenage pregnancy: A school-based cluster randomised control trial,' *The Lancet* 388/10057, pp. 2264–2271.

Bunting, M. (2020) *Labours of Love: The crisis of care.* London: Granta.

Caine, R. and Caine, G. (1994) *Making Connections: Teaching and the human brain.* Parsippany, NJ: Dale Seymour Publications.

Caine, R. N. et al. (2009) *12 Brain/Mind Learning Principles in Action: Developing executive functions of the human brain.* Thousand Oaks, CA: Corwin Press.

Claxton, G. and Lucas, B. (2012) 'Is vocational education for the less able?' in Adey, P. and Dillon, J. (eds), *Bad Education: Debunking myths in education.* Maidenhead: Open University Press, pp. 17–36.

Coe, R. et al. (2014) *What Makes Great Teaching.* London: Sutton Trust.

Coe, R. et al. (2020) *Great Teaching Toolkit Evidence Review.* Evidence Based Education. Available at: https://www.cambridgeinternational.org/Images/584543-great-teaching-toolkit-evidence-review.pdf. Accessed 5.04.22.

Coffield, F. (2012) *Learning styles: Unreliable, invalid and impractical and yet still widely used*, in Adey, P, Dillon, J (eds) *Bad Education: Debunking Myths in Education.* Berkshire: Open University Press, 215–230

Cole, L. (2020) *Who Cares Wins.* London: Penguin.

Coles, M. and Gent, B. (2020) *Education for Survival.* London: University College London Press.

Crawford, M. (2009) *The Case for Working with Your Hands.* London: Penguin Viking.

Crehan, L. (2016) *Cleverlands.* London: Unbound.

Curry, A. and Hodgson, A. (2008) 'Seeing in multiple horizons: Connecting futures to strategy,' *Journal of Futures Studies* 13/1, pp. 1–20.

Csikszentmihalyi, M. (1997) *Finding Flow.* New York: Basic Books.

Csikszentmihalyi, M. (2002) *Flow: the psychology of happiness: The classic work on how to achieve happiness.* London: Rider.

Csikszentmihalyi, M. and Csikszentmihalyi, I. S. (eds) (2006) *A Life Worth Living: Contributions to positive psychology.* Oxford: Oxford University Press.

Day, C. et al. (2009) *The Impact of School Leadership on Pupil Outcomes.* Nottingham: Department for Children Schools and Families. Available at: https://dera.ioe.ac.uk/11329/1/DCSF-RR108.pdf. Accessed 5.04.22.

Deary, I. J. (2001) *Intelligence: A very short introduction.* Oxford: Oxford University Press.

De Botton, A. (2019) *The School of life.* London: Hamish Hamilton.

De Bruyckere, P. et al. (2015) *Urban Myths about Learning and Education.* London: Elsevier Academic Press.

Desforges, C. and Abouchaar, A. (2003) *The Impact of Parental Involvement, Parental Support and Family Education on Pupil Achievement and Adjustment: A literature review.* Nottingham: Department for Education and Skills. Available at https://dera.ioe.ac.uk/6305/1/rr433.pdf. Accessed 5.04.22.

De Villa, A. (2017) 'Critical thinking in language learning and teaching,' *History Research* 7, pp. 73–77.

Dewey, J. (1984 [1926]) 'Individuality and experience' in J. A. Boydston (ed.), *The Later Works of John Dewey, 1925–1953. Vol. II.* Carbondale and Edwardsville: Southern Illinois University Press, pp. 55–61.

Dhillon, J. K. (2009) 'The role of social capital in sustaining partnership,' *British Educational Research Journal*, 35/5, pp. 687–704.

Diamond, J. (2011) *Collapse: How societies choose to fail or succeed.* London: Penguin.

Dunbar, R. (2021) *Friends.* London: Little Brown.

Durant, W. (1961) *Story of Philosophy.* New York: Simon and Schuster.

Dweck, C. (2006) *Mindset: The new psychology of success.* New York: Ballantine Books.

Education Endowment Foundation, *Teaching and Learning Toolkit.* Available at: https:// educationendowmentfoundation.org.uk/evidence-summaries/teaching-learning-toolkit. Accessed 5.04.22.

Eliot, T. S. (1934) *The Rock.* London: Faber & Faber.

Facer, K. (2011) *Learning Futures: Education, technology and social change*. London: Taylor & Francis.

Feinstein, L. (2003) 'Inequality in the Early Cognitive of British Children in the 1970 Cohort Development,' *Economica* 70/277, pp. 7397.

Fernbach, P. and Sloman, S. (2017) *The Knowledge Illusion*. London: Penguin Random House Audio Publishing Group.

Flintham, A. (2010) *Reservoirs of Hope: Sustaining spirituality in school leaders*. Cambridge: Cambridge Scholars Publishing.

Fullan, M. (2007) *The New Meaning of Educational Change*. 4th edn. New York: Teachers College Press.

Fullan, M. (2019a) 'The unity of the human race: Our precarious future,' *Education Weekly*, 25 August. Available at: http://blogs.edweek.org/edweek/finding_common_ground/2019/08/the_unity_of_the_human_race_our_precarious_future.html. Accessed 7.11.19.

Fullan, M. (2019b) 'Most examples of deep learning are not deep enough,' *Education Weekly*, 28 August. Available at: http://blogs.edweek.org/edweek/finding_common_ground/2019/08/most_examples_of_deep_learning_are_not_deep_enough.html. Accessed 7.11.19.

Fullan, M. et al. (2018) *Deep Learning — Engage the World, Change the World*. Thousand Oaks, CA: Corwin Press.

Gardner, H. (1999a) *Intelligence Reframed*. New York: Basic Books.

Gardner, H. (1999b) *The Disciplined Mind*. New York: Simon & Schuster.

Gardner, H. (2006) *The Development and Education of the Mind*. Abingdon: Routledge.

Gawande, A. (2003) *Complications: A surgeon's notes on an imperfect science*. London: Profile Books.

Gilbert, S. and Green, C. (2021) *Vaxxers*. London: Hodder and Stoughton.

Gladwell, M. (2006) *The Tipping Point: How little things can make a big difference*. Boston, MA: Little, Brown.

Gladwell, M. (2008) *Outliers: The story of success*. Boston, MA: Little, Brown.

Glatter, R. (1997) 'Context and capability in educational management,' *Educational Management & Administration* 25/2, pp. 181–92.

Goldacre, B. (2013) *Building Evidence into Education*. Available at: http://media.education.gov.uk/assets/files/pdf/b/ben%20goldacre%20paper.pdf.

Goldsmith, E., et al. (eds) (1972) 'A Blueprint for Survival,' *The Ecologist* 2/1. Available for download at https://www.resurgence.org/magazine/ecologist/issues1970-1979.html. Accessed 23.12.21

Gompertz, W. (2015) *Think Like an Artist.* London: Penguin Books.

Goodall, J. (1990) *Through a Window.* Boston, MA: Houghton Mifflin.

Goodhart, D. (2020) *Head, Hand, Heart: The struggle for dignity and status in the 21st century.* London: Penguin Books.

Gopnik, A. (2016) *The Gardener and the Carpenter: What the new science of child development tells us about the relationship between parents and children.* New York: Macmillan.

Gorard, S. (2009) 'Serious doubts about school effectiveness,' *British Educational Research Journal* 36/759, pp. 745–766.

Gray, B. (1989) *Collaborating: Finding common ground for multiparty problems.* San Francisco: Jossey-Bass.

Green, F. and Kynaston, D. (2019) *Engines of Privilege.* London: Bloomsbury.

Groves, M. and West-Burnham, J. (2020) *Flipping Schools!* Suffolk: John Catt.

Groves, M. et al. (2017) *Leadership for Tomorrow.* Carmarthen: Crown House.

Guba, E. G. and Lincoln, Y. S. (2005) 'Paradigmatic controversies, contradictions, and emerging confluences,' in N. K. Denzin and Y. S. Lincoln (eds), *The Sage Handbook of Qualitative Research.* London: Sage Publications, pp. 191–215.

Gutman, L.M. and Schoon, I. (2013) *The impact of non-cognitive skills on the outcomes of young people. Literature review.* London: Education Endowment Foundation.

Hammersley, M. and Atkinson, P. (1989) *Ethnography. Principles in Practice.* London: Routledge.

Hansen, M. T. (2009) 'When Internal Collaboration Is Bad for Your Company,' *Harvard Business Review* 87/4, pp. 82–88.

Harari, Y. N. (2011) *Sapiens: A brief history of humankind.* London: Vintage.

Harari, Y. N. (2018) *21 Lessons for the 21st Century.* London: Jonathan Cape.

Hargreaves, D. H. (2010) *Creating a Self-improving School System.* Nottingham: National College for School Leadership. Available at: https://assets.publishing.service.gov.uk/government/uploads/system/uploads/attachment_data/file/325873/creating-a-self-improving-school-system.pdf. Accessed 6.5.22.

Hargreaves, A., & Harris, A. (2011) *Performance Beyond Expectations.* Available at https://dera.ioe.ac.uk/10022/. Accessed 5.5.22.

Harris, A. and Hargreaves, A. (2015) *Schools Performing Beyond Expectations.* Nottingham: National College for School Leadership.

Harris, A. and Jones, M. (2020) 'COVID 19: School leadership in disruptive times,' *School Leadership & Management* 40/4, pp. 243-247. Available at: https://doi.org/10.1080/13632434.2020.1811479.

Hart, R. (1992) *Children's Participation: From tokenism to citizenship.* United Nations Children's Fund. Available at: https://www.unicef-irc.org/publications/100-childrens-participation-from-tokenism-to-citizenship.html.

Hattie, J. and Zierer, K. (2017) *10 Mindframes for Visible Learning: Teaching for success.* London: Routledge.

Hochschild, A. (2005) *Bury the Chains: Prophets and rebels in the fight to free an empire's slaves.* Boston, MA: Houghton Mifflin.

Huxham, C. and Vangen, S. (2005) *Managing to Collaborate: The theory and practice of collaborative advantage.* Hove: Psychology Press.

Intergovernmental Panel on Climate Change (2018) *Global Warming of 1.5°C: An IPCC Special Report on the impacts of global warming of 1.5°C above pre-industrial levels and related global greenhouse gas emission pathways, in the context of strengthening the global response to the threat of climate change, sustainable development, and efforts to eradicate poverty.* Geneva: World Meteorological Organization. Available at: https://www.ipcc.ch/sr15/.

Intergovernmental Panel on Climate Change (2021) *Climate Change 2021: The Physical Science Basis. Contribution of working group I to the sixth assessment report of the Intergovernmental Panel on Climate Change.* Geneva: World Meteorological Organisation. Available at: https://www.ipcc.ch/report/ar6/wg1/.

James, O. (2016) *Not in your Genes.* London: Vermilion.

Jerome, L. and Kisby, B. (2019) *The Rise of Character Education in Britain: Heroes, dragons and the myths of character.* Cham: Palgrave Macmillan.

Joyce, B. R. and Showers, B. (2002) *Student Achievement Through Staff Development*, vol. III. Alexandria, VA: Association for Supervision and Curriculum Development.

Jukes, I. et al. (2010) *Understanding the Digital Generation.* Thousand Oaks: 21st Century Fluency Project.

Kahane, A. (2010) *Power and Love.* San Francisco: Berrett-Koehler.

Kelly, G. J. (2008) 'Inquiry, activity, and epistemic practice,' in R. Duschl and R. Grandy (eds) *Teaching Scientific Inquiry: Recommendations for research and implementation.* Rotterdam: Sense Publishers, pp. 99–117, 288–91.

Kettlewell, K. et al. (2020) *International Early Learning and Child Well-Being*

Study (IELS): National report for England: December 2020. London: Department of Education. Available at: https://assets.publishing.service.gov.uk/government/uploads/system/uploads/attachment_data/file/1000508/IELS_national_report_FINAL_Dec_2020_revised.pdf.

Kohn, A. (1997) 'How not to teach values: A critical look at character education,' *Phi Delta Kappan* 78, pp. 428–39.

Kolbert, E. (2006) *Field Notes from a Catastrophe.* London: Bloomsbury.

Krznaric, R. (2011) *The Wonderbox: Curious histories of how to live.* London: Profile Books.

Krznaric, R. (2020) *The Good Ancestor: How to think long term in a short-term world.* New York: Random House.

Kynaston, D. and Green, F. (2019) *Engines of Privilege: Britain's private school problem.* London: Bloomsbury.

Lamott, A. (1995) *Bird by Bird: Some instructions on writing and life.* New York: Anchor Book Press.

Lancy, D. L. (2017) *Raising Children.* Cambridge: Cambridge University Press.

Largo, R. (2019) *The Right Life.* London: Allen Lane.

Lauchlan, F. et al. (2012) 'Bilingualism in Sardinia and Scotland: Exploring the cognitive benefits of speaking a 'minority' language,' *International Journal of Bilingualism* 17, pp. 43–56.

Law, S. (2006) *The War for Children's Minds.* London: Routledge.

Lasker, R. et al. (2001) 'Partnership Synergy: A practical Framework for Studying and Strengthening the Collaborative Advantage,' *The Millbank Quarterly* 79/2, pp. 179–205.

Layard, R. (2005) *Happiness: Lessons from a new science.* New York: The Penguin Press.

Leadbeater, C. (2004) *Personalisation through participation: a new script for public services.* London: Demos.

Leithwood, K. et al. (2006) *Teaching for Deep Understanding.* Thousand Oaks, CA: Corwin Press.

Lieberman, M. (2013) *Social: Why our brains are wired to connect.* Oxford: Oxford University Press.

Lucas, B. (2021) *Rethinking Assessment — The Case for Change.* Victoria: Centre for Strategic Education.

Lupton R. and Hayes, D. (2021) *Great Mistakes in Education Policy.* Bristol: University of Bristol Press.

MacAskill, W. (2015) *Doing Good Better.* London: Guardian Books.

Major, L. E. and Machin, S. (2018) *Social Mobility: And its enemies.* London: Penguin.

Marks, E. et al. (2021) 'Young People's Voices on Climate Anxiety, Government Betrayal and Moral Injury: A global phenomenon,' *Lancet Planetary Health* 5/12. Available at: http://dx.doi.org/10.2139/ssrn.3918955.

Marian, V. and Shook, A. (2012) 'The Cognitive Benefits of Being Bilingual,' *Cerebrum* 13.

Marton, F. et al. (eds) (1984) *The Experience of Learning: Implications for teaching and studying in higher education.* 3rd edn. Edinburgh: University of Edinburgh, Centre for Teaching, Learning and Assessment.

Maslin, M. (2021) *How to Save our Planet.* London: Penguin Books.

McEachen, J. (2017) *Assessment for Deep Learning.* Ontario: New Pedagogies for Deeper Learning.

Meadows, D.H. et al. (1972) *The Limits to Growth: A report for the Club of Rome's project on the predicament of mankind.* New York: Universe Books.

Mehnedbegovic, D. (2016) *Education Talks: Bilingualism in education.* Erasmus Interviews Online Platform. Available at: https://www.schooleducationgateway.eu/en/pub/viewpoints/interviews/education-talks-bilingualism-.htm. Accessed 6.04.22.

Miller, P. (2010) *The Smart Swarm: How understanding flocks, schools, and colonies can make us better at communicating, decision making, and getting things done.* New Jersey: Avery Publishing Group.

Millis, B. J. (2014) 'Using cooperative structures to promote deep learning,' *Journal on Excellence in College Teaching* 25/3 and 4, pp. 139–48.

Mlodinow, L. (2018) *Elastic: Flexible thinking in a constantly changing world.* London: Penguin.

Monbiot, G. (2017) *Out of the Wreckage.* London: Verso.

Mukherjee, S. (2016) *The Gene: An intimate history.* London: Vintage.

Muuri, M. (2018) 'Six key principles that make Finnish education a success,' *Edsurge.* Available at: www.edsurge.com/news/2018-07-31-6-key-principles-that-make-finnish-education-a-success. Accessed 5.04.22.

National Advisory Committee on Creative and Cultural Education (1999) *All Our Futures: Creativity, culture and education.* Available at https://sirkenrobinson.com/pdf/allourfutures.pdf. Accessed 6.04.22.

Nowak, M. A. (2012) 'Evolving cooperation,' *Journal of Theoretical Biology* 299, pp. 1–8.

Oates, T. (2018) 'Skills versus Knowledge,' *Impact* 4. Available at: https://my.chartered.college/impact_article/skills-versus-knowledge-a-curriculum-debate-that-matters-and-one-which-we-need-to-reject/. Accessed 6.04.22.

Obama, B. (2006) *The Audacity of Hope*. New York: Random House.

Ofsted (2010) *Finnish Pupils' Success in Mathematics*. Available at https://dera.ioe.ac.uk/1144/. Accessed 6.04.22.

Ofsted (2019) *School inspection Framework*. London: Ofsted. Available at https://www.gov.uk/government/publications/school-inspection-handbook-eif/school-inspection-handbook. Accessed 5.5.22

Organisation for Economic Cooperation and Development, (2001) *Back to the Future of Education*. Available at: https://www.oecd.org/education/back-to-the-future-s-of-education-178ef527-en.htm. Accessed 23.05.22.

Organisation for Economic Cooperation and Development (2018) *Equity in Education: Breaking down barriers to social mobility*. Paris: OECD Publishing. https://doi.org/10.1787/9789264073234-en. Accessed 6.04.22.

Organisation for Economic Cooperation and Development (2019a) *OECD Future of Education and Skills 2030: OECD Learning Compass 2030*. Available at: http://www.oecd.org/education/2030-project/teaching-and-learning/learning/learning-compass-2030/OECD_Learning_Compass_2030_concept_note.pdf. Accessed 6.0422.

Organisation for Economic Cooperation and Development (2019b) *OECD Future of Education and Skills 2030: Student Agency for 2030*. Available at: http://www.oecd.org/education/2030-project/teaching-and-learning/learning/student-agency/Student_Agency_for_2030_concept_note.pdf. Accessed 6.04.22.

Perkins, D. *Future Wise Educating our children for a changing world* (2014) San Francisco: Jossey Bass

Petrie, P. et al. (2006) *Working with Children in Care — European Perspectives*. Maidenhead: Open University Press

Pinker, S. (2011) *The Better Angels of our Nature*. London: Penguin Books.

Pinker, S. (2015) *The Village Effect*. London: Atlantic Books.

Plomin, R. (2018) *Blueprint*. London: Allen Lane.

Postman, N. (1982) *The Disappearance of Childhood*. New York: Delacorte Press.

Pring. R. (2015) *Philosophy of Educational Research*. London: Bloomsbury.

Putnam, R. (2000) *Bowling Alone*. New York: Simon and Schuster.

Raworth, K. (2017) *Doughnut Economics: Seven ways to think like a 21st-century economist.* Vermont: Chelsea Green Publishing.

Ridley, M. (2020) *How Innovation Works.* London: 4th Estate.

Rovelli, C. (2018) *There Are Places in The World Where Rules Are Less Important Than Kindness.* London: Allen Lane.

Sabates, R. and Dex, S. (2012) *Multiple Risk Factors in Young Children's Development.* CLS Cohort Studies Working paper 2012/1, Institute of Education London.

Sacker, A. et al. (2002) 'Social inequality in educational achievement and psychosocial adjustment throughout childhood: magnitude and mechanisms,' *Social science and Medicine* 55/5, pp. 863–80.

Sammons, P. et al. (2014) *Influences on students' GCSE attainment and progress at age 16: Effective pre-school, primary and secondary education project (EPPSE).* London: Department of Education. Available at: https://dera.ioe.ac.uk/20875/1/RR352_-_Influences_on_Students_GCSE_Attainment_and_Progress_at_Age_16.pdf. Accessed 5.04.22.

Sahlberg, P. (2015) *Finnish Lessons* 2.0. 2nd edn. New York: Teachers College Press.

Sandel, M. (2020) *The Tyranny of Merit. London*: Allen Lane.

Savage, M. (2015) *Social Class in the 21st century.* London: Penguin.

Schlechty, P. C. (2002) *Working on the Work.* San Francisco, CA: Jossey-Bass.

Schneider, M. and Stern, E. (2010) 'The cognitive perspective on learning: Ten cornerstone findings,' in *The Nature of Learning: using research to inspire practice,* Dumont, H. et al (eds). Paris: OECD Publishing, pp. 69–90.

Sennett, R. (2008) *The Craftsman.* London: Allen Lane.

Sennett, R. (2012) *Together: The rituals, pleasures and politics of cooperation.* New Haven, CT: Yale University Press.

Shafak, E. (2020) *How to Stay Sane in an Age of Division.* London: Profile books

Sharp, C. et al. (2020) *Schools' Responses to Covid-19: The challenges facing schools and pupils in September 2020.* Slough, National Foundation for Educational Research. Available at: https://www.nfer.ac.uk/media/4119/schools_responses_to_covid_19_the_challenges_facing_schools_and_pupils_in_september_2020.pdf. Accessed 5.04.22.

Schleicher, A. (2018a) *World Class: How to build a 21st century school system.* Paris: OECD Publishing.

Schleicher, A. (2018b) *Valuing Our Teachers and Raising Their Status.* Paris: OECD Publishing.

Senge, P. (1999) *The Dance of Change: The challenges of sustaining momentum in learning organisations.* London: Nicholas Brealey.

Sims, E. (2006) *Deep Learning 1.* London: Specialist Schools Academies Trust. Available at: https://webcontent.ssatuk.co.uk/wp-content/uploads/2014/08/14142830/02-Deep-learning-1-Emma-Sims.pdf . Accessed 5.04.22.

Social Mobility Commission (2020) *Monitoring Social Mobility 2013 to 2020.* Available at: https://www.gov.uk/government/publications/monitoring-social-mobility-2013-to-2020. Accessed 5.04.22.

Standing, G. (2014) *A Precariat Charter: From denizens to citizens.* London: A&C Black.

Staricoff, M. (2021) *The Joy of Not Knowing.* London: Routledge.

Starko, A. J. (2017) *Creativity in the Classroom: Schools of curious delight.* London: Routledge.

Sternberg, R. J. (1990) *Wisdom.* Cambridge: Cambridge University Press.

Strauss, D. (2002) *How to Make Collaboration Work.* San Francisco, CA: Berrett-Koehler.

Syed, M. (2019) *Rebel Ideas.* London: John Murray.

Sylvester, R. (2021), 'The AI revolution can supercharge learning in schools', *The Times*, 26 November. https://www.thetimes.co.uk/article/the-ai-revolution-can-supercharge-learning-in-school-xnv0vql8r. Accessed 2.5.2022

Taylor, M. (2013) 'Falling in love with the C-word,' *RSA*. Available at: https://www.thersa.org/discover/publications-and-articles/matthew-taylor-blog/2013/09/falling-in-love-with-the-c-word. Accessed 30.12.21.

Tett, G. (2021) *Anthrovision: How anthropology can explain business and life.* London: Random House.

Thomas, G. (2009) *How To do Your Research Project.* London: Sage.

Thunberg, G. (2019) *No One is Too Small to Make a Difference.* London: Penguin.

Timms, H. and Heimans, J. (2018) *New Power.* London: Macmillan.

Toynbee, P. and Walker, D. (2008) *Unjust Rewards: Exposing greed and inequality in Britain today.* London: Granta.

Vygotsky, L. S. (1978) *Mind in society: The development of higher psychological processes.* Cambridge, MA: Harvard University Press.

Wallace-Wells, D. (2019) *The Uninhabitable Earth.* New York: Columbia University Press.

Waters, M. (2013) *Thinking Allowed: On schooling.* Carmarthen: Crown House Publishing.

West-Burnham, J. (2007) *Leading Personalised Learning in Schools.* Nottingham: National College for School Leadership.

West-Burnham, J. and Coates, M. (2005) *Personalizing Learning.* Stafford: Network Educational Press.

Wilkinson, R. G. (1996) *Unhealthy Societies: The afflictions of inequality.* London: Routledge.

Wilkinson, R. G. (2005) *The Impact of Inequality.* New York: New Press.

Willingham, D. T. (2009) *Why Students Don't Like School.* San Francisco, CA: Jossey.

Zeldin, T. (1996) *An Intimate History of Humanity.* London: Harper Collins.

Zhao, Y. and Watterston, J. (2021) 'The changes we need: Education post covid-19,' *Journal of Educational Change* 22, pp. 3–12. Available at https://doi.org/10.1007/s10833-021-09417-3. Accessed 5.04.22.

INDEX

A

B

C

G

H

I

J

K

L

M

N

O

P

R

S

T

U

V

W

X

Z